FUGITIVE

Michael O'Farrell is an investigative journalist who was born in Los Angeles in 1974 and grew up in the Irish midlands. A journalist for over two decades, he has reported widely on matters of public interest from across the globe and at home. A graduate of Trinity College and Dublin City University, he began his career in the *Irish Examiner* before joining *The Irish Mail on Sunday* where he is currently the paper's Investigations Editor. In November 2023 he was named Campaigning Journalist of the Year at the Irish Journalism Awards for his work with whistleblowers, and he also took home the Feature Journalist of the Year award. In previous years he has been named Investigative Journalist of the Year, Business Journalist of the Year, News Analysis Writer of the Year and has also won the Scoop of the Year category. A keen fly fisherman, Michael lives in rural Ireland with his wife and four children.

FUGITIVE
THE MICHAEL LYNN STORY

Michael O'Farrell

MERRION
PRESS

First published in 2024 by
Merrion Press
10 George's Street
Newbridge
Co. Kildare
Ireland
www.merrionpress.ie

© Michael O'Farrell, 2024

978 1 78537 367 1 (Paper)
978 1 78537 174 5 (Ebook)

A CIP catalogue record for this book is available from the British Library.

Typeset in Minion Pro 11/17

Cover design by riverdesignbooks.com

Merrion Press is a member of Publishing Ireland.

To my family – past, present and future.

Contents

PART THREE   JUSTICE?

Prologue

The first car arrives at the rendezvous location two hours before sunrise. There are four men inside. Then an unmarked van pulls up. And another. Next, a dog van arrives, distinguishable by its roof vent. As the final few vehicles assemble, officers huddle together in the darkness. They are tense. Excited. Primed for the raid they are about to conduct. Enveloped in a cloud of their own freezing breath, they speak in hushed tones. Every detail is double-checked. Soon they will move out in convoy towards their target.

Out of sight, just over the rolling hills of Wicklow, the home of Michael Lynn is ablaze with outdoor Christmas fairy lights. Everything is silent and still. Inside, Lynn's wife, Brid Murphy, and the couple's four children are fast asleep. Soon their home will be swarming with gardaí.

Lynn's is not the only family due a rude awakening this morning. Elsewhere, at locations across two other counties, additional search teams have also assembled in the darkness. They will simultaneously raid the homes of two associates of Lynn's and a rural lock-up linked to him.

In his Dublin penthouse apartment, one of these associates – a Bulgarian national who oversees a network of new companies and bank accounts – will refuse to provide passwords for his computers and phones. But he has been under observation for months now. Secret court orders have already provided the authorities with access to the accounts. They know precisely who has access to the funds within. Before the day is over substantially more than €2 million, suspected of being linked to Lynn's crimes, will be frozen.

In Wicklow, the huddle breaks up. Officers pull on stab vests and garda windbreakers. They are ready to move out.

It is 9 January 2024 – sixteen years since Michael Lynn first turned fugitive and just three weeks since he was found guilty of stealing millions. The story of the intervening period is one of the most extraordinary episodes of criminal justice Ireland has ever known. It is an odyssey that, even today, is still throwing up fresh twists as the hunt for Lynn's millions continues. Awaiting sentencing, Lynn – not for the first time – has spent Christmas behind bars. He will not learn of today's raids until they are long over.

PART ONE
MANHUNT

1

Bring Him Before Me

THE PASSENGER WAS A BUSINESSMAN IN a hurry. He needed to get to the airport. Clearly worried about missing his flight, he kept asking the driver to speed up.

It was only later, as he watched the evening news, that the astonished taxi driver realised just who his early morning fare had been. The hassled-looking executive who had flung himself into the back of his cab at 6 a.m. on Wednesday, 12 December 2007, with just a small suitcase and a leather briefcase, was Michael Lynn – on his way to becoming Ireland's most renowned white-collar criminal.

That morning Lynn should have been preparing to testify before the High Court in Dublin where, at 11 a.m., he was to face questions about a string of multimillion-euro loans. Eighty million euro had been borrowed from high-street banks. Hundreds of clients had paid for apartments abroad that did not yet exist. Regulators had uncovered disturbing evidence of fraud and misconduct. Still, everyone hoped – and Lynn had promised – that he could explain it all away.

Instead, after weeks of relentless thoughts churning around his skull like bricks in a tumble dryer, he had made the biggest decision of his life – to vanish. And so he had fled.

This was not a fate Lynn had ever envisaged. He saw himself as an upstanding lawyer and millionaire, an international property mogul, an honest and good-natured husband, a songwriter and singer, a dealmaker – not a criminal or a fraudster. Yet innocent men seldom run – and he had run.

Now his fate was to be hunted across the globe, exposed as a greater fraud than anyone had ever imagined and eventually brought home in shackles to face multimillion-euro theft charges.

Before that though, he'd suffer the shame and physical pain of festering in a sordid Brazilian jail for years amid violent rapists and murderers. He'd see his second, third and fourth children for the first time from behind bars, and watch them begin to grow up without him. He'd miss his mother's funeral. Angela Lynn would die after a long battle with Alzheimer's in the summer of 2015, eight years after her youngest son's dash from the law earmarked the Lynn name for ignominy.

But all that was in the future. For now, investigators seeking to find Lynn would begin by trying to pinpoint the flight he'd been racing to catch that morning. There were several flights he could have taken. Aer Lingus flight EI562 to Barcelona taxied towards the runway shortly after Lynn was dropped at Dublin Airport. Another flight departed for Malaga, in the south of Spain, at the same time. Both routes would have provided ample onward connections for Lynn and either would have done. So, too, would a private jet. All the better since it would leave no public trace or trail to follow. And Lynn had access to just such a jet thanks to a €250,000 down payment he'd made to exclusive provider NetJets in September – enough for fifty hours' flying time.

Whichever option he chose, there was no turning back. Michael Lynn had sealed his fate.

As his plane banked steeply through a mid-winter's dawn, the orange sodium vapour streetlights of Dublin ringed the darkness of the city's bay below. On the northern tip of that shoreline lay what was, perhaps, Lynn's most ostentatious folly – his dream home, Glenlion House – purchased just months earlier for €5.5 million with his new wife, Brid Murphy.

It was Brid – until recently a nurse at St Vincent's Hospital on a salary of €47,000 – who had spotted the ad for the Howth mansion as she leafed through a newspaper on board a business flight with her new husband between Slovakia and Armenia. 'We both thought it looked really nice,' she would later say.

With a classical garden modelled on the ruins of Pompeii, Corinthian columns and carved stone tablets, the home boasts a private beach and striking views across the Irish Sea. Brid would later swear under oath, as she went to court to secure her share of the property's value as Lynn's wife, that she didn't know her husband had fraudulently secured three mortgages worth €12 million on the house.

The hapless banks didn't know either. Each thought they had sole claim to the asset in the event of a default. If Lynn failed to make repayments, they thought they could simply repossess Glenlion to recover their money. But that would require their loans to be legally registered against the property – a task typically trusted to an independent solicitor. But what if that solicitor's undertaking was a lie? What if it was a forgery? And what if the person behind that deception was Michael Lynn himself? Soon the banks would be scrambling to deal with this very nightmare.

As Lynn's flight left nothing more than a pair of evaporating vapour trails in its wake, it was precisely that purchase – and mounting evidence of an astonishing array of other fraudulent loans – that the President of the High Court, Judge Richard Johnson, was preparing to hear about. In anticipation of the hearing, listed for High Court No. 6, a phalanx of over 100 lawyers had gathered; most of them representing the scores of banks duped out of tens of millions.

Reality quickly dawned as the court registrar rose to call the subject to the stand. Michael Lynn was not present.

'Bring him before me! At 2 p.m. sharp!' thundered Judge Johnson. Ears pricked, reporters brought pens to notebooks to capture his anger. Barristers rose to scurry out, exchanging sideways glances – all with the same explosive thought.

Everyone knew. Two p.m. was just a formality. Lynn had done a runner.

2

Go Get Him!

I HAD BEEN DREADING THIS CALL – yet knew it was likely to come.

'Sebastian wants you to find Michael Lynn,' the chirpy voice of news editor Neil Michael barrelled down the phone line.

Sebastian Hamilton was my editor at *The Irish Mail on Sunday*. When he said, 'find Michael Lynn', what he actually meant was find him, get him to speak exclusively on the record and secure photos from various different angles. No pressure.

'He's that solicitor who legged it last month,' Neil continued. 'Lord knows where he is, but if anyone can find him, we can.'

I didn't agree. The man had absconded. He could be anywhere – literally anywhere – in the world. There were reports he was utilising a private jet. For all I knew he could be dead. And if we did find him, he was hardly going to speak to a journalist.

Plus, I knew nothing of the case and had never written or read a word about the man, despite growing news coverage of his affairs. Truth be told, I had ignored the story altogether and hoped to keep it that way. Anyone tasked with finding Lynn was very likely doomed to failure. But now I had no choice in the matter.

'Sure, no problem. I'll do my best,' I replied, slumping back on my home office chair, cursing silently to myself. How was I going to pull this one off?

It was January 2008 and Lynn had already spent Christmas on the run. He had a good month's head start.

Outside a flash of white against black caught my eye as a lone magpie swooped down from a bare ash tree to the frozen lawn. Great, I thought. One for sorrow. Not the omen I needed. I cast my eyes further afield, trying to spot another one, and got lucky. 'Two for joy', I mouthed and clicked through to Google.

Just weeks earlier, few people had ever heard of Michael Lynn. Now he was notorious.

Born in 1969 to Hugh Gerard Lynn and his wife, Angela, Michael's childhood was spent on the family's 100-acre farm at Gortnor Abbey, on the shores of Lough Conn near Crossmolina, County Mayo, in rural Ireland. Lynn was the youngest of five, the joker of the pack, the one who got away with everything.

Perhaps he learned a trick or two from his fun-loving mother, who had once decided on a whim to go about her daily business in Crossmolina dressed in a white wig, pretending to be someone else – a tale that was recalled fondly at her funeral. He will also have learned from his father's astute dealings at the Mayo Sligo Mart in Ballina – not a place for the tame-hearted or foolish – and at the Crossmolina Agricultural Show, where Hugh was chairman for decades until his death in 1995.

But Michael Lynn was never destined for the life his father led. Hugh dreamt of winning the Crossmolina Agricultural Show's perpetual trophy for best pedigree Friesian Cow – a prize for which he was always in the running – sponsored by Allied Irish Bank. His youngest son, though, would develop different plans for that particular bank.

Lynn's early school life at Crossmolina Boys' National School and at the convent of Jesus and Mary, Gortnor Abbey, was unremarkable. Described as pleasant, popular and bright, he had a passion for music and Gaelic football. He entered talent competitions, such as the Pioneer Total Abstinence Association's annual talent show and the GAA's Scór na nÓg. Early headlines about him in the *Western People* newspaper chart the success of his

Crossmolina Ballad Group – a world away from the scandal that would one day see his name splashed across newspaper front pages for a very different reason.

Together with a Crossmolina contemporary, Marc Roberts, Lynn spent his teenage weekends playing the organ and singing at church weddings. In 1997, Roberts would go on to represent Ireland in the Eurovision song contest, securing second place.

In 1987, Lynn began studying law at Trinity College, graduating in 1991. An apprenticeship with Dublin law firm Moran and Ryan followed, before he set up his own legal practice in Blanchardstown in West Dublin. His specialty – conveyancing and property.

Professional photos commissioned by Lynn at the time show a fresh-faced, proud-as-punch young man standing before his firm's nameplate on the wall outside. Beneath a family crest-type logo containing the letters ML in swirling calligraphy, designed to look sophisticated, the sign read: 'MICHAEL LYNN & CO. Solicitors and Commissioners for Oaths'. A series of posed shots from inside the office show him dressed in a neat waistcoat and tie, perched on a desk, his hand resting on a pile of leather-bound law volumes. Michael Lynn had arrived.

So, too, had the Celtic Tiger, with its fool's gold property boom that Ireland would rush to embrace, and fail dismally to regulate. Right at the starting gate, perfectly positioned to lead the charge, was Michael Lynn. A tearaway spark was about to meet gasoline.

In the early years Lynn focused on building his law practice and dealt with routine legal matters of a general nature. Like any small-time local solicitor, he handled whatever came in the door and charged an appropriate fee. Much of the work, such as drafting wills, was routine, formulaic – and easy money. But increasingly, as Ireland lurched towards a looming property boom, he found himself completing more and more paperwork on property deals for homebuyers, investors and the banks. It was important but mundane work, much of it completed by Lynn's growing number of staff, which would peak at seventeen in 2006.

Soon Lynn began to dabble himself, but quickly found he needed something more. In partnership with one of his clients – developer and businessman John Riordan – Lynn began investing in UK and Irish property. In June 2003 the pair incorporated a new firm called Kendar Holdings Ltd. Typically of Lynn, a songwriter and former wedding singer possessed with a strong sense of melancholy, the Kendar name was derived from those of two childhood friends – Ken and Dara – who were killed in separate tragic accidents.

With Kendar, Lynn stepped into the big leagues, buying a €5-million development site in the sleepy fishing village of Cabanas, just a short distance from the Moorish Algarve town of Tavira. A plan for 272 apartments in three staggered construction phases was rolled out. A glitzy sales drive led by footballer Rui Costa, then a Portuguese international and AC Milan midfielder, was kicked off with champagne and canapés in Dublin's Four Seasons Hotel in December 2003.

In 2004, other sports personalities, such as former Irish soccer international Ray Houghton, retired rugby international Victor Costello and former Mayo footballer Willie Joe Padden, lent their names to the Kendar dream. Padden and a host of other well-known GAA stars would travel throughout the country using their status to achieve sales for Lynn. As the foundations were still being laid in Portugal, deposits flooded in for the Algarve development, which Lynn had named Costa de Cabanas.

By 2005, with the first phase of seventy-six apartments built, Lynn bought out Riordan and ploughed on alone, ramping up his activities with new acquisitions in Bulgaria, Hungary, Slovakia and elsewhere. Nothing, it seemed, could stop this runaway train. As quickly as his team could source new sites – and print new brochures to market them – the developments sold out. Often nothing had actually been built. Often nothing ever would be.

In 2006 Lynn secured an unprecedented publicity coup, appearing on *The Late Late Show*, Ireland's best-known and most-watched prime-time chat show. Astoundingly he gave away a €105,000 penthouse apartment in one of Kendar's planned developments in Bulgaria. The competition was co-sponsored by *The Sunday Business Post*, Ireland's property and business bible.

The prize, located in the Bulgarian ski-resort of Bansko, was the single most valuable prize ever to be given away by the show.

In a blaze of publicity, Lynn whisked the winners, David Timlin and Olivia Joyce from Mayo, to Bulgaria to see the location of their new holiday home. The site they saw remains vacant to this day. Aside from a hole in the ground where the earth was once stripped in preparation for foundations, the location – a hilltop perch surrounded by ancient pine trees and pristine snow-topped mountain peaks – remains devoid of development.

Vacant, too, were Lynn's supposed words of wisdom when he spoke to *The Irish Times* in June 2006 to warn investors about getting carried away: 'There are opportunities in all of these countries. You come home and you're punch-drunk with opportunities. You almost have to go to bed for a week,' he enthused. 'My advice is to take a breather before signing anything. In Ireland, it is said there are three factors to ensure success in the property market – location, location, location. With overseas property, it's investigate, investigate and investigate.'

The problem was that if you were buying from Lynn, he did the investigating for you – and no one was investigating him. He cornered all sides of the property transactions he dealt with by setting up a dedicated legal firm – Overseas Property Law – to dole out advice and manage foreign conveyancing for Kendar's buyers.

Above the din of the Celtic Tiger's roar, no one was listening when those worried about the conflicts of interest they saw tried to speak up. On 4 September 2006 – more than a year before Lynn would ever face any questions about his affairs – worrying comments were stacking up on the website rateyoursolicitor.com. One client wrote: 'This guy conveys property alright but the fees are astronomical and he'd cut your nose off for a penny. Advice: Cheque [*sic*] every inch of your invoice (although he takes cash) and never lodge money with him as his client account funds his property deals. He runs a property development company selling apartments in Spain/Portugal. Buys a block of 20 for 1 million and sells each unit for 250,000.00 (plus VAT and outlay). Oh he's a gangster.'

Such concerns were echoed a day later in a post from another concerned individual: 'It would not hurt the Law Society to ensure that there was no conflict of interest arising from his property dealings.'

On 28 February 2007 – more than six months before any action was taken against Lynn – a worried solicitor posted to the site: 'Absolute disgrace, never replies to correspondence or returns phone calls. Law Society, where are you?'

3

The Beginning of the End

LIZ DOYLE SIGNED THE VISA AUTHORISATION form, punched in the New York fax number and hit send. There was a satisfying whirr as the paper slid through the machine. Outside two air-conditioning units on the side of the building sent a steady drip to the ground below.

Short and busy, with wisps of blonde hair prone to spreading across her face, Liz, a hard-working and ambitious mother of three, had been a legal executive and Michael Lynn's personal assistant for years. Intuitively primed to her boss's needs, Liz took care of everything she was asked to – drafting legal correspondence, overseeing assignments, making bank lodgements, and procuring concert and match tickets, hotel bookings and flights for Michael and Brid. Nothing was too large or too small to trust her with. Flowers at the last minute for an important London client? No problem. Chauffeur-driven limousine in Lisbon? Sure. First-class flights to Rio first thing? On it.

Today she was booking a six-night stay for Michael and Brid in New York's St Regis Hotel – one of the most famed and exclusive establishments on the planet, just a heartbeat away from Central Park. Normally based in Lynn's Dublin HQ, to which she commuted from a comfortable home in the suburbs, on this occasion Liz was helping out temporarily at the Algarve headquarters of Lynn's international property firm, Kendar.

Despite the climate control and a soft breeze blowing inland from the Gulf of Cadiz, it was hot. Just about right for mad dogs and Englishmen, as the locals would say. 'And Irish Buckaleiros,' Lynn might add – his favoured term for the small-time investors from whom he specialised in soliciting cash deposits.

Far faster than it had drawn the sent page into itself, the fax machine spewed out a send receipt. The time: 5.37 p.m. on 5 July 2007 – six months before Michael Lynn would flee justice in Ireland.

Buoyed by millions secured from obliging banks throughout Europe and the US, Lynn was in the midst of an astonishing whirlwind spending spree that would see him lavish millions across the globe. In 2007 alone, he completed forty property deals, adding to an already substantial portfolio that now spanned nine countries including Slovakia, Bulgaria, Hungary, China, the US and the UK.

Not content to merely stay in the five-star St Regis – which Liz had booked for six days from 15 July – Lynn bought a piece of the place. He came away from his stay having purchased a $640,000 timeshare apartment at the hotel's Residence Club. Previous owners included Marlene Dietrich and Salvador Dali. John Lennon had once given a performance from a bedroom there. Dietrich, Dali, Lennon ... Lynn. Perhaps the out-of-control solicitor, caught in a delirious credit warp, felt his name belonged on that list.

The St Regis property was Lynn's second Big Apple investment. The previous Christmas he'd picked up an apartment in the Cove Club Condominium, Battery Park, thanks to a Deutsche Bank loan.

With new loans – often secured on the same assets – being generated almost weekly, Lynn's life was becoming a blur. Bent on a mission no one else understood, Lynn was Icarus in a pinstriped suit and silk tie soaring towards the sun oblivious to the consequences.

'The banks couldn't get enough of me,' he would later declare when I became the first person to catch up with him since he had absconded.

At times those around him felt he was impossible to keep up with. His momentum through life, driven by an unparalleled determination, seemed unstoppable. The flash drive of his mind was hard-wired to monitor every element of his growing property empire – perhaps too much so. He meddled in the smallest and largest details, putting his staff under ferocious pressure. He could recall contractual small print at will, summon up the mobile numbers and email addresses of brokers, bankers, buyers and builders from memory, and make a snap decision worth millions on a dime. It would have seemed almost delirious had it not all been delivered with such apparent authority and assurance.

Meanwhile, his staff, many of whom fell by the wayside worn out and exhausted, did their best to keep track of their boss by compiling constantly changing lists: his property purchases in Ireland and, globally, his travel itinerary, his hotel bookings, his multiple mortgage applications and the contracts and agreements he would dictate or scrawl down by hand on sheets of A4 paper for others to decipher.

Even his busy social life required a list as he and Brid indulged in a hectic schedule of entertainment between business and pleasure trips abroad. In the first six months of 2007 alone, concerts booked for the couple included Moving Hearts, Michael Bolton, Snoop Dog/P. Diddy, Westlife, Lionel Richie, Meatloaf, Il Divo, Justin Timberlake and Rod Stewart. They rarely attended alone and frequently paid for as many as ten guests to accompany them. On 19 May that year, Lynn met Bobby Robson, Glenn Hoddle, Sven-Göran Eriksson and Jack Charlton when he attended the FA Cup Final between Chelsea and Manchester United in Wembley. Increasingly the lines between business and pleasure became blurred as personal expenses were charged to Lynn's companies.

Lynn also splashed out on personal property, demonstrating some expensive tastes in the process. On 24 January he bought an antique burl veneer bookcase from a bespoke antique dealer in Dublin, perhaps for his then €1 million period home in St Alban's Park in Sandymount, a wealthy suburb of Dublin city. He'd moved there with Brid after their April 2006 marriage at the historic five-star Dromoland Castle in County Clare. The price of this one piece of furniture – a cool €8,910.

Two days earlier Brid had signed a memorandum of understanding with a Hungarian firm to renovate a historic Budapest apartment Lynn had bought near the capital's fashionable theatre district. A few months later, in June 2007, Lynn agreed to purchase properties in Dubai, reserved three villas with pools in Croatia and had his staff arrange an apartment purchase in Panama. 'I have spoken this morning with my colleague in Panama and forwarded him a copy of Michael's credit card. The unit is now officially being held in his name,' Jason Higgs of www.luxuryhotelhomes.com confirmed to Lynn's office.

During the remainder of the summer, further advances were made for three apartments in Spain, a home in Calgary, Canada, and two apartments at the Ocean View Complex in Portland, Dorset. But the centrepiece of Lynn's extravagant purchases was to be 'Bungalow V17' in the Punta Perla resort in the Dominican Republic. The waterside bungalow boasted its own splash pool and private yacht mooring, while the wider resort promised attractions such as three signature golf courses, a casino, a heliport, four international five-star hotels, an equestrian centre, spas, beach clubs and on-site designer shopping.

With a purchase price of $1,105,000, the Punta Perla home should have given Lynn and Brid access to one of the finest golf, marina and spa resorts in the Caribbean. There is a twisted irony in the fact that the development was never finalised and has become a legal quagmire ever since, with hundreds of investors losing out.

On 10 August 2007, before flying off on holiday to Rome with Brid, Lynn made a written offer of €5.8 million to Portuguese developer Luis Ferreira in a bid to purchase an entire apartment complex in the Algarve town of Tavira. Perhaps Lynn planned to flip the development, turning a quick profit. Instead, it was Lynn's life that was about to turn upside-down. Rome would be the last holiday he would take for quite some time.

By now the end was near. Michael Lynn's precariously balanced house of cards was about to tumble spectacularly.

On 10 September, Fiona McAleenan – a solicitor working for Lynn's law firm – resigned suddenly and reported him to the Law Society. She claimed to have found irregularities involving loans from different banks pledged against the same properties.

To Lynn this felt like a betrayal – one he would never forgive. Returning from holiday in Rome two days later, he launched himself into tackling the crisis. But it was too late. The Law Society's chief investigator, accountant

Mary Devereux, arrived at Lynn's offices on 24 September. Despite attempts to lead her astray, Devereux – who had a no-nonsense reputation and years of experience ferreting out financial secrets – soon knew that something about Lynn's affairs was seriously amiss. After just five days she reported that the accounts of his legal firm were 'totally unreliable' and that there had been a free flow of funds between Lynn's law firm and his property firm, Kendar.

Deceptively and suspiciously, Lynn had been using bank drafts. Unlike personal or business cheques, bank drafts don't identify from whom or from where the money to buy them has come. Lynn took advantage of this to maintain a perilous illusion. He could buy a draft from one bank with funds borrowed from another and pay it into a third to settle a debt or fund a deposit on another property. Drafts were also obtained with money belonging to family members and clients as Lynn ran rings around the rules.

When asked to explain these transactions, he either produced what Devereux believed were forged papers, or made promises – never to be fulfilled – to deliver what she was asking for at a later date. It soon became clear that he had drawn money from clients' accounts to help finance personal transactions worth millions. Moreover, mortgage funds obtained to fund property deals in Ireland were, instead, quickly wired abroad – often to purchase overseas properties for Lynn. His assurance, given as a solicitor, that loans would be secured against the intended property assets was a devastating lie.

When the dust settled, the astonishing scale of Lynn's deception through-out 2007 became apparent. In January, he had drawn down a €1.4 million loan from Irish Nationwide, which he would top up in April by a further €4.125 million. In February, he borrowed €600,000 from Ulster Bank. In March, National Irish Bank gave him €1.33 million and Anglo Irish Bank loaned him €1.14 million. In April, Bank of Scotland advanced €3.85 million and in June Permanent TSB lent him €3.725 million. In August, ACC Bank gave him €3.78 million.

Few of these loans were secured against the properties being purchased, as Lynn had promised they would be. Instead, most of the banks, deceived by false legal undertakings from Lynn's firm, were left exposed to huge losses. On the day he received the €4.125 million from Irish Nationwide, Lynn used part of it to purchase anonymous bank drafts worth €2.45 million. No one knows what he used these drafts for. The money would never be seen again. In February 2008, just ten months later – and with Lynn now on the run – Irish Nationwide accepted the inevitable. 'We wrote off the loan and took the loss,' Killian McMahon, the bank's internal auditor, confirmed with a shrug when Lynn's case finally came to court in the spring of 2022.

In all, Lynn had drawn down €26.3 million from January to August 2007 in Ireland alone. Most of it was unsecured and would never be paid back. International banks on several continents had lent further millions.

The banks were not the only ones to suffer. To pay the deposit on Glenlion, his dream home in Howth, he had used €550,000 belonging to a client's account in his law firm. In all, Lynn's multiple loans and dishonest manoeuvres over the purchase of Glenlion saw him pocket €6.25 million.

Even Lynn's sister Anne – a one-time partner in the Crossmolina Ballad Group – saw monies belonging to her redirected. In December 2006, €250,000 was received into Anne's client account in Lynn's office. The money was intended to pay for apartments she was buying in Prague. But one day after the money was lodged, some of it was used to buy two bank drafts for €21,000 each. Investigators believe Lynn used the drafts as a deposit for a property in Dublin.

On 10 October, the Law Society acted. It secured a High Court order to freeze Lynn's Irish accounts, telling the court that money belonging to his clients was missing, that the accounts of his law firm were 'totally unreliable' and that 'acts of dishonesty' had been perpetrated with client funds.

Lynn's myriad deceptions were unravelling fast. He was as good as bust and the banks, now beginning to realise they'd been conned, wanted their money – and an explanation. In response, lawyers for Lynn assured the courts that he was prepared to cooperate fully. Lynn, they said, hoped he would be able to meet his liabilities if his properties were sold in 'an orderly way', and not in 'a fire sale'.

After Lynn absconded, the front door of his law firm was locked and sealed by the Law Society. The files and computer servers within would be needed by the authorities as they pieced together Lynn's labyrinth of deceit. The law offices, a crucial location from which one of Ireland's biggest ever thefts had been masterminded, should have been preserved as a crime scene. No one should have had access. But by the time a criminal fraud investigation got under way, crucial files and a computer server had mysteriously vanished. Someone had removed everything they could.

4

The Trail Begins

RYANAIR FLIGHT FR7032 BANKED SHARPLY TO the right and descended towards Faro. Below, the Algarve's Ria Formosa lagoon – a nature reserve of mudflats and white sandy beaches – sheltered the shoreline from the wildness of the open Atlantic beyond. Behind the lagoon's calm inner channel, dozens of tourist resorts were sprinkled with cyan blue swimming pools and luscious green golf links speckled with golden sand bunkers.

To the east – just 48 kilometres distant and close to the Spanish border – the crystal salt drying beds of the Moorish town of Tavira flashed back blinding rays of sun. A few kilometres beyond lay the village of Cabanas with its fleet of small, brightly painted fishing boats bobbing on the lagoon's inner sanctum. It was here I hoped to find a trail that would lead to Lynn.

The hunt had begun. It was 24 January 2008.

Hardly speaking, Sean Dwyer and I disembarked and pushed through the small, single terminal airport. Focused. Alert. Determined. Sean, a vegan-veg-munching-early-morning-jogger, was a veteran press photographer with the stamina and focus of a military sniper and an attitude to match.

We knew the airport itself was as good a place as any to stumble across Lynn, Brid or someone connected to them. We scanned the throng of tourist guides and drivers crowding around the arrivals doors. Nothing doing.

Same at the check-in desk for the return flight to Dublin. Retired sun-burnt golfers. Painfully Irish-looking. The odd mixed-race family with kids dividing their time between countries. Nothing more.

Time to move on.

Just to be sure, I approached the information desk. Everything is worth a shot at times like these.

'Could a Mr Michael or Brid Lynn approach the information desk,' the announcement rang out through the public address system. 'Michael or Brid Lynn to the information counter please.'

No luck. This time.

The smells of jet fuel, salt air, duty free, freshly ground coffee and rental car air freshener gave way to the dusty musk of the region's dry earth as we sped east towards Cabanas on the A22 motorway, a snake of twisted, baking asphalt running parallel to the Algarve shore. At Sean's feet his Nikon lay prepped and ready in the footwell of the passenger seat. My digital dictaphone, with new batteries and enough memory for twenty hours of recording, was tucked into a breast pocket.

A lucky break could see Lynn pop up at any moment. A flick of a record switch, a click of a camera shutter and we'd be on the next flight home. Job done.

Half an hour later, we sat silently in our car, eyes fixed on the Cabanas office of Lynn's firm Kendar. A little more than 100 metres away, staff came and went, each captured with a single shutter click of Sean's camera. Another face to memorise, another car registration added to the list. Piece by piece a picture would form.

Two weeks of blind calls to every associate of Lynn that I could trace had confirmed this was the beating heart of his operation. Locals said Lynn had just purchased a new landmark office in the town square of nearby Tavira and was in the process of moving his operations there. Some said they'd seen him there just a week earlier.

We knew Lynn maintained a villa in the hills somewhere nearby but, problematically, no one had been able to say precisely where. Finding it would have to wait. For now the focus remained here in Cabanas and on the new office in nearby Tavira where staff still dealt with his affairs on a daily basis. If he wasn't in either of the offices or nearby right now, he might be sometime soon. Someone inside knew where he was and was in contact with him. They might go to meet him at a safe house, deliver an important document, pick him up at the airport, or meet him for lunch. One way or another there were clues here. Something would give. It always does.

Within a few days we felt we had the measure of the place. Knew the marks to hit. Were familiar with the streets, exits and entrances to Tavira and Cabanas. Had learned the rat runs which locals took for shortcuts. Knew the nearest ATM, pharmacy, petrol station – any of the points everyone sooner or later has to visit.

After surprisingly little time – even just a few days – any community begins to reveal its patterns and habits. Pretty soon you can sense a place inhale and exhale to the rhythm of those who live and work there. Soon we knew which car would leave for work at a certain time, when the retired lady in the villa across the road would go for her daily walk, when the kids were let out of school, when the postman did his rounds and which men would be sitting in the seafront cafés nursing a measure of port at midday. For Sean and I, predicting these routines became a game – a way to pass the time as we took turns circulating from dawn to dusk in separate rental cars as the other watched from static vantage points, lying in wait.

Something else, though, was becoming clear. Strolling around Cabanas on foot, a nagging sixth sense told me that of all the places Lynn may have owned property, this would be his favourite.

Lynn would later confirm this hunch.

'It's nice here, isn't it? When I came out here in 2003 and I saw Cabanas I thought – this is it,' he told me.

With its sleepy white, blue and yellow tiled cottages along the lazy cobblestoned shorefront and the brightly painted wooden boats of octopus fishermen who set their pots in the lagoon beyond, Cabanas was a step back in time to a simpler age, especially in winter and spring when the tourists were absent. Just behind Lynn's Costa de Cabanas development lay endless fields of alternating olive groves and almond orchards stretching down to the water's edge, speckled here and there with whitewashed farmers' cottages that had stood there for generations. Atop a flourishing carpet of wildflowers and self-seeding herbs, the heavenly scented blossoms of ancient almond trees mixed on the warm sea breeze with the aroma of wild fennel and camomile. Inland, the blazing orange hills of burnt sienna soil were divided by pristine streams gurgling through hidden valleys where goats grazed free among orange and lemon groves, oblivious to the breathtaking view of the coastline below.

At Lynn's favourite seafood restaurant in Cabanas – the shore-front Ristorante Pedro – delicious soft goat's cheese is served with local sour bread and olives as a default starter, and the fish is carried, still dripping from the sea, direct from boat to grill. Here, life follows a more relaxed pace than in the busy resorts along most of the Algarve. Here, just as in nearby Tavira, a fugitive could very pleasantly lie low in exile almost endlessly – if he were allowed to.

It was close to 10 p.m. and Nuno Paulino was still at work at the Costa de Cabanas office. Usually, all the staff leave before six. Something unusual was going on.

Tanned and sharply dressed, with slicked, dark, greased-back hair, Paulino was Lynn's right-hand man in Portugal. Since Lynn had fled it was Paulino, a trained accountant, who appeared to be running Kendar's local operations.

Sitting in our car, alert and silent, we monitored the building from afar, afraid to pull up closer in the deserted street outside. Suddenly a jet black Audi Q7 – a make and model Lynn was known to drive – rounded the corner at speed and roared past us, setting the street ablaze with its distinctive LED headlights. It pulled up outside the Kendar office in the middle of the street, engine idling and facing away from us.

A figure appeared from the Kendar office, a stack of paperwork in his hands. Time stood still as he leaned towards the driver's window, speaking and passing documents in and out, oblivious to our presence. Some paperwork was put aside on the dashboard, but many documents were quickly torn up by the person in the Audi and handed back through the window before being stuffed roughly into plastic shopping bags.

Lynn might have been just several hundred metres away, but there was nothing we could do. A photo was impossible in the pitch-black and it was pointless trying to approach the car. I would not get a word in before it sped away.

A moment later, Paulino turned back towards the office and the Audi raced off, its distinctive red tail lights disappearing into the night.

And then it happened – fate opened up a brief opportunity and something gave. As he returned towards the office, the figure inexplicably discarded the bags of torn-up paperwork that had been passed to and fro through the car window into a pile of cardboard boxes left out for recycling. It was ours for the taking.

5

Paper Trail

ROOM 514 OF THE PORTA NOVA Hotel was a mess. Literally everything – from the floor to the twin beds and the bathroom sink – was covered with jagged strips of torn paper.

At the height of his success Michael Lynn revelled in holding fort, playing piano and singing on the rooftop bar of this Tavira hotel. Now, a couple of floors below, in my room, documents pertaining to the remnants of Lynn's property empire lay strewn across every available surface. And it all had to be sorted before the cleaners knocked on the door in the morning.

First I piled up torn pieces of paper that seemed to be from the same page in little bundles around the room before painstakingly fitting the torn edges together, piece by piece, to reveal a complete page where possible. Then each complete jigsaw was photographed whole before being disassembled and tucked away to be handed over to Fraud Squad detectives and Law Society investigators later.

The process took virtually all night but was utterly absorbing and exhilarating in equal measure as, one by one, some of Lynn's secrets began to emerge for the first time.

Since he'd fled Dublin in December, Lynn had been forbidden, by High Court order, from transferring money from his Irish accounts, and his law firm accounts were frozen. The banks, meanwhile, were seeking to trace Lynn's personal and business assets across Europe in the hope of recouping their losses before they were moved out of reach. Yet here, among the documents pieced together in my hotel room that night, was a copy of a €20,000 bank draft – dated 10 January 2008 – from Kendar Portugal to an associate of Lynn's. Clearly Lynn still had access to funds. And he was moving them.

A handwritten A4 sheet entitled 'Money Transfers 2007' detailed four bank transfers in August and September of that year. Could this be evidence of Lynn moving cash beyond reach of clients, creditors and the law? The first transfer – for €1.5 million – on 10 August, appeared to have been made from an account in Lynn's law firm containing client funds. The last transfer – of just under €500,000 – was also from the law firm's client account and seemed to have been made on 11 September, just as the Law Society was about to investigate Lynn in Dublin.

Other transfers listed involved millions going to Kendar Slovakia and a mysterious, previously unknown company called 'Caviarteria Tec' in Liechtenstein. In all, €3,966,414 had been transferred in a four-week period between August and September 2007 – €2 million of it relating to funds held in the client account of Lynn's law firm.

Just as intriguing was another handwritten document which, judging by the scrawled writing, had been penned by Lynn's own hand. 'If I could make you a million would you be interested?' it read. 'Let me show you my model.' The page appeared to detail a property-based investment scheme heavily reliant on leveraged borrowing. Was Lynn still trying to secure money from others with new hare-brained schemes even as the authorities in Ireland hunted him down? I could imagine him making the pitch to some Celtic Tiger investor who was already mortgaged to the hilt several times over.

The document cache also included recent fax reports showing outgoing faxes to Lynn's Bulgarian lawyer in Sofia and the Crowne Plaza Hotel in Bratislava in the previous weeks and days – possible clues about Lynn's movements and activities. A call to the Crowne Plaza confirmed Lynn had been there for three days in January.

There were letters and messages from concerned investors and lawyers in Ireland, who had called, emailed, faxed and written desperately seeking information about their investments. What would they think if they knew their worried correspondence had ended up unceremoniously dumped without a second thought? Should I tell them? That decision would have to wait. Like a thousand others.

There was also a post-it note with my name and mobile number, left for Paulino by a receptionist weeks before when I telephoned to speak with him. He never returned the call. At least I knew not to bother trying again.

Strip by strip, piece by piece, the documents which had been carelessly cast aside gave invaluable glimpses into Lynn's dealings as the Kendar property empire imploded.

There was a draft letter to Irish investors dated 16 October 2007, which Paulino had written two days after concerns about Lynn's affairs first became public. 'You will be aware by now of the recent press concerning Michael Lynn,' it read. 'I would like to advise you that Kendar Portugal is operating as a separate entity, with a new board of directors and a new structure. Our team here are working hard to guarantee that all aspects of Costa de Cabanas is running efficiently and that Costa de Cabanas 2 and 3 are still proceeding and will be delivered within the timeframe agreed.'

The letter, it appears, was never sent, but the new structure referred to was already in place.

One of the documents – a complex organisation chart for Lynn's business in Portugal – referred to two new anonymous companies without naming them. Astonishingly the chart appeared to reference new projects previously unheard of that were now in development.

A title page entitled 'Vantea Sales Manual' was puzzling as the rest of the manual was missing. What was Vantea and how was it linked to Lynn and Kendar? Clearly something was going on. But what?

The answer came the next day as we once again began to circulate between Lynn's planned new office in Tavira and the old office in Cabanas. Whereas the day before a sign outside the Cabanas office had borne Lynn's Kendar logo, it had now been replaced with a new logo for Vantea.

No one knew it yet – and no one had warned any investors – but Kendar Portugal was no more. Instead a new corporate structure, designed to disguise any involvement by Lynn, had been quietly implemented. This process began on 16 January, when Kendar Portugal was renamed Vantea at the office of company registration in Lisbon.

Something else had changed too. The ownership of the company had been transferred to two new companies – Nota Breve and Numero Misto – leaving Kendar Holdings with just a 2 per cent stake. The new firms had been registered in Portugal on 6 December 2007, just days before Lynn fled Ireland. The names of these new entities – translated as Brief Note and Mixed Number – seemed typical of Lynn's passion for music and sense of humour. But for now their ownership remained a mystery.

Listed at nondescript apartment addresses in a residential city 100 kilometres away, the firms now in control of the newly rebranded Kendar were completely anonymous. It was pointless to chase them down, but when I later did, the occupants of the addresses said they knew nothing. A man at the address for Nota Breve gave his name only as João and claimed he knew nothing of Lynn or the new company. He said he had rented the apartment from 1 January and did not know who the former tenant was. A woman who answered a listed number for the building's administrator hung up when asked about the firms. Staff at a nearby restaurant said they recognised photos of Lynn but had not seen him for a while.

Five steps ahead of those pursuing him, Lynn appeared to be still very much in control, although nothing could be linked back to him anymore. From now on, anyone seeking the return of their money for an apartment never delivered by Kendar had no hope. But the business and its newly secret owners clearly intended to carry on. A new website – www.vantea.com – was registered on 13 December, the day after Lynn absconded. This redirected the user to another new website – www.costadecabanas.eu – registered a month earlier. The ownership of the two sites could not be traced.

However, files from the cache discarded outside the Cabanas office revealed the intentions of those behind Kendar/Vantea. Kendar's management may have been ignoring certain calls from Ireland, but even as Lynn became the focus of investigation and suspicion in Dublin, staff were being directed to achieve sales elsewhere. In October and November 2007, Kendar signed four new real estate mediation agreements with Portuguese estate agents, who were to promote and sell the still unbuilt Costa de Cabanas stage two, where earth movers had just recently prepared the ground for new foundations.

Looking further afield, one employee had compiled a list of international property fairs throughout the coming year at which Vantea could advertise and sell units at Costa de Cabanas. Vantea was particularly interested in the Moscow International Investment Show in March 2008, for which travel and booking costs for a team of two had already been estimated. Correspondence between the show's organisers and Lynn's staff showed Kendar/Vantea sought to rent a €4,500 stand at the exhibition. A torn-up email from the Moscow organisers – sent two days after Lynn left Ireland – spelled out the advantages: 'The Russian market is now expanding fast and the Moscow International Investment Show will provide a professional platform and the most effective method to target and meet with wealthy Russian buyers.'

It was clear what was going on. Despite being on the run, Lynn had managed to remain in the real estate business selling the same properties by a different name – this time targeting wealthy Russians.

6

Lynn's Lair

'OBRIGADO,' I THANKED THE WAITRESS AS she brought a new round of espresso and freshly squeezed orange juice.

'*De nada*,' she replied with a curious glance. I could sense that she wanted to ask why I'd been sitting there all day, but she didn't. I gave her a tip – the largest so far – and she moved away almost reluctantly. We were going to have to move on soon.

Across the freshly laid cobblestone square, beyond a bubbling fountain, civil servants ambled in and out of the arches of Tavira's town hall at a quarter of the pace of those on private business. Adjacent to the municipality's headquarters, in the corner of the square, lay Lynn's new office: a three-storey stone edifice draped in green mesh. The premises had received its planning permission on 6 January and renovations appeared to be at an advanced stage.

According to local associates, Lynn himself had been spotted here in recent weeks and throughout the day I had seen Paulino and other staff from the Cabanas office coming and going with files and boxes. All we needed was for Lynn to show up and a split second later he'd be in Sean's sights as I cut across the square to confront him.

But as it was, we were almost through our second week and though we had learned a lot, we had not yet sighted Lynn. At least not in daylight.

My gut told me he was coming and going from his hilltop villa to international locations and being careful not to be seen in public. But we still had no idea where the villa was. A property search had not yielded any results and the best anyone could say was that the home was somewhere on a hilltop overlooking Tavira.

The pressure was on to produce something for Sunday's paper. If not a photo of Lynn himself, the first snap of the fugitive's sun-kissed hideaway might suffice for the front page. If only we knew where the damn thing was.

And then it hit me. Sometimes the solution is too obvious to be true. Embarrassingly so.

Directory enquiries, the phone book, I thought with a start. Perhaps Lynn was listed. Why wouldn't he be?

With us was Daniel, a local student we occasionally employed as a fixer and translator.

'Yes, Mr Michael Lynn – in Tavira,' he asked in Portuguese when directory enquiries picked up.

'*Obrigado*,' we heard him say as he scribbled down the number. 'Can you give me the address?'

Sean and I waited, hardly daring to breathe. Back home data protection rules mean directory enquiries will not provide an address under any circumstances. But a moment later I punched the air with joy and high-fived Sean as Daniel wrote down the words 'No. 3 Quinta do Perogil'.

We were there in minutes, cameras and recorders at the ready. This could be it.

The view was stunning. From the Quinta do Perogil hilltop, the old town of Tavira, with its red-tiled rooftops, was splayed out below on both sides of the glistening Gilão river. Beyond that the river cut a swathe through the lagoon, piercing the mud and sand reef, before succumbing to the open Atlantic.

Lynn's modern villa, tall, angular and glistening white, was sublime. In the immaculately kept garden, young palm trees were set among tended flowerbeds watered by automatic sprinklers. Pink flowering vines spilled forth from trellises on boundary fences. Behind the building a blue dolphin statue standing on its tail housed an outdoor shower alongside a blue-tiled swimming pool and sea-facing veranda. A swing sofa reclined in the shade beside stone pillars at the front door. On the roof a satellite dish pointed skyward, providing a vital link to Irish TV news.

However, the villa seemed empty. Every window was closed with the white, slated wooden shutters pulled shut. There was no sign of life.

Standing outside the gate I dialled the phone number and could hear the phone ringing inside the house. It was answered by the voicemail of a woman with an Irish accent. Brid.

I rang the buzzer on the gate pillar. Nothing.

Neighbours confirmed for us that Lynn had been there in recent days, but that he came and went frequently, driving his black Audi Q7. We'd missed him. This time.

The Portuguese postal system does not have the world's best record when it comes to missing mail – something I was soon to become thankful for. Every day in 2008 the Correios de Portugal delivered more than six million items and every day 2,000 or so would inexplicably go missing.

One such envelope, containing Lynn's detailed phone bill, should have been delivered to his Tavira villa. Instead, it wound up in the letter box of another Irishman with a similar-sounding surname in nearby Cabanas, who opened it before he spotted the error. Then he threw it on the sideboard in his kitchen with all the other misdelivered mail he'd received and forgot about it – until I knocked on his door. I did so blindly as I canvassed the homes of any Irish resident I could find before I flew home. Thankfully, the mistaken recipient of the phone bill, angered at the damage Lynn had done to the reputation of Irish expats in Portugal, was happy to hand it over. Some breaks are lucky, but most involve shoe-leather work like this.

We might have failed to find Lynn this time but, as a result of my latest find, this first trip had at least thrown up an insight into his first weeks in exile. Now I could see that just thirteen days after fleeing Ireland, he was calling family back home as he endured his first Christmas on the run. Lynn, it appeared, had stayed in Tavira for the entire holiday period, from Christmas Day until 1 January, making telephone calls. Selling assets. Moving money. Leaving clues for investigators.

Lynn's phone bill showed that two calls were placed on Christmas Day from his villa – one to his sister Anne, who lives in Clane, County Kildare with her husband Patrick Jordan, then the multimillionaire chief operating officer of Siteserv PLC.

'They were private calls. Don't expect a call back,' a curt and angry Mrs Jordan told me when I later phoned to query the contact with Lynn.

Like her brother, Anne was passionate about music. She'd been a member of her brother's ballad group in Mayo and now sang in local choirs. For that reason, Christmas was a particularly magical time. Usually. 2007 would be different. The tumultuous events involving Lynn were still red raw and had entirely engulfed the Lynn family.

The other Christmas Day call was to the Tulla, County Clare, home of Brid's father, Teddy.

'I am Brid's father and I have nothing to say,' was all Murphy would say when approached about the contact. His voice was firm, defiant and proud. Christmas Day is Brid's birthday.

It appears from this call that Brid was with Lynn in Portugal throughout Christmas. A two-and-a-half hour call to the mobile of a former nursing colleague on 30 December solidifies the likelihood that she spent Christmas with Lynn.

'I have nothing to say,' the St Vincent's University Hospital nurse told me when I enquired about the call.

A second call to Anne from Lynn on New Year's Eve lasted an hour. A third call was placed to her mobile. Three more calls were also placed to Teddy Murphy in the last days of the year, culminating in a New Year's Eve call, placed just minutes before midnight, that rang in 2008.

Torn between her father and her husband, a life in Ireland or a life on the run, these calls must have been tough for Brid and tougher still for her father, who would pass away within two years having been robbed of precious time with his daughter and seen his dreams for her dashed.

Whether or not Brid rang in 2008 with Lynn in Tavira, it was certainly going to be a very different year to the one she must have imagined just a few months earlier. With each errant decision that Michael Lynn made came consequences for others. Sometimes quickly, sometimes not for years, sometimes for those close to him, sometimes to those unknown. But in the end, the waves his actions set in motion always washed ashore. They continue to do so.

Meanwhile, despite the holiday period, Lynn was busy. Calls to associates in the UK, Dubai, Ireland and the Ukraine were made as he frantically sought to sell property, liquidate assets, make travel plans and hide his continuing involvement in his Portuguese development company Kendar.

'He wanted to sell some property. He had several conversations with me,' an employee of Dubai firm www.gowealthy.com, who identified himself only as Arshad, told me when I contacted him about calls he'd had from Lynn on 27 December. Interestingly, Arshad's firm also specialised in the provision of expert advice to those wishing to move assets offshore.

That same day, Lynn dialled New York's Country Bank, a small Irish-focused institution led by Bill Burke, one time St Patrick's Day parade Grand Marshal. A native of Tubbercurry in County Sligo, Burke is fond of boasting that most young Irish New Yorkers who want to set up their own business come to him for advice and loans.

'If you walked in here to this office you would probably walk out the door again in half an hour with a cheque in your hand. We are very good at it because we make quick decisions,' he once told an interviewer. Lynn's kind of bank.

Burke said he could not comment on whether or not Lynn was a customer. 'He's not a person we are looking for because I would know. I'm not too sure if the banks here are, but I couldn't even confirm or deny that if I knew.'

A third call by Lynn that December day was to the Dexania Bank in Luxembourg, an institution that featured large in the documents detailing transfers from Lynn's client account that had been carelessly discarded at his Cabanas office.

After a call to a local security company and a final thirty-three-minute call to the home of his sister Mary, the calls from Lynn's villa stopped at precisely 22.10 p.m. on 1 January 2008. He'd clearly moved on and, for now, the trail had gone cold.

7

Into the Balkans

THE STREET WAS DESERTED AND FOREBODING. Pools of struggling illumination, from lamps hung too far apart over the centre of the road, failed miserably to meet in the middle. The shadows made me nervous – so did the vacant shop fronts and overflowing bins along the pavement.

Nothing felt right. Just nothing. Not least this spot as a meeting point. The fact that this was Sofia, one of Europe's most mafia-ridden and corrupt cities, didn't help either.

'It's him,' said my fixer as a blinding pair of headlights belonging to a jet-blue Mercedes approached at speed and screeched to a halt on the other side of the road.

Recruiting fixers abroad is always a lottery. With this guy it was beginning to feel more like a game of Russian roulette.

From within the car a thumping Russian disco beat pulsated through the German bodywork and bounced around the asphalt outside. A hand – attached to a wrist bearing a gold Rolex – beckoned us forward. The fixer took the front seat, gesturing to Sean and me to sit behind.

The car jolted, wheels spinning, and cut across the street, darting between two industrial-type metal bins, into a blind alleyway before shuddering to a halt in the shadows.

What the fuck? screamed Sean's eyes as I gripped the door handle, the scent of leather seats, chewing gum and cheap aftershave in my throat.

'This is Nico,' enthused my guide. 'The good guy I told you about.'

Nico thrust his hand between the seats offering a business card. No handshake – just an indistinguishable grunt. Jet-black and glossy, the card featured a large silver Scorpion, its tail poised to strike. Underneath Nico's name was a description relating to 'security' and a Bulgarian mobile number.

As far as I could tell from behind, Nico was mid-thirties, slim but gym-toned and dark-skinned. He looked and felt every inch the greasy gangster dressed in a dark suit jacket with a black open-necked shirt underneath and tight jeans. I couldn't see his feet but, in the same way I knew he had tattoos somewhere on his body, I knew his shoes were leather-soled and pointy.

'You speak English?' I asked.

'No,' Nico replied as I watched him remove his shades and fix his eyes on me through the rear-view mirror.

'Deutsch?' he suggested, turning down the thumping disco music. The blue graphic equaliser lights on the dashboard kept dancing away in silence.

'*Nein, nur ein bißchen, es tut mir leid,*' I apologised.

The fixer took over. His instructions were to explore the feasibility of securing some CCTV footage of Lynn, who, police sources claimed, had been spotted in Bulgaria in recent days. Any further information, so long as it was legally obtained and legal to possess, would also be gladly accepted. But nothing untoward could be tolerated. We would not, under any circumstances, get involved in anything shady.

'He needs €250 now and €250 after,' said our fixer, after some animated discussion on his part and deadpan nods and monosyllabic responses from Nico.

'I think that's the price of exiting this car,' breathed Sean. I counted out five fifties knowing I'd never see Nico or the money again.

'Velcome to Sofia,' said Nico with a smile as he took the cash. 'You need woman?'

It was now June 2008, six months since Lynn had absconded. In the interim, news reports, many of them unreliable and fanciful, had him sighted everywhere from Premiership soccer matches in London to the beaches of Rio. The only confirmed sighting occurred ten days after he rang in the New Year from Portugal.

On 11 January 2008, border police at Newark airport detained and questioned Lynn as he disembarked from a flight from Lisbon. He was released and after three days disappeared again.

Lynn now faced forty-eight charges of professional malpractice, and fifty-five civil High Court cases were being taken against him. On 23 May 2008 he had been struck off the roll of solicitors.

'Mr Lynn has brought deep disgrace upon himself and disrepute on his profession through systematic abuse of the trust placed in him as a solicitor,' declared Law Society president James MacGuill.

But he was still on the run. Still moving assets and still not subject to any criminal charge. Maddeningly for those he deceived, the absence of a criminal warrant meant Lynn remained free to conduct affairs without fear of arrest so long as he stayed away from Ireland.

If the law is an ass, Lynn was riding it roughshod. Reacting to tip-offs from contacts forged in Cabanas and Tavira, Sean and I had made several frantic dashes to Portugal when Lynn was spotted in the area – always arriving too late. Lynn, ever paranoid, never stayed in one location for long, making it exceptionally difficult to catch up with him from afar.

Now it was time to do some digging in Bulgaria.

As well as Portugal, Lynn's company Kendar had offices in Sofia, on the sixth floor of the Bellissimo Centre – a landmark building on Bulgaria Boulevard. The gleaming twelve-storey edifice of reflective glass dominates the Sofia suburbs, reflecting the steep forested and snow-capped slopes of the nearby Vitosha mountain on its facade. In addition to this office, Kendar owned a ninth-floor apartment and a development land bank in the nearby Boyana district – Sofia's most exclusive neighbourhood.

From Monday 16 June we watched the office carefully, alternating our two local rental cars every couple of hours and replacing them every day to avoid suspicion. Some businessmen came and went from the building in armoured cars accompanied by armed bodyguards. Security on the building itself was also armed. Not the kind of place to be caught loitering with intent.

When it became clear that Lynn was not present, I ventured inside. Outside his locked sixth-floor office door, a pile of Kendar Bulgaria brochures was scattered on the marble floor. No one answered when I knocked. Inside all was silent and still. In the lobby downstairs a security guard recognised a photo of Lynn immediately.

'Yes, he was here Friday,' he said. 'Not since.'

We'd missed him by forty-eight hours. Again.

8

The Web Thickens

THE MCCARTHY-DUNDON CRIME GANG FROM Limerick consider themselves pretty tough. And they are. In 2007 they could hold their own against anyone in their own stomping grounds. And that's saying something. Limerick's murder rate that year, seven homicides per hundred thousand residents, saw Forbes Magazine describe the city as the 'murder capital of Europe'.

But in the port city of Varna, on Bulgaria's Black Sea coast, only one thing happens when you flash thick wads of dollars when you've come to a gun range for weapons training.

And so it was. The Irish gang members soon found themselves at the wrong end of a gun barrel and liberated from their cash, watches, mobile phones and a sizeable chunk of gangster ego. That was September 2007.

Now, it was our turn to sample the edginess of Varna, a city where it was rumoured Lynn had planned a beach-front resort.

Strategically positioned between the Balkans, Russia and Western Europe, Varna is a hub of criminal activity sandwiched amid an arching seafront dominated by freight cranes and marine activity. It is also the nerve centre of a burgeoning underground tobacco, drug, car and people-smuggling network run by competing gangs of Chechen, Russian and Bulgarian mobsters. Many of the criminal outfits in Varna count past members of various Special Forces and State agencies from the former USSR among their numbers. People who get the job done. No questions asked.

Whatever Lynn was up to here, it was sure to prove interesting. More interesting, in fact, than we could ever have imagined.

'You want him disappeared?' The former detective gestured casually, cocking a chubby index finger to his temple.

Beside him his three colleagues – also former members of the Bulgarian Murder Bureau – remained motionless. On the table, seven glasses of Kamenitza beer fizzed into the summer sunshine. Time stood still.

'No, no,' I nearly choked on my drink. 'We want to talk to him, take his photo.'

The detectives look bemused and disappointed. Even more so when we declined to pay anything upfront and insisted no laws be broken. This time – having learned from the meeting with Nico in Sofia – the encounter would only cost the price of a round of drinks.

Absurdly, this face-to-face had come about precisely because of my desire to avoid scenarios like the one in Sofia – yet Bulgaria kept delivering them.

Arriving in Varna, I'd overruled our fixer's hare-brained preferences and insisted on going straight to police HQ to file an official request for information about Lynn. In a city with near daily gunfights, I wanted to declare my presence and intentions rather than risk being mistaken as something other than a journalist.

We found the chain-smoking press officer for the police in a dimly lit basement room beneath the headquarters. A white desk fan swung slowly from side to side, glowing up the ember of her cigarette and scattering ash across the table. Somewhere behind her, a police radio crackled and beeped, bringing life on the streets into the room in bursts of urgent static.

Our fixer spoke. She listened and nodded, occasionally smiling at Sean and me as if to keep us in the loop. We smiled back. They might as well have been sharing recipes for blackberry jam for all we knew. It would have been more productive.

Three hours later, at the third of a series of hatches – before which came a maddening sequence of queuing for official stamps and authorisations – our written request was accepted with a grunt and a promise of a response in two weeks.

That was the official route. Officially we're still waiting for an answer.

Unofficially, we found ourselves quickly talked into buying drinks for ex-police officers available for hire, whose services we politely declined. As always, it was old-fashioned shoe leather, tyre rubber, door-knocking, document-searching and question-asking on our part that got the job done.

We started asking those questions at Shkorpilovtsi, located just off the E87 coastal highway, twenty minutes' drive south of Varna. This was where we'd heard Lynn had planned his resort. Nothing of that plan had ever been made public in Ireland.

Shkorpilovtsi is a protected nature reserve featuring ancient rolling forests along one side of a low-lying valley pierced by the almost chocolate-brown Kamchia river as it empties into the sea. At the shore, a lone, ramshackle beach bar of wrapped cane windbreakers and sun umbrellas was empty. The barman, who looked as if he slept behind the counter, was wary.

'An Irish guy? Kendar? Resort here? … Couldn't say. Not sure.' Each utterance delivered with a shrug.

Across the road, three workmen were preparing a boundary wall at a vacant property. As we began to ask questions of them, the atmosphere suddenly bristled with tension. A phone call was made. Our fixer looked nervous.

A BMW with blacked-out windows appeared. The suited occupant listened. Sized us up. Decided we weren't worth his time and drove off in a cloud of dust.

I peeled off my shoes and socks and ambled down to the water's edge, the warm sand between my toes. Staring intently towards the horizon, knee-deep in salt water, I mulled it all over. What was there to do? What had Lynn planned here? Where the hell was he? What could this place tell me about him?

The coast was abandoned as far as the eye could see in each direction. To the south, the sand petered out into rocks and crumbling cliffs. To the north, a wide arc of sand dunes was wedged between the shore and the rising slopes of the nature reserve's forest. Beside me a crumbling concrete frame of an abandoned pier stretched far out into the deep water – a one-time dock for ships, it seemed. Today its only occupants were a fisherman, with a rod and bucket by his side, and his two boys.

'Communista holiday platz,' he said, gesturing towards the dunes and trees when I asked about the location. We fishermen can always communicate, whatever the language. What he was trying to explain was that this place – the last stretch of undeveloped Black Sea beachfront in Bulgaria – was once a famed Communist Party holiday camp for teenagers from throughout the Soviet Bloc.

'Kaput.' He gestured breaking an imaginary stick with his hands.

'Communista system kaput,' I agreed.

'Bulgaria kaput,' he shot back. 'Mafia. Everything Mafia. No good.'

Soon after, we chased down the property deeds. Shkorpilovtsi – or at least vast tracts of it on one side of the Kamchia river – was owned by Lynn. And he had some interesting neighbours. The other side of the river mouth was being developed by the then Mayor of Moscow, Yury Luzhkov, and his billionaire wife Yelena Baturina – Russia's richest woman. 'Little Moscow' locals called it.

Michael Lynn and the Mayor of Moscow side by side on the shores of the Black Sea. There's a saying in Bulgaria that all countries have a mafia – but only in Bulgaria does the mafia have a country. How on earth had a country boy from rural Ireland wound up in this place? And what had he done to get here?

Lynn had planned a massive development called Longosa Beach in Shkorpilovtsi – by far his biggest and most ambitious project. There were to be 1,000 apartments in eleven building complexes, hotels, restaurants, bars, swimming pools, state-of-the-art gyms, a cinema and a supermarket. Had it been completed, Longosa Beach would have realised a €50 million profit for his Kendar company. The site alone, with planning permission and building permits, was worth more than €19 million.

But it had already been sold.

Just as in Portugal, Lynn had moved quickly. His Bulgarian assets had already been secured or cashed in and hidden behind a web of new offshore firms. Lynn's local firm – Kendar Bulgaria – was no more. Like its Portuguese counterpart, it, too, had been quietly given a new name – GLS Property Bulgaria – on 4 April, just eight weeks before our visit. GLS Property Bulgaria in turn was fully owned by another company, S and A Services – an offshore company recently registered in Panama and designed to keep its owners' identities secret.

As ever, Lynn was streets ahead of the authorities, his assets vaporising into thin air like steam from a kettle. GLS Property Bulgaria had already sold one of Lynn's developments to a newly established Sofia firm called Vagner Bulgaria, which in turn was fully owned by an anonymous company of the same name in the tropical islands of the Seychelles. This sale, which had just been completed, involved the development site in Bansko, which Lynn had publicised with his brazen *Late Late Show* apartment giveaway. It was worth €7.2 million.

The Black Sea land had been sold just three weeks previously. This time the buyer was Boyana Estates, another new firm with an address in Sofia. It, too, was owned by an anonymous offshore firm, this time in Cyprus, called Caviarteria Technologies. Just months earlier, I'd recovered evidence in the papers discarded at Lynn's headquarters in Cabanas of millions being transferred to a 'Caviarteria Tec'.

Mayor Borislav Natov's mouth dropped open in astonishment. Somehow the word 'gobsmacked' seemed to have been invented specifically for his face at that very moment. No one had told him Kendar was no more. He had absolutely no idea Michael Lynn was on the run and that his lands at Shkorpilovtsi had just been mysteriously sold offshore.

Flustered, he rose from his desk and began heaping thick folders on a table from a filing cabinet, opening out maps and technical drawings of building after building – the entire case file for Lynn's Black Sea resort. As Mayor of Shkorpilovtsi, Natov saw these plans as the key to finally opening up his impoverished rural community to the tourism income enjoyed by the rest of Bulgaria's Black Sea resorts.

'They came to us and they asked us to speed up the procedure for changing the land from agricultural land,' he said. 'Kendar made a donation and helped to repair the church in the town, so we did this for them. They received their construction permits in the autumn of 2007. We are just waiting for it to begin – we were sure it was a serious investment.'

A day later and 700 kilometres away, the Mayor of Bansko, Alexander Kravarov, was similarly shocked at the news that Lynn's planned mountain resort had been sold: 'This Kendar company has been smearing Bansko's reputation as a location for investment. We want real investors here, not fraudsters. I hadn't realised he has sold up. That's news to me.'

It would be news, too, for the hundreds of Irish people who had paid Lynn tens of thousands for their Bansko apartments. Fearing the worst, Lynn's customers had pinned their diminishing hopes on promissory notes issued by Kendar Bulgaria in January.

'We at Kendar Bulgaria apologise for the delay in providing you with the most current information about your investment in Bulgaria,' read the 23 January email with the promissory notes attached. 'Following recent publicity surrounding Michael Lynn in Ireland, we at Kendar Bulgaria wish to distance ourselves from these events. Kendar Bulgaria Ltd is working in a full capacity with regards to the project Bansko All Seasons resort in Bulgaria. The construction has started and is proceeding as planned.'

Heading back to Sofia, I sought out Kendar's Bansko site. Against the treeline, a huge Kendar billboard, yellowed by the sun, still advertised the 'final release' of 333 units. The phone number on the sign had long since been disconnected. A thick blanket of tall weeds had begun repopulating earth once stripped in preparation for building. The place was as empty as Michael Lynn's word.

9

An Ominous Meeting

It's 2.30 a.m. in Sofia. There's a rustling outside my hotel room and a white envelope slides beneath the door. Inside is a handwritten message in blue biro on a neatly folded sheet of A4 paper. 'KENDAR – info. 8pm 28/06/2008. LOBBY BAR – PRINCESS HOTEL' is all it says.

Through the peephole I can see nothing.

I call through to reception. 'Did you deliver a note to my door just now?'

'No sir.'

I sit on the bed, mind racing. The previous day we'd visited the offices of Legacom, a Sofia law firm where GLS Property Bulgaria – formally Kendar Bulgaria – is registered. A Legacom solicitor – Julian Todorov – was listed as a manager of GLS, so we figured there was a chance Lynn may show up if Legacom was assisting with his affairs. The listed addresses of the other new companies that had just bought Lynn's Bulgarian developments in Bansko and Shkorpilovtsi had proved to be fake.

'I'd like to speak to Julian Todorov,' I told the receptionist at Legacom.

'I'm afraid he's busy. Do you have an appointment?'

'No. Here's my card. I believe he can tell me about GLS Property Bulgaria.'

'GLS?'

'Yes it's the new company of Michael Lynn. It used to be called Kendar. It's registered at this address. I'd like to ask about the recent sale of its assets.'

The receptionist left to speak in hushed tones to an unseen person in a side office and returned.

'I'm afraid Mr Todorov is in a meeting now.'

'That's okay. I'll wait.'

'It may last all day.'

'I'm a patient man. I'll wait all day if I have to and come back tomorrow,' I smiled, sitting down on the leather couch in reception.

Todorov never appeared. I was politely asked to leave as the office closed for the day.

Now, just hours later, a note had appeared under my hotel-room door. What bothered me most was that I hadn't told anyone where I was staying.

I choose a table close to reception and wait.

Passing through the hotel's revolving glass doors he picks me out immediately and strides quickly across the polished marble floor.

A firm but friendly handshake. Purposeful eye contact. His name is Peter. No surname asked for or given.

'Let's go out, I know a good place nearby,' Peter suggests, gesturing towards the darkened street outside. I can see two policeman chatting with taxi men, the bright neon lights of the hotel's casino reflected on the metallic paint of their squad car.

'Let's not. I'd prefer to stay here, if you don't mind. Drink?'

'No – not on duty,' he says, ordering a beer.

In his early thirties, Peter is trim and fit with a rash of dark stubble, slicked-back hair and the same dress sense as all those swooshing around this city in dark-windowed BMWs and luxury jeeps: slim-fit jeans, pointy leather shoes, expensive open-neck shirt, gold chain, black, single-breasted jacket, designer watch and silver money clip. Confidence and cockiness ooze from his pores.

I can't tell whether or not he is armed under the jacket, though I think not.

'You're interested in Kendar?' he opens. His English is flawless.

'I'm interested in Michael Lynn.'

'So are we. Maybe we could help each other.'

'Maybe. But who's "we"?' I ask. The answer is not what I expect.

'I work for DANS – the Bulgarian Secret Service.'[1]

Over his shoulder I see Sean order a coffee and open a newspaper at a table in the corner. Wherever this is going, I'm glad he has my back. All I know about the Bulgarian Secret Service is that in 1978 they had famously assassinated dissident Georgi Markov on a London street using a ricin pellet delivered via a specially engineered umbrella.

'Can I see your ID?' I ask.

'I can't do that. This is an unofficial meeting. My bosses are powerful people with powerful friends – friends in Moscow who have asked for help. Nothing we talk about is official. This meeting did not happen.'

A pause. He fixes me with his stare. I nod and take a deep breath. Where the hell is this going?

'We'd like to find Anthony Cantwell,' he says, pausing again to gauge my reaction.

I knew the name but little more. Cantwell was a relative newcomer to the Kendar family, yet he'd quickly become Lynn's right-hand man in Eastern Europe. Lynn had even signed over power of attorney to Cantwell, giving him complete control of certain assets and firms. I had one such document, with an Irish address for Cantwell, in my room upstairs.

'I've come across him,' I reply, 'but my main interest is finding Michael Lynn.'

'That's not a problem. We can find Lynn like this,' Peter says, clicking his fingers like a magician.

---

1   Formed in January 2008 – just a few months before my meeting with Peter – DANS is an amalgamation and modernisation of three former Soviet-era Bulgarian security agencies and is responsible for national security in Bulgaria. In 2009, the agency was engulfed in controversy when it emerged it had, almost from its inception, launched a secret spying operation on prominent journalists. Named 'Galeria', the operation was illegal because it had not been instigated in response to any particular national security threat. As part of Operation Galeria, agents monitored the lives of journalists, wiretapped their phones and occasionally spoke with them in order to 'dissuade' the publication of certain stories.

I wondered if 'we' could make people disappear just as easily.

'Can I ask why these Russians want Mr Cantwell?' I venture. 'Is it connected to the asset sales and transfers that have been taking place? Cantwell had power of attorney for Lynn, didn't he?'

'Let's say he owes my bosses' friends a lot of money. I mean a lot,' comes the response. 'He sold a promissory note and walked away with a suitcase of money. It was a double-cross, a trick. The money is gone. People are angry. Important people.'

He names two other Lynn associates also involved – both Irish citizens of whom I'm unaware – but Cantwell is clearly his main focus.

I speak vaguely about Cantwell. Try to play coy rather than dumb – which is far closer to the truth. In turn, he gives nothing away about Lynn, other than his capacity to find him in an instant if he so wishes. We reach a tacit agreement to keep in touch to our possible mutual benefit. He provides an email address for that purpose.

Business done we both relax – a little – and over a few more beers begin to chat about our respective jobs. To convince me of his authenticity, he speaks enough about the bureaucracy he has to deal with and the challenges he's faced in investigations. From the way he speaks, his background is clearly in financial fraud. His office is under pressure to show the EU, which Bulgaria has just joined, that corruption can be eliminated. We both ignore the fact that his presence here likely runs counter to that task.

We both speak of work we have been proud of and cases lost. There is common ground to be found. Shit happens, to journalists and spooks alike. Frustration is universal. Griping about it a good cure. There's something about him I like – a calmness, a secure presence, a geniality, the way he clearly loves his country.

But I'm left in little doubt that if found, Anthony Cantwell will be killed.

10

Snake in the Midst

THE RUSSIANS WEREN'T THE ONLY ONES seeking Anthony Cantwell. The US Marshals Service, responsible for apprehending American fugitives across the globe, were trying to find him too. Only they knew him by his real name: James Patrick Holcomb.

Once an award-winning weatherman for western Pennsylvania's WJAC-TV, Holcomb was a married father of three. He was also several other things. A veteran of the US Navy, he'd attended the University of Maryland, the Naval Meteorology School and the University of Tennessee. He was a crook too. And a paedophile. And now, astonishingly, he was a fugitive living under an assumed identity who had inserted himself into the very heart of Michael Lynn's empire.

Born 7 December 1965, Holcomb was a native of Fayette County, West Virginia, where he began his TV career on the local station WOAY-TV. On air, where he used the name Jay Patrick, he fit the role perfectly. Bespoke-suited, square-jawed, neatly cropped hairdo, steady confident air, a quip to sign off and a killer smile to fade.

But off screen Holcomb had a dark side. In 2004, he pleaded no contest to a felony charge of aggravated indecent assault and two misdemeanour counts of indecent assault and indecent exposure. The victim told police the abuse had started in 2000 when she was four and continued until April 2003.

Placed under house arrest, with an electronic ankle bracelet monitoring his every move, Holcomb worked at the Upper Yoder Township nursery while he awaited sentencing. On the day he was to be sentenced – 25 September

2005 – he disappeared. So, too, did a chequebook belonging to the nursery. On the run, Holcomb would forge and cash cheques worth $7,547 from this to fund his escape. The only trace he left behind at the nursery was a busted ankle bracelet. He was now officially a fugitive.

Immediately federal agents from the US Marshals Service began to chase down leads across the US. Soon they extended their search to Asia and Europe. But Holcomb – like Lynn – was streets ahead of the law. By November 2006, he'd somehow made it to Ireland – thanks possibly to a desperate internet post left on a forum used by adoptees and their mothers.

In 1999, Noreen Drake Stoker, the mother of the real Anthony Cantwell, had posted a heartfelt plea online: 'Anthony you have always been on my mind. If you are out there I want you to know that I made the best decision I could have made at the time only with your future happiness in mind. I hope it has worked out that way. Please get in touch if you feel this is right for you. You will always have a special place in my heart.' The message added that Anthony Joseph Cantwell had been born in Dublin in June 1966, with the adoption papers signed in the UK.

The fate of that child is unknown. But a new Irish passport – number PT0087252 – was issued in his name on 16 November 2006 in Dublin. Holcomb was now Cantwell, an Irish citizen with an address in Dún Laoghaire – a wealthy suburb of Ireland's capital. If anyone had checked, they would have realised the address was that of a temporary hostel for travelling students.

With his new identity, Holcomb was hired as a sales manager by Kendar in 2007. Inexplicably, Michael Lynn would soon hand him power of attorney for all of Kendar's affairs in Hungary and Bulgaria. Later, he would prove anxious to distance himself from Holcomb, telling his lawyers to issue a statement saying he'd played no role in hiring him.

'We didn't know that Cantwell was not Cantwell. He had power of attorney and he misused this and sold some of the properties and took money from bank accounts,' Lynn's Hungarian lawyer Zoltan Kristian said.

Holcomb's time ran out in March 2009. Acting on a tip-off, Federal Marshals apprehended him in the Ukrainian capital Kyiv. He had gone back to his roots and was starting a new weather channel there – a project he'd been associated with before he went on the run. He'd married again too and, at the time of his arrest, was expecting a child with his new wife. Like Lynn, he'd see his child born from behind bars.

'I wanted to make some money and come back to fight the [sex-abuse] case,' Holcomb told reporters when he was returned home to the US. 'I kind of fell in love with it there,' he said of Kyiv.

But he hadn't bargained on the determination of the US Marshals Service.

'It's important for the public to know that when a defendant with charges such as these flees, all efforts are made to take the person back into custody and bring that person to justice,' said District Attorney Patrick Kiniry. 'This is an example of how defendants who run from the law are never forgotten about in the system. Although the wheels of justice sometimes move slowly, they do turn. Justice delayed is not necessarily justice denied.'

Holcomb was sentenced in September 2009 to four to ten years for sexual abuse, forging cheques and fleeing the country. He was also ordered to undergo mandatory treatment and endure a lifetime of registration as a sexually violent predator under America's Megan's Law. The court heard that because of the victim's young age when the abuse took place – and because it continued over an extended time – Holcomb met the definition of a paedophile. Psychologist William Allenbaugh also told the court that Holcomb had shown traits of being a pathological liar. Holcomb told him, 'Before, I had an image to uphold. I'm better now. Lying was the easiest road to travel.'

Holcomb was paroled from prison in the summer of 2013. Shortly afterwards, on 23 August, he was dead. Found at home in Fayette County, he appeared to have taken his own life. Soon afterwards the death was confirmed to local reporters by the local sheriff's department. However, the department does not release details of suicides, so the precise circumstances of how Holcomb died remain unknown. I had to wonder, had the Russians finally caught up with Anthony Cantwell? We will never know.

Michael Lynn, though, was still on the run.

11

Chasing Shadows

It's MORNING RUSH HOUR AT THE junction of Budapest's Grand Boulevard and Andrássy Avenue. A warning bell sounds. Tram number 4 – a long yellow tube heaving with humanity – slides to a halt. Passengers extract themselves from the vehicle, rushing to beat the sharp, electric buzzer as the doors snap shut.

On each corner of the intersection, steel-rimmed steps lead down to the city's Millennium metro line. Warm air is sucked in and exhaled out to the rhythm of arriving and departing trains below. This is Oktogon, one of the busiest transport hubs in Budapest, so named because of its eight-sided design.

On one of those sides, above a bio food store and a cheap wristwatch shop is Michael Lynn's Hungarian hideaway – a luxury fourth-floor apartment recently renovated by a local tradesman to Brid's taste. The apartment is accessed through an arched doorway leading to an internal courtyard ringed on each floor by a thin, wrap-around balcony with intricate wrought-iron rails.

A few doors away, on the corner, a Subway sandwich franchise does a busy trade. Outside, a small wooden plinth with flimsy chairs and tables, offers a view in every direction. This is where Sean and I sat scanning the crowds for a face long burned into our retinas.

It was 10 September 2008 – a quiet news week – and as good a time as any to see if we could catch Lynn off guard with an impromptu trip to one of his bases. We'd been seeking him now for eight months solid. Soon there'd be no lack of news back home. Soon things would change utterly. But for now, with no sign of Lynn in Budapest, we flew back home not knowing the world was just about to change.

A day later, in New York, a chief financial officer by the name of Ian T. Lowitt signed his name at the base of a three-page document and tried to comprehend the scale of what was about to happen. On the morning of 15 September that piece of paper – a Chapter 11 petition for bankruptcy protection in the name of Lehman Brothers Inc. – was filed at the offices of the United States Bankruptcy Court Southern District of New York. The Lehmans' bankruptcy remains to this day the largest ever corporate collapse.

Within weeks, the ensuing tidal wave washed ashore in Ireland. In the dead of night a panicked and hopelessly unprepared government scrambled. By morning on 30 September, Ireland's banks had been guaranteed by the taxpayer. The die had been cast.

Now, for sure, the Celtic Tiger party was over. The rules had just changed. It was time to suffer the hangover. It was time to pay the price. Now every citizen of Ireland would pay back the loans Lynn and others left behind.

'He's here right now,' the voice of a trusted source breathed down the line. 'Clear as day it's him. You gotta get over. Now!'

By the autumn of 2008 we had developed a good network of sources in each jurisdiction where Lynn was active and we received frequent reports of sightings. It was getting there fast enough to confront him that was the problem. Sometimes we'd flown to one country only to receive word of a sighting in another upon landing. We were always at least twenty-four hours behind him.

In September 2008 we'd dashed to Portugal on receipt of a tip-off that Lynn was dining in a village restaurant with the Mayor of Tavira. And he was. We'd arrived the next day, only to receive a photo from an Irish tourist in Budapest of Lynn shopping with Brid. He had spotted the couple on the corner of Oktogon and followed them. Dressed in an oatmeal linen suit, with sunglasses perched on his head, Lynn had bought sun cream in a pharmacy and a carton of milk in a twenty-four-hour convenience store around the corner from his apartment. 'Mike!' the tourist had called out, at which a startled Lynn scurried away with his wife. A photo snatched from behind clearly showed Lynn and Brid, who was clutching the same distinctive handbag she had held when accompanying her husband to court in Ireland, before he chose a different path.

That time, instead of blazing off to Budapest to chase down the sighting, we'd stood down and flown home. Lynn would not have hung around Budapest in the wake of being approached, especially since we'd published the photo. Once disturbed, a pool is best left alone to be fished another day.

There were other considerations too. For close to a year Lynn had been the central villain of Ireland's failing fortunes, a poster boy for the boom whose true colours had been exposed. But now, interest in Lynn was dwarfed by an astonishing flow of shocking revelations and events as Ireland's economy spiralled out of control in the wake of the Lehman Brothers collapse.

On 19 December 2008, Anglo Irish Bank's chief executive, Seán Fitz-Patrick, resigned after admitting he had concealed from shareholders a total of €87 million in personal loans by temporarily transferring them to a rival bank. He'd done this each year just before publication of Anglo's annual report, in which he was legally obliged to disclose his borrowings to shareholders. Revelations were emerging about a golden circle of prominent businessmen who had participated in a desperate Anglo scheme designed to hide the fact that Ireland's richest man – Sean Quinn – had gambled disastrously by assembling a secret 28 per cent stake in the bank.

On 21 December, Ireland's Minister for Finance, Brian Lenihan, announced the government would recapitalise Ireland's three main banks – Allied Irish Bank, Bank of Ireland and Anglo Irish Bank. But for Anglo, recapitalisation was not enough. On 15 January 2009, the entire bank was taken into State ownership. Other banks, such as Irish Nationwide, would follow.

The casualties and calamities just kept on coming. In the opening weeks of 2009, virtually all of Ireland's banking CEOs – and the Financial Regulator, Patrick Neary – would resign. And each and every step of the way, the risks those in business and banking had taken were socialised. Their debts became everyone's debts.

The enfolding drama saw Ireland's Fraud Squad – at that point a team of no more than a dozen under-resourced officers – besieged with new priorities. Scandal after scandal swamped police with new financial investigations, all of them politically pertinent. However important any investigation into Lynn might have been beforehand, it was now firmly mothballed. Interpol blue notice alerts – resulting in routine notifications to the Irish police of Lynn's comings and goings across international borders – still trickled through to detectives in Dublin. But no one paid much attention.

I swung onto the motorway towards Dublin Airport and floored the accelerator. Minutes beforehand the latest tip-off had come through. The hunt had resumed.

Lynn might not have been a priority for the authorities just then, but for us he remained a target. After more than a year on the run, he was gaining confidence, secure in the knowledge that the focus of the Irish authorities was elsewhere. Increasingly he was getting brave – cocky, even – and taking less care not to be seen.

Privately, as he would reveal to me later, he was scoffing at the mayhem back home, using it to realign his battered self-belief. It wasn't just him who'd erred. Everyone was at it. He'd been one horse among a stampede at the trough. Now the world might see that he wasn't so bad after all.

If only. If only he hadn't run. If only he'd allowed himself to be checked in the one time he was about to seek help – a dazed and emotional wreck in the foyer of a Dublin mental hospital days before vacating his homeland. But he hadn't been ready for that and all the self-awareness and honesty to which it would have led. Yes, he had participated in the feeding frenzy. But he'd done more than that. And he couldn't face the world knowing that. So he ran.

And here we were again, rushing to get in front of him.

Or not.

'I know you won't want to hear this,' my editor, Sebastian Hamilton, began. He'd called my mobile as I hurtled towards the airport. There were to be no more frantic dashes abroad. We'd spent enough time and blown our expenses budget far into orbit. It was over.

I pulled off the motorway and parked, the thrill of adrenaline quickly subsiding as a vacuous downer took its place. We had failed.

A text beeped through to my phone. It was Sebastian again. 'Listen I know how much you've put into this and I'm sorry to have had to call it off. If we can say for certain where Lynn is going to be at some point we can go. But only then. We need cast-iron certainty. No more chasing shadows.'

12

Last Chance

THE ROAR FROM THE CROKE PARK stadium crowd was deafening. Irish captain, Brian O'Driscoll, had just broken through the French defence, sidestepped two tackles and scored a try that would go down in history as one the best of his career. The date: Sunday, 7 February 2009.

In Beckett's Irish bar, on the corner of Budapest's Bajcsy-Zsilinszky street, Michael Lynn felt good. With a half-empty pint in his hand, he leaned against the bar counter beaming at the game on a large TV in the corner. He watched the scoreboard update: Ireland 18–France 10, with forty-three minutes on the clock. Perfect.

Not long ago he'd have watched the match from a tax-deductible corporate box in the stadium. In 2007, Kendar had spent €35,000 on such hospitality – including €4,245 for a Croke Park game between Ireland and England. But those days were over. Still, it felt good to be Irish in an Irish bar watching an Irish team. Better still, that life seemed to be slowly returning to normal and that no one seemed to notice him at all.

Except they did. With the lights dimmed in the lounge, Lynn, busy socialising with Brid and some friends, failed to notice the figure on the balcony above him taking photos. Two days later those images, dark and grainy but unmistakably of Lynn, were offered to us via an intermediary. They'd be perfect for Sunday's paper. Fugitive Michael Lynn enjoying the match with a pint as the economy back home imploded – that was always going to be newsworthy.

For many though, it was more than just news. Behind each stark headline were real families suffering devastating consequences as a result of Lynn's actions. They could not leave their troubles behind as he had done. On 9 February 2009 – two days after Lynn was seen enjoying himself in Budapest – one such family went before the High Court in Dublin.

The young family, whose identity the court protected, had bought their home from Lynn in December 2005 and paid for the €500,000 property by taking out a new mortgage. They didn't know Michael Lynn was the owner. They didn't even know who Michael Lynn was, or that he'd undertaken to lodge the proceeds of the sale with Bank of Scotland to clear his own mortgage on the home. But he never did so and now the bank – also a victim of Lynn's deceit – was applying to repossess the home.

The family had never missed any of their mortgage repayments. They'd done nothing wrong. Like all of Lynn's victims they'd been secretly and silently robbed. 'He mightn't have used a gun,' the head of the family said of Lynn, 'but he still took my money.'

The following month, Ms Justice Elizabeth Dunne would grant a repossession order, with a six-month stay, in favour of Bank of Scotland. 'Notwithstanding my very, very great sympathy for the defendant, I must abide by the law,' she said.

The family, who still faced paying their own monthly mortgage repayments back for decades for a house they were being kicked out of, could hardly comprehend how they'd wound up here. But they knew exactly what it would mean.

'The judge didn't have a choice but to hand the property over to the Bank of Scotland,' the father said. 'But I'm going to be homeless in six months.'

On a nationwide level the news was just as grim. Two days later – on 11 February 2009 – a stony-faced Brian Lenihan addressed the nation, imparting yet more bad news. Recapitalising the country's two largest banks – Allied Irish Bank and Bank of Ireland – was now going to cost tax-payers €3.5 billion for each institution.

With each passing day, Michael Lynn felt more comfortable – and became less cautious. Therapy helped. Especially since the counsellor he attended in the Algarve allowed him to speak without fear of judgement. The support of his wife and family was also vital.

'I have seen my family,' he'd later tell me. 'My own family have been so loyal and that's something that I appreciate hugely from them and it can't be easy for them either.'

In its own way, the increasingly calamitous news back home helped too. No one viewed the collapse of Ireland's banking system with as much fervour as Michael Lynn. Each new bailout, each new banking scandal and every new appalling twist in Ireland's unfolding economic Armageddon meant something different to Lynn than to most people.

'The place is fucked,' he'd later tell me, as a generation's wealth poured away like blood on the streets, each drop diluting his own sense of guilt. With others now firmly established as public enemy number one – Lynn could sit back almost forgotten and watch with interest from afar.

True, his actions had exiled him from the country he loved most – and he missed Ireland painfully. That longing was evidenced by the Mayo GAA flags kept locked up among his most important files, and the ballads he'd find himself humming as he walked the salt marshes of Tavira like he'd once walked the shores of Lough Conn near his birthplace. But it was easy enough for friends and relatives to nip over for flying visits to Portugal. And anyone who rented a room in the little B&B across the street from Vantea's Tavira office – as we had routinely done before being stood down – could sit in the first-floor windows and watch them come and go.

From that uncomfortable perch I'd once seen Lynn's mother, Angela, and a female companion slip out into the main square. They'd ambled across the warm cobbles, over an ancient, arched pedestrian bridge, then through a narrow passage beneath an archway to the left. Beyond the archway, overlooking the gurgling waters of the Gilão river, the Black Anchor – Tavira's Irish pub and restaurant – was located. Lynn, lying low, never went there, but no one would recognise his mother.

From a bench outside the building's facade, beneath an open porthole window, I could easily hear the conversation inside. 'Will you have a cup of tea?' Mrs Lynn was being asked by her companion as the barman greeted the pair. But Lynn was in the news that day and a copy of the *Irish Independent*, with his face on the front page, lay on the counter. Worse – the six o'clock TV news from Ireland was being beamed from a flat-screen in the corner. And it, too, featured Lynn.

'Some bollox,' said an out-of-town punter at the bar, blissfully unaware of the identity of those present. 'He's living it up anyhow – wherever the feck he is. There's a lot of fellas would love to know where that cowboy got to.'

Angela Lynn never got her cup of tea that day. Instead she left, hurrying off towards a nearby taxi rank to hail a cab. I watched her pass directly in front of me as she exited the bar, unsettled and upset. I marvelled at how close to Lynn I could get, yet have no chance of actually meeting him. And I could only guess what a mother would feel hearing her son spoken of in those terms everywhere she went. I could also only wonder about Lynn's motivation and how he thought the shame he had brought on his family was worth the price they were paying.

It was Lynn himself who set in train the events that would soon allow me to ask him myself. Not only was he beginning to feel comfortable enough to attend matches in Irish bars in Budapest, but he was back openly dealing with matters at the Costa de Cabanas resort in the Algarve – despite having gone to great lengths to ensure his continued involvement would remain untraceable.

One such matter involved plot 10, the pool and bar area in the corner of the resort. Those lucky enough to have bought one of the development's completed apartments from Kendar believed the use of the pool area came with the deal. Not so, Lynn now insisted, as he told the resident's management committee they would have to pay €40,000 to ensure access to the pool. The dispute meant both sides would have to meet face to face. And when that happened, we'd know where Lynn would be for sure. No more chasing shadows. No more second-guessing.

It happened mid-afternoon on Thursday, 12 February 2009. Finally, the call came through.

'He's meeting us at 10.30 a.m. tomorrow,' the voice of a trusted committee member breathed down the line. 'Vila Galé Hotel, Tavira. You've got to get over now.'

I knew the place well – had stayed there half a dozen times by now. Just off Tavira's town centre and built around a splendid open pool, the hotel had just one entrance and would be easy to watch. Anyone arriving there would be a sitting duck. If we could just get there on time.

The timing could not have been worse. Since 1 February, Ireland and the UK had been besieged by the largest snowstorm in decades. Airports were repeatedly shutting down. Dublin and London were at a standstill and the tip-off had come too late for all direct flights to Faro from Ireland that day.

Not sure how we'd make it to Tavira on time, I headed straight for Dublin Airport, calling Claire Hyland in the office en route.

'Claire, I'll be at the airport in thirty minutes – Sean too – we've got to get to Faro any way possible.'

An invaluable part of the news-desk team, Claire was used to our impossible and invariably last-minute demands for flights, rental cars and hotels all over the globe.

'Sure thing,' said Claire. 'On it.'

And, as ever, she was. We made flight EI172 at 3.30 p.m. to Heathrow with minutes to spare. Claire had sourced last-minute tickets from the London airport to Lisbon that should have had us in the Portuguese capital by 8 p.m. with an onward connection to Faro before midnight. But, agonisingly, snow grounded us in Heathrow and it was late into the night by the time we took off. At 10 a.m. the following morning – with just half an hour to spare – we reached Tavira, having driven from Lisbon through the night. We parked facing the main entrance of the Vila Galé.

Sean stayed put, setting up his gear as I hurried down the street to pay for the parking. Missing this shot because an over-eager parking warden chose the wrong moment to intervene would be unforgivable.

Fifty metres down the street I nearly bumped headlong into Michael Lynn on the narrow, cobblestoned footpath as he came from the other direction towards his scheduled meeting. Dressed in worn sneakers, jeans and a football jersey, he looked unkempt, stressed and menacing. Taller than he appeared in photos, with a puffed-up face like someone who'd been drinking too much and not sleeping enough, he did not seem like someone to mess with.

Instinctively, I stepped off the kerb to let him pass, every fibre in my being shot through with adrenaline, the hairs on the back of my neck standing rigid. This was what fourteen months of work had boiled down to. The time was now.

I watched from behind as Lynn strode past Sean in our car, crossed the street and entered the hotel. Scouting around for Lynn's car, I found it nearby, tucked into a tight parking spot by the kerb. The soft-top Audi A5 was where he would have to come back to after his meeting.

Now all I had to do was get him to speak when he came out and catch it all on tape. That's all.

To do so I had perhaps 200 metres-worth of walking time between the hotel and the car during which I could make my case, but I had to wait until I was sure Sean had his photos in the can before I pounced. Everything would happen in the space of a few seconds. My chances of getting him to speak were next to nil. But we'd know soon, one way or the other. This was it.

It was less than a week since Lynn had watched Brian O'Driscoll's famous try from Beckett's bar in Budapest. Now, on the other side of Europe, it was my turn to get the ball over the line.

13

Snared

THE URGENT WHIRR OF SEAN'S NIKON tore through the tense silence in our rental car like a sudden burst of muffled gunfire.

An hour and a half after entering the Vila Galé Hotel, Michael Lynn had just exited through its revolving door and into our sights. Head down, looking stern and preoccupied, he was moving quickly towards his car. At a speed of eight frames a second, Sean's camera shutter captured every moment.

'It's definitely him,' whispered Sean after several shot bursts of the camera.

I remembered to breathe again.

One way or another the story was now in the can. The photos, alone, were a result. Anything else would be a bonus. But there was still more to play for.

Checking the red record light on my dictaphone to make sure it was recording, I set off after Lynn, sliding the device into the breast pocket of my jacket. Sean took the opposite side of the street. Darting behind parked cars and doorways, he stayed within shot but out of sight lest he spook Lynn and ruin any chance of him speaking.

'Michael,' I call out from a few metres away, just as he reaches his car. 'Can I grab you for a second?'

My tone and pitch are casual, non-threatening. The last thing I want is to appear threatening. I'm sure the dictaphone in my breast pocket is capturing the sound of my heart thumping with every word spoken.

'Who are ya?' Lynn asks suspiciously.

'Michael O'Farrell is my name.'

'How ya doin'?' he responds warmly, mimicking my easy-going approach.

'I'm a journalist. I work for the *Mail on Sunday*.'

'Yes,' he replies, the realisation and relief dawning on his face. 'I know you.'

He knows now he's not in any danger – physically at least – and that I'm not an angry creditor or debt collector – something of a hazard of late for Lynn.

'Forgive me – I'm out of breath,' I splutter, trying to catch some air. 'Can we have a coffee?'

'Yeah, sure,' comes the seemingly easy reply.

His body language suggests otherwise.

'You need to get fit – no more than myself,' Lynn jokes. Though his voice remains jovial, his physical demeanour is almost menacing.

He turns to face me and I look him in the eye. Here it is. Here and now. Months in the making, everything will come down to the next few milliseconds. It's as if we are in a car that's skidded to a halt and is rocking perilously on the edge of a cliff as a butterfly hovers above the bonnet contemplating a landing that will tip us over the edge.

Synapses firing in overdrive, I hold his gaze and try to ooze benevolence. We are two minds reaching to read the other. One of us will get it wrong. Whatever non-verbal cues are being transmitted between us, Lynn must rely on intuition to decipher them and make a choice. The butterfly will land or dance away. A judgement will be made – to trust, to deceive, to take a measured chance or to turn and run. It's up to him.

I lean up against Lynn's car placing myself in between him and the vehicle's door, forcing him to turn sideways from where I judge Sean to be. If I've got it right, Sean could now shoot without drawing Lynn's attention, yet still capture his target. Also, if he wanted to flee, I was now in the way. He'd have to move me to open the door. And I wasn't going anywhere.

'Can we sit down?' I nod towards a nearby café.

'Yeah of course,' he begins, before stumbling through a series of half-formed excuses. 'I'm going to … I'm not trying to avoid you, it's just … Could I meet you in …? I need to meet somebody now,' he finally trails off, looking at his wristwatch.

The butterfly touches down. The balance of weight begins to shift. I've lost him, I think. He's off. Shit. I'll have to resort to shouting pointless questions at him as he gets into the car and speeds away.

'Relax. Relax,' he reads my concern intuitively. 'I know everything you've written about me, okay – blah, blah, blah. Some of it's right and some of it's completely wrong.'

'Well, if we can sit down and go through it all–'

He cuts me off. 'Yeah – I'm not going to give you an interview, Michael, honestly.'

The rejection is spoken in a what-kind-of-idiot-do you-take-me-for? tone. I'm not sure what my next play can be.

Then it happens. There's a pause. He's considering something. It's as if a coin spinning in the air in his thoughts has just landed lucky side up and clicked him into impulsive mode.

'Actually – I'll have a quick cup of coffee with you.'

Snared.

'I've been looking for you for a long time,' I tell him as we stroll side by side towards the café. 'The air travel was nice and you occupy some nice parts of the world – so I have no complaints.'

Lynn chuckles. 'Where are you from, Michael?' he asks.

'I'm a Kildare man – from Maynooth.'

'Ah very good,' he nods. 'It's pretty bad over there – in Ireland,' he proffers gravely.

'We were all driven to make profits, profits, profits. I was the rising star.'

These are not the words of Michael Lynn, though they might as well be. Instead, they are those of infamous stock trader Nick Leeson – the man whose deceit brought down one of Britain's oldest banks.

In 1995 Leeson's errant stock market trading sparked losses of £827 million for Barings Bank – twice the bank's available trading capital. At the time Barings, founded in 1762, was the United Kingdom's oldest merchant bank. It had funded the Napoleonic Wars, counted the Queen as a client and was seen as virtually indestructible. Until Nick Leeson came along.

Although their crimes and backgrounds are different, there are parallels between Leeson's story and that of Lynn – something I had spoken about with my editor, Sebastian. Leeson, a derivatives trader for Baring's Singapore division, secretly gambled away hundreds of millions before his deceit was unmasked. Like Lynn, his response to reckless losses was to gamble more and then to flee. The pressures and stresses he endured – both as he battled to recover his spiralling debts before being exposed and then as a fugitive – must have been similar to those Lynn now faced.

'I'm sorry,' Leeson had scrawled on a note left on his desk as he went on the run. He was soon apprehended in Germany after a global manhunt traced him through Thailand to Frankfurt. He was extradited back to Singapore after a nine-month legal battle, jailed for six and a half years and languished in a violent, gang-ridden prison. Lynn would endure a similar fate.

But, crucially, Leeson's story ends well – and this was something we reckoned Lynn would appreciate. Released in 1999, Leeson eventually moved to Ireland, settling in Barna, County Galway. There he became something of a celebrity – a profile that was enhanced further by his involvement in Galway United Football Club, where he rose to become CEO. His story – detailed in his bestselling autobiography *Rogue Trader* – was made into a movie of the same name starring Ewan McGregor and Anna Friel.

Today Leeson is a regular guest on the keynote-speaking circuit around the world and, in 2013, he appeared on the TV show *Celebrity Apprentice Ireland*. He has been rehabilitated and given a second chance. For Lynn, still on the run and facing jail time of his own, the Leeson saga would offer hope – we thought.

And we were right. Lynn had, it turned out, seen the movie.

'Do you know what I think strikes me?' I ask as we reach the café. 'I've looked at you for some time now and I can't help but think of Nick Leeson. He was in trouble for a lot more money than you are and now he's back in Ireland running a football club. He sorted it out – he fixed it.'

Lynn nods and purses his lips. I can see this has struck a chord. He's thought the same himself and, as our relationship develops in the months to come, he, too, will raise the comparison repeatedly.

Now though there's some delicate business to be done.

'How do you want to deal with this – or how do you want to treat me?' I ask as we enter the café.

'I'll treat you with respect,' he replies, ordering an espresso and a café con leche.

We take a table in the back of the premises, out of earshot of the bar, and I hang my jacket on a chair between us. I'm conscious that the background music, hum of conversation, steam jets from coffee machines and clanking of dishes will make the dictaphone recording very difficult to follow. But it will have to suffice.

Soon three things become clear. Firstly, Lynn remains stubbornly self-delusional – or is lying completely – about his intentions.

'I'm reaching a point where I will have all the investors secured. That's my primary goal,' he says, apparently in earnest. 'You can have an opinion – was I out to fuck the investors? Absolutely not. I'm not Robin Hood and I'm not Mother Teresa, but I'm not a guy who would do that.'

Secondly, he's a wit who likes to charm and crack one-liners – however inappropriately.

'What do you have to say to the banks?' I ask at one point.

'Thank you for the money,' comes the cheeky response.

And thirdly, he has a large, wounded ego that, having taken a hammering, seems desperate for reassurance that he's really not the fraudster he's been portrayed as.

'What do you think of me?' he asks.

'I think you got in over your head at some point,' I begin.

'Yes,' he exclaims, sitting back in satisfaction.

'And then it all started to go wrong – like Nick Leeson,' I continue. 'And I think that maybe you'd like to rectify everything that went wrong. And who knows? Maybe you can be a character like him, who in a few years' time, is back living in Ireland.'

He's nodding in agreement, clearly tempted by the thought.

'I don't know though – to be honest with you – whether any of your actions were fraudulent, because a lot of them look like it,' I continue. 'So I'm going to maintain an open book on that. But I do believe at the beginning you got in–'

'I was bold,' he interjects. 'I was naughty,' he repeats in a childish, mocking tone.

I envisage an impetuous child before me, caught red-handed with his hand in the cookie jar and ready to say sorry if it means he'll get away with it.

'You certainly took advantage of situations you were in, I'm sure. I can see you were taking advantage of banks who were–'

'I was a businessman,' he breaks in again. 'Listen, the first house I bought in 1997 for €76,000. The second house I bought for €110,000 in 1999 and I borrowed €125,000. I was twenty-eight years old. I represented a bubble, everything that was good in Ireland about the Celtic Tiger era. I never intended this to happen. Honestly. Never.'

After more than an hour, we've spoken about many topics and I push again for a formal interview.

'Everything you've said – what's wrong with it?' I ask.

'There's nothing really – but I've gotten so used to saying nothing,' he replies, before typically adding a musical reference. 'You know that song – "You say it best … when you say nothing at all".'

Then comes a touch of mock vanity of the type that betrays precisely such a vice.

'But I'm not giving pictures. Look at me,' he says pinching his football shirt between his thumbs and forefingers as if it's too dirty to hold and letting it fall back on his chest. 'My problem with journalists – my mistrust – is that I'm here now, for instance, being sincere with you and that you'd go back and write: "Lynn in football T-shirt".'

I struggle to comprehend his priorities. Is this his biggest concern? Why on earth would he care about his image at a time like this? But I hold my tongue.

The thought of the tabloid headline reminds him of other media gripes – such as the manner in which his use of the private jet firm, NetJets, has been portrayed. Soon after he absconded, it was widely reported that he had booked €250,000-worth of flying time with the exclusive company just before going on the run. Reports of the private jet use fuelled a certain perception of Lynn as a money-guzzling, out-of-control executive. Now he wishes to counter this image.

'NetJets – fuck that shit,' he spits. 'I used NetJets because it's efficient. When you have eight people on a plane it costs x amount and you get more work done in five days … you know what it's like to travel.'

I continue to push for a full interview, seeking to reach an agreement. By now he's entered negotiation mode. He begins to behave just like a businessman cutting a deal.

'Can we agree this?' he asks. 'You do out a list of questions.'

'I'd rather have you talking spontaneously,' I reply. 'At some point I will have to ask hard questions and you can just say "no" and we move on.'

Eventually, our unlikely negotiation is close to concluding, though he's still refusing to pose for a photo – not knowing we have taken dozens already, not knowing we'll take dozens more when this meeting ends. In return for a promise of further interviews, he demands to see the article in advance.

'What I'm saying to you, Michael, is if you fuck the first one up, don't come near me ever again,' he says.

'Then there has to be a picture of some kind,' I counter.

Though I can hardly believe it – and don't understand why – I can sense he's there to be pushed over the line.

'There has to be,' I continue. 'We can doctor it. We can do whatever you want – we can put tits on you if you like.'

He giggles at the thought and finally our last barter is made. He'll pose for photos – so long as we don't reveal his precise location and he'll get a written guarantee that he can see the article before publication. Not change it, just see it.

'Okay, talk to your editor,' he agrees. 'Is this going to be the front page – yeah?'

'Unless the government falls overnight,' I respond.

'Oh dear God,' he sighs.

'Out. Everyone!'

Sebastian had been overseeing an afternoon news conference at Associated Newspapers HQ in Dublin when I called through to his mobile.

'I'm sitting here with Michael Lynn and he's agreed to do an interview,' I tell him. 'I'm going to put you on to him now.'

'Do we have photos?'

'Yes.'

'Does he know that?'

'No – he's agreed to be photographed. He needs reassurance that we'll keep his location secret.'

Lynn takes the phone and typically begins with a wisecrack.

'Hi, Sebastian. The only thing I'll say to you is you'll have to give Michael a budget for a gym because he was very out of breath when he ran after me.'

There's a pause as Sebastian speaks. Lynn nods and listens.

'Sound,' I hear Lynn say, nodding his head.

I know Sebastian is now speaking of Nick Leeson and seeking to engage with Lynn on a human level. By the sound of Lynn's side of the conversation, he's succeeding.

'I think, Sebastian, you've hit the nail on the head,' Lynn finally says. 'I never intended for this to happen. If I could have envisaged that I would find myself in this position I would have remained at home.'

After a year of silence, Lynn appears relieved to be speaking. The more he talks the more he unburdens himself. I can see he earnestly wants Sebastian to understand. He earnestly wants everyone to understand.

'It's taken all my own strength to remain mentally right,' he continues. 'So you're talking to a normal human being who just – as a businessman – has been engaging in self-fantasy over the last fucking year and I made a balls of it. I made huge mistakes. I was over-ambitious and I was greedy. That's a fact. And people have suffered as a result of it. And I deeply, deeply regret it. And to me, the mark of a man is when you're in the shit do you run or do you stay to try to sort it out, and that's what I'm doing.'

After twenty minutes Lynn is still going. As I listen, I picture Sebastian back home in Dublin, writing furiously, taking note of every word.

'Why did I get the fuck out?' Lynn is saying. 'I got the fuck out because of the investors. I could not get somebody to represent me. I could not get anyone to take into account the investors.'

Faced with the prospect of receivership, Lynn realised his bankers – rather than any creditors he may wish to favour – would take priority. That was the law. Those are the rules when you go bust. But Lynn didn't like it. He thought he could do better. He wanted to make his own rules.

'Let's look after the lofty thrones – the little people they'll have to suffer.' Lynn, now more animated than I've seen him, is telling Sebastian of the banks' attitude. 'Well, I'm sorry. I am a little person. I'm still fairly grounded – all sixteen stone of me – and I was fucked if I was going to double fuck these guys because they were down in a situation where they didn't know what was happening,' he says of the smaller investors. 'I assured them the assets could be secured so that they could be looked after.'

After what seems like an age, Lynn signs off with Sebastian and, though I can hardly believe it, agrees to the terms we have discussed. We agree to meet in an hour in the Vila Galé Hotel and I rush off to book a room. Part of me doubts he will show up at all, but another part tells me he just might.

PART TWO

IN EXILE

14

On the Record

'HOW MUCH DO YOU OWE?'

Sitting in a hastily booked room in the Vila Galé Hotel, still dressed in the same tatty trainers, jeans and football jersey, Lynn is halfway through his promised interview. It's just an hour since we'd made our deal and, though we doubted he'd appear at all, he's actually shown up early.

At first he laughs at the question.

'Sorry for laughing. Don't put that in,' he hastily adds.

Then he knuckles down.

'Let me give it to you jurisdiction by jurisdiction,' he begins.

Outside the window, palm trees rustle in the light breeze. Beyond the hotel car park, fishermen tend to their colourful boats, sea gulls ducking and diving in the air above their nets. On a small circular table between us my dictaphone is counting the seconds and laying down Lynn's words.

'In Portugal, investors are owed approximately – in or around – €3.2 million,' he begins. 'In Bulgaria, €5 million. Slovakia, €60,000. Budapest, €4.2 million.'

'Those are the [personal] investors?'

'That's correct.'

'In addition to a figure for the banks – what's your figure for this?' I ask, seeking to understand how much he has borrowed before absconding.

A grin creeps across his face. He bows his head and looks up with his eyes like that cheeky child again.

'I don't want to be flippant,' he begins, putting on a faux-meek voice. 'But I understand €80 million. That's what I understand.'

The €80 million Lynn owes to banks has been splashed across headlines ever since he fled. And he's smiling now. Enjoying the absurdity. He's hovering between being ridiculous and sincere – a combination that's served him well to date. Being a joker wins friends and disguises intent. Appearing sincere wins trust, loans and buyer deposits.

He sees the flippant approach has perturbed me and seeks to contextualise the debt.

'Can I just say one thing about this? Everywhere in the press you see: "Michael Lynn fugitive who absconded with €80 million." The last statement of affairs that I sent in [to worried creditors and banks seeking answers] from my accountants and financial adviser showed my assets to be worth approximately €65 million.'

As the interview progresses, I ask about these assets – Lynn's personal homes and the properties in Portugal, Bulgaria and elsewhere that I have traced as they were moved from Kendar into a labyrinth of secret offshore structures beyond the reach of creditors.

'I own absolutely no assets,' he answers blankly, his face betraying not a flicker of a tell even though he's just spoken of being worth €65 million. 'The bank – AIB and a few other geniuses – have seized in Portugal the property that I own as an individual. They also seized the 50 per cent interest I own in my own home here in Portugal and they are trying to sell that as well.'

'People are going to doubt that,' I say. 'Just as people are going to doubt that you never committed fraud. What do you say to those people? Did you ever deliberately set out to take money from people and not give it back?'

'Absolutely not. Absolutely not. Absolutely not,' he says firmly. 'It's highly unlikely that I would put all of the companies in my personal name, all shareholdings in my personal name, that I would be the face of the business and potentially steal money.'

Instead, Lynn says his ill-timed 'vision' for Kendar was to create a global, leveraged, mushrooming snowball of real estate projects that could be sold on to an equity fund as one monumental investment – with Lynn as its property manager. 'My plan was to build, to provide apartments. My plan was to sell to funds,' he explains. 'I never had a plan to steal from people.'

His exile has been forced and impromptu, rather than a choice or planned strategy, he says. 'I'm Irish, I'm from Mayo – I want and would have wanted to have lived in Ireland. Yes, I had an intention to live abroad for a period of time during the sale and the fund takeover, but I never intended to be as I am at the moment. You know when you go to a country and say: "God I'd love to live out there"? Try living out there and not being allowed the choice of returning.'

I ask again about mortgage fraud.

'The common perception, alleged countless times, every time a bank goes to court, is that mortgages were claimed against the same properties from different banks. Did that happen?'

'You're not going to let up on that point are you?' he smiles, before pausing to reach into his pocket for a packet of gum. 'Would you like a chewing gum?' he asks, unwrapping a piece for himself as I await an answer to my question.

'They clearly allege that happened and it sticks in people's minds and the document trails are apparently there to show it,' I push.

'It's true that the borrowings I had were extensive against the portfolio. But in order to understand that, it's critical that you understand the advice received and the agreements which were in place with the banks and that's a matter between me and the banks. The only thing I admitted was that I owe them money.'

I bring up Vantea – the anonymous firm now controlling Lynn's Costa de Cabanas resort. Who owns the firm and why is this secret?

'My understanding, in relation to Vantea, is the beneficial owners are two European companies,' he begins. 'And if the company's office is checked, I understand there are two companies named who own it and that's all part of a fund.'

'There may be two companies named, but because the true owners are kept secret we can't see who owns them,' I point out.

'You can actually, when they make a tax return at the end of the year.'

'But I am asking you, who owns them?'

'My answer is I don't know,' he begins. 'Honestly. I don't own them if you're asking me that specific question. Do I own Vantea? Absolutely not. I sold my interest and my shareholding to those companies. If they are anonymous or if they're standard companies or whatever, that's their business. It's not my business. What is my business, and the reason that I am constantly travelling throughout Europe at the moment, is to try and realise the one thing that's important to me, which is to honour the investor commitments, in so far as it is reasonable and physically and financially possible to get all or part of their money back, or the apartment they wanted to get. And, secondly, to go to the Irish banks and reach a deal. I owe the Irish banks money. I acknowledge that debt. I don't deny it.'

'But it looks as if you are managing Vantea,' I respond. 'You are in and out of the office. People around here seem to think you are responsible for the company. They seem to come to you if they have an issue or problem with the apartments. What is your relationship with Vantea? Are you a manager – do you help them? What's going on?'

'I am a consultant to the company occasionally,' he concedes. 'There is a contractual commitment to the investors which they haven't honoured fully yet and I want to see that through, and when that's done I will feck off. Don't put "feck off" – I don't like cursing. In relation to me going into the office, it's true, I go to the office. I don't deny that I've gone into the office, but it's very difficult for me to put in place the obligations for the investors unless I go into the office and have meetings.'

As always, nothing about Lynn's affairs is straightforward. His truth changes depending on the situation, much like a tree casts a different shadow as the sun revolves around it. He maintains that he, personally, owns nothing but appears to exert considerable influence over assets worth millions. He claims not to know who the hidden owners of Vantea are but admits working for them as a consultant. He acknowledges debts of €80 million to the banks but jokes about these as if they're meaningless. Everything is an elaborate construction of smoke and mirrors that only he can explain. To believe any of it you must believe he is telling the truth without any other agenda at play.

And that's a difficult ask due to his actions since he went on the run. There is precious little, if any, credibility left on Michael Lynn's balance sheet. But he's still trying to trade on it.

15

A Personal Toll

THE SONG BEGINS WITH A SLOW country backbeat and a lingering piano riff. Then, after a weeping slide guitar blends into the mix, Michael Lynn begins to sing. The lyrics are about a young boy whose mother tells him to follow his destiny, not to be one of the crowd.

Lynn has a surprisingly good voice and the refrain – from an album of his given to me by an associate – rolls through my mind as I listen to him speak, particularly at one point in the interview when he chokes back tears. After the second verse, a bass kicks in as the tune builds to an emotional chorus in which the boy – now an adult in need of help – pleads for understanding from his mother.

The melancholic track was written and recorded long before Lynn went on the run. But it seems strangely apt now as I watch him struggle to come to terms with what he's done. Though the detail of our interview has been technical, there's a good deal of emotion, regret and shame on display too.

'I was on my own personal drug of ambition, fuelled by the desire to succeed. Today I look in the mirror and ask myself who he was. I am disappointed that I lost some of my own fundamentals that I was given as a young fella. I have let my family down and I have let myself down. And that's difficult and I need to live with that all the time. But that's my problem, that's my bed and I have made it. The mistakes that I have made, I have to live with the consequences.'

There's regret for the suffering he's caused.

'I have to also understand the consequences that this has had for other people. I am aware of how I have affected other people's lives – the investors who invested with me, and I am truly sorry that the plan, the vision I had, was interrupted, because I never intended them to suffer as they have.'

There's a sense of feeling sorry for himself.

'I have no property in Ireland. The only hope I have of having any property in Ireland is that my brother will let me walk on the farm in Crossmolina. I have lost everything in Ireland.'

There's a desire to be understood.

'I think it's important that people understand that, regardless of the image of the individual who borrowed this extensive amount of money, there is a human being behind it. And that when this occurred it was just like a major, major shock and then suddenly they are taking your property left, right and centre.'

There's homesickness.

'The truth is I want to go back. The life that I am leading and the pressure … I have a wonderful wife. She has been extremely loyal to me and loyal to us as a couple. I am extremely lucky and Ireland is where I am from. It's my home. It's like one long Good Friday when you can't have a drink. So every day is like Good Friday. I can't go back to Ireland and that's not really the way that I want to live my life nor is it the life that I wish to impose on other people, family and others.'

There's seemingly sincere contrition.

'You know I have to say sorry, but I have to do something about it as well. So abject apologies are important, but it's important to have something behind it as well.'

There's a raw recollection of his lowest moment.

'There was one Friday when I came home to my wife. There was a rugby match on. But I didn't see a rugby match. I saw nothing. I sat in front of the TV and I stared at it and I was lost. My wife contacted her doctor and we ended up down in St Pat's psychiatric hospital, and they were going to admit me. And I was there for two hours touching my nose, touching my ear and all those kinds of things, you know.'

There's the pivotal moment he pulled himself together and refused to be admitted.

'I decided, no, I'm not going in there. Absolutely not. They can take every asset of mine, but they are not going to defeat me mentally. I will survive this, and I will survive it because I must. And I have. It was very difficult emotionally and personally. And it still is.'

There's a desire to return to normality.

'I don't think I really ever want to achieve celebrity standing. That's one thing for sure. Perhaps I have, for all of the wrong reasons. I read some of the papers and look on the internet and I think: "God, I'd love to meet that fellow they're writing about because it is not me." The high-flyer they call me. I'm sitting here. I've got a dirty T-shirt on. I'm an ordinary guy who had huge ambitions and who made huge mistakes. So I don't want celebrity status. I do want to have a normal life if possible and I can only do that when I have done the right thing. I have to do the right thing first.'

There's defiance.

'I don't know what it's like to be in prison. I have only watched *Prison Break*. I wouldn't see any reason why I would have to go to prison and the one thing I want to make clear is I am not going to be a scapegoat for others. Absolutely not. I am not going to be used as an example for what was recognised as an acceptable form and practice of business by bankers, lawyers, accountants and auctioneers. I am not going to be the poster boy who ends up in prison to my cost alone.'

There's anger at the authorities.

'Hang on a second here. These guys want to morally, commercially beat me into a pulp until I simply go: "Take me, I am wrong, I'm totally wrong" and I just collapse.'

And there's an apparent determination to make amends.

'I do not intend to lie down until such time as I have ensured that I can retrieve as much of their money as I physically and humanly can, or can provide them with adequate security in terms of build-out of the product which they honestly entered into a contract with Kendar to obtain. These people did no wrong. I am sorry for what happened to them and I believe that right now the key issue for me is that if I am sorry I have to show it by actions as opposed to just words, because that's just bullshit – words.'

Sean takes out his camera and begins to take some shots. He's timed it well so as not to interrupt the flow of our dialogue. Immediately Lynn is again conscious of his image.

'Don't do a side profile – there's a fellow in Crossmolina – I walked into the pub one evening and he looked at me and said, "Lynn you're as stout," he jokes self-deprecatingly in a put-on Mayo drawl.

Then he raises the question of his clothing.

'Am I going to be like this, in the jeans and the football shirt? What do you think lads – honestly?'

The issue is resolved when I lend him a new Boss shirt from my suitcase, which he changes into in the bathroom. The shirt will forever remind me of this absurd moment.

'Ye lads must have great craic, do ye – going around the world?'

Interview concluded, Lynn is almost jubilant as we take the back stairs down to the hotel's underground car park, to take photos away from prying eyes. The thought does not strike Lynn, but Sean is quietly delighted at the brooding darkness of the location. Little could better portray the sense of a man in hiding than an empty, underground silo, shadows stretching into the darkness.

With the serious business now behind him, Lynn chats comfortably with Sean, who, he has established, lives in Wicklow.

'Your hurling team's showing promise,' he tells him.

Sean agrees and asks Lynn to stand below a florescent lamp beside a grey concrete pillar. The light is on a timer and, as Sean clicks away, I have to keep jogging over to the sensor by the door to trigger the switch.

In less than twenty-four hours Sean's photo – with Lynn peering intently and defiantly at the lens – will roll off the printing presses in Ireland, emblazoned across the front page of hundreds of thousands of newspapers bound for every shop in every town and village in the country.

'Do you still play music?' I ask him as Sean works away.

'I do yeah.'

'Do you have a piano at home?'

'I have a keyboard. Creatively I've been fairly stunted over the last year. Did you ever find you can't write music when you're … do you know there's two sides of the brain … you guys are creative so you know what I mean.'

'Well, I could never write music when I was happy,' I say. 'You can't have been happy this year.'

'No – I wrote one song. But I'm useless with words. I can't write words.'

'What's the song about?'

'I've no words to it. And anything that I recorded I had to write the words literally under pressure. I work much better under pressure.'

'I think you like being under pressure.'

'That's true. I do. I like pressure. I think I operate better under pressure but not the type of pressure I've experienced in the last fifteen months. I wouldn't wish this on anybody, because it's not the kind of thing you want.'

Then his mind switches. He's back to the banter. Back to concerns about his image.

'How do I look? How's the hair on my nose?' he pouts at Sean, shuffling on his feet as he does so. 'Jesus – can you allow me to work with you on the selection of the photograph please? Cause there's one there – did you see the one on the *Irish Independent* the other day?' he says in mock horror, asking if I know the journalist who wrote the story.

'I don't tend to mix with journalists,' I tell him.

'Yeah – I was the same with lawyers. And now I definitely don't mix with them,' he adds.

The truth is, he'd abandoned any real practice of law years ago – though he took massive advantage of the trust placed in him precisely because of his reputation as a lawyer.

'What do you want to be?' I ask.

'I don't want to be a country and western singer,' he says with a surprisingly loud laugh that serves to completely negate the idea, were anyone thinking it. 'I still think I have talent in business and I still have a belief in myself and I think I know who I am. This has been – this is – a very difficult journey, but, at least for me, what's most important is that I am willing to put up my hand and say, "I was responsible and I was captain of the ship."'

He does want to spread the blame, though, when the time is right. 'I am not wasting time engaging in finger-pointing and I'm trying to find solutions. Finger-pointing can wait. But I won't leave that without revisiting it.'

16

Devil's Scripture

JUDGE RICHARD JOHNSON RAISED HIS BUSHY eyebrows, pursed his lips tightly, folded his hands and fixed his gaze on the lawyer before him. That lawyer – Peter Bredin, representing Bank of Scotland – shifted uncomfortably. He knew better than to interrupt the President of the High Court until he had expounded whatever was on his mind.

It was 24 February 2009 – just a week since the interview with Lynn had been published and fourteen months since Judge Johnson had first issued an arrest warrant for the errant solicitor in December 2007. Since then, despite repeated requests for updates from an irritated Johnson, the authorities had failed to act and a criminal file appeared nowhere near ready to be sent to the Director of Public Prosecutions (DPP).

Instead, Lynn was engaging in what those investigating him believed to be a self-serving game of cat and mouse with the authorities. Through his lawyers he repeatedly set up meetings abroad where he said he'd answer Fraud Squad questions. 'I haven't spoken to them, but my lawyer has spoken to them on a number of occasions and has made them aware that I am available for a meeting,' he'd told me. 'We have no problem meeting them to answer the questions that they wish to put to me.'

In all, four different meeting dates were agreed between November 2008 and October 2011. Lynn even secured a promise from the authorities that an EU arrest warrant would not be issued until at least four weeks after any interview. But each time, Lynn cancelled at the last minute, buying himself more time.

Meanwhile, dozens of solicitors and barristers appeared before the commercial section of the High Court each Monday morning as the banks they represented jostled to limit their exposure to the loans they had afforded Lynn. As soon as these Lynn cases had commenced, Judge Johnson had begun to ask some astute questions of the banks – 'curiosities on my part' he called them.

'I made a request when this started that I be given details of bonuses paid to the officials when the banks paid the money,' he had reminded the court to no avail in June 2008 when Lynn had been on the run for six months.

Four months later – in October 2008 – he'd asked again.

'I want details of who are the bankers who got bonuses and who authorised the loans … will they [the banks] kindly take note,' he'd demanded, adding that his request referred to 'all the banks and building societies'.

That was all before Lynn's interview, in which he'd described the banks as 'being very interested in my story'.

'They were very excited, as were my professional advisers and fellow directors,' Lynn had said, 'very excited by the amount of money that could be made and we were all – including myself – following the trend. I was the Celtic cub out of control in hindsight. And I was greedy and over-ambitious. But yes, there were other parties involved. They didn't conspire; we were all part of a mythical illusion.'

Perhaps with these words from Lynn's interview ringing in his mind, Judge Johnson tried again. The answer he got this time – that there were 'legal and commercial difficulties' to providing the names of bankers who got bonuses – did not sit well.

'I take it the reasons were that revealing the truth can be very often difficult and embarrassing for bankers,' Judge Johnson replied.

In response, Peter Bredin could do little but refer to data protection requirements.

'The devil can quote scripture for his own purposes,' the exasperated judge growled.

Two days later I flew to meet Lynn in secret in Budapest. The location – a high-end café in the theatre district – was his choice. But the purpose of the meeting had been set by me. Like Judge Johnson, I, too, wanted to know about Lynn's bankers. And now he was in the mood for talking.

In our interview two weeks previously, I had asked Lynn if his bankers had overlooked little things while processing his loan applications.

'They were overlooking huge things,' he'd responded without hesitation. 'What they wanted was cash flow – repayment capacity in terms of perception – and then it was: "How do we give you the money?"'

Right there, in just six words that should never belong together in economics – repayment capacity in terms of perception – Lynn had smartly encapsulated both the cause of Ireland's banking crisis and the reason for its inevitable conclusion. The whole thing had been an illusion, a trick of perception. And one of the most adept at the sleight of hand required to make the trick work was Lynn.

None of the subsequent reports or investigations into Ireland's banking collapse – compiled at a cost of millions to taxpayers – would achieve such a succinct and concise explanation. Repayment capacity in terms of perception. Simple as.

In our interview in Portugal, Lynn had been conscious of being contrite. He had tempered his views for public consumption. This meeting had a different purpose. Now, Lynn – still proud, self-assured and stung by the criticism and venom heaped upon him back home – wanted to spread some of the blame. Like a desperate and cornered viper backed into a burrow, he wanted to lash out wildly. That meant heaping dirt on his financiers and associates, and lifting the lid on his dealings with them.

'Not one bank that lent to me refused the commission or the plaudits that would have been gained by bank managers for the loans that they extended,' Lynn had said in his interview.

Now it was time to learn the details.

Soon I was struggling to keep up as he ran through a list of his bankers and business associates throughout Europe and beyond, spewing out names, email addresses, landline and mobile numbers from memory in a remarkable display of mental agility. This was the Michael Lynn employees had described to me as I'd hunted for him months earlier. He was assured and confident, completely on top of his brief. Sharp. Dogged. Decisive.

There was something else too, though. He was angry. Bitter. Venomous. And more determined than ever to spread the blame. Now that he'd gone public – to virtually no positive reaction – he wanted to lash out at those he blamed for his plight.

Some of those he mentioned were the kind of people Judge Johnson was so eager to hear about: the people who had shared in a commissions' bonanza of up to 1 per cent – or €10,000 for every million – lent to Lynn. With €80 million borrowed in Ireland alone, that meant as much as €800,000 in commission could have been distributed to Irish lenders and brokers for agreeing that Lynn's 'perceived ability to repay' was solid.

Aware of the value of his business to these bankers, Lynn had actively used the commission as a carrot. Sometimes he'd openly discussed it with brokers and lenders.

'I was trying to get you commission … but to be honest we need to be careful,' he'd written to an intermediary about one multimillion-euro loan at 1.34 a.m. on Monday, 8 January 2007. The email, sent as Lynn enquired if finance had been approved for two other property purchases, is telling. Not only does Lynn appear fully aware of the motivating power of commission – he seems to be conspiring with others to abuse it.

There were other ways of staying close to lenders and associates. Some of the bankers and businessmen, Lynn said, had been invited to stay at his flagship Costa de Cabanas resort in Portugal. Still more had given him valuable wedding presents and asked for favours Lynn could provide. Several had availed of his corporate hospitality at international matches and concerts. Others, Lynn maintained, were in a different league and had privately sought backhanders or a cut of the action for themselves.

'We'd expect something for ourselves,' is how Lynn described one key figure putting it. And Lynn had obliged, he said. But could it be proved?

Days later, back in Ireland, I sought to place myself in front of one such banker hoping the element of surprise would see him slip up enough to implicate himself. First, I tried dropping into his office on spec – a tactic that works more often than you'd think. When that failed, I pulled his home details from the Land Registry and duly found myself climbing the granite steps to his plush, multimillion-euro home to press the intercom. Through the speaker, the executive's wife assured me her husband was not in.

I left a business card in the letter box and strolled away across the driveway's crunchy designer gravel. On impulse I paused at a bus stop just down the street. This seemed a perfect place to hang about inconspicuously – and it was close enough for me to intercept my target before he reached his front door once he arrived home.

Leaning on the wrought-iron railings beside the bus stop, I mulled over everything. Lynn was admitting bribery. He'd paid kickbacks and granted valuable favours for loans. Had others done the same – and how could I prove it?

In the manicured drives along the street, new Jaguar, BMW and Mercedes cars glistened in the cold. Gardeners, childminders and cleaners came and went. It was a world far away from the lives being lived by the folk occupying the heaving buses pulling up before me every few minutes. Behind grimy windows fogged up with condensation, security men, secretaries, nurses and shop assistants endured another rush-hour trip back to the suburbs and their negative equity homes.

My phone rang. A private number. I snapped back into the present and answered.

'Hello.'

It was the head of PR for the bank at which my target worked.

'You've been to the office of our employee. You've been to his home and you've been waiting outside for hours.'

'Correct. I'd like to speak with him,' I replied, chuckling to myself inside.

I wondered if my man was waiting around the corner to come home for his tea. Part of me hoped so.

'Can we help you in the press office?'

'It's a private matter,' I replied. 'It would not be correct of me to speak with third parties about it.'

But the game was up. Any element of surprise was lost. We both knew it. I agreed to send a query by email.

As we rang off, the diesel engine of a departing double-decker shook the pavement as it pulled off into traffic with a roar. For a moment a flood of memories from the past year flashed through my mind: the rapping of car tyres on the cobblestoned streets of Tavira, the bells of the yellow trams outside Lynn's Budapest apartment, the crunch of gravel underfoot at Kendar's unbuilt Bansko site in Bulgaria and the urgent whirr of Sean's camera. I shook the memories off and prepared to submit my questions to the bank's press office.

The prompt reply included a letter alleging I'd libelled the banking official by sending queries to his bank. He had retained an expensive and high-profile legal firm.

It was time to try elsewhere.

I walked up to the front counter and asked for him by name, leaving my own name in return. Having gotten nowhere with my initial attempt to speak to one of Lynn's bankers, it was time to try again. Someone else was in my sights.

The person I sought was busy, I was politely told. Perhaps later. Same again when I'd returned once or twice throughout the afternoon.

I left my details and waited, deliberately positioning myself in full view outside. Banks have security protocols and anyone appearing to be carrying out covert surveillance might trigger a call to the police – something I wanted to avoid. I didn't want to appear suspicious or sneaky, just polite, patient and determined. Plus, I wanted to see if the man I was seeking would try to avoid me and, if so, to what lengths he would go.

My purpose here was simple. This was the very branch where Michael Lynn had once applied for a loan worth millions. My target had initiated the loan and Lynn said he'd received a valuable kickback in return.

I mulled all this over as I sat waiting outside. I imagined Lynn, ebullient in his boom-time prime, popping through the branch door to sign the paperwork a couple of years earlier. I imagined the chit-chat, the backslap, the all-but-obligatory reference to the latest GAA match, and Lynn's hearty laugh as he cracked a joke or two.

I could picture Lynn trying to sell apartment units to staff, leaving bro-chures for them to consider. And I could see him casually dropping the offer of a free holiday into the conversation as if it were nothing. As if it didn't matter.

'If you ever need a break just give me a tinkle,' I imagined him saying.

But was it true? I was here to find out. And I'd have to get the lender concerned to speak about it, to acknowledge it. Otherwise, I could prove nothing. Getting in front of him, however, wasn't proving easy.

As the early spring sun dipped low, closing time came and went. Still no sign. My man it seemed, had left by the back entrance. A voice on the other side of the bank's intercom confirmed his departure. Time to try something else – like a knock on his home door.

I'd researched where he lived – a newly built, stone-fronted house outside town in the countryside. En route, I touched base with our legal team to make them aware of my movements. There can be a fine line between what's appropriate and what's not when it comes to approaching people at home and at their workplace. The line can be particularly difficult with people like bankers, who have legitimate fears about being targeted for robberies or their families being held hostage by tiger gangs.

As I approached the house an elderly lady was out enjoying the end of the day with a walk along the road. I'd looked up the property in the Land Registry and cross-referenced local planning records, ordinance survey maps and satellite imagery to locate it. I was sure I had the right place.

'No, you're in the wrong place altogether,' the lady replied, without a second's hesitation, when I asked. She was suspicious. Her taut, upright posture betrayed it. But she kept her tone neutral. Falsely so.

One assured set of very specific but utterly fictitious directions, and half an hour later I was hopelessly lost in a warren of country lanes as darkness fell. Hemmed in by wind-beaten hawthorn hedges and a rural landscape crisscrossed by meandering back roads, I knew I'd never find anything after dark. About to give up, I pulled into a farmyard open to the road, intending to ask for new directions.

I never got a chance. Horn beeping, a car shot from the glum dusk, skidding to a halt beside me. It was my target. And he looked angry.

It seemed he was beckoning me to follow. Driving fast, he sped away in the direction he'd come from. I fell in behind, struggling to keep up on the unfamiliar narrow road. He led me straight back to the home I'd earlier been directed away from, sped through the gates, down the driveway, completed a hasty three-point turn and shot back up to the gate, blocking the entrance.

I pulled up in front of him and made to get out of my car.

'Stay there,' he roared, rolling down his window.

'I just want to talk about Michael Lynn,' I shouted as best I could between cars, indicating who I was. A tense to and fro ensued, during which he asserted his innocence of any wrongdoing or conflict of interest.

'I took a holiday and I paid for it, and you can quote me on that. I didn't do anything wrong here,' he said. 'I have a Visa statement to say that I paid for my flights. Everything else was paid for in cash.'

He promised to provide his Visa statements, but when I followed through with a call to his mobile the next day, he referred all queries to the bank's press office instead. Later, in a statement, the bank said it had 'satisfied itself that there is sufficient evidence to demonstrate there was no conflict of interest as suggested'.

There is no evidence to demonstrate otherwise – other than the word of Lynn – the word of a crook. A banker had been offered a free holiday but had correctly insisted on paying. Whether or not he received any commission for his role in the loan remains unknown. If he did, he was perfectly entitled to it. Those were the rules of the game.

Judge Johnson never found out who received commissions for processing loans to Michael Lynn and his businesses. Those names remain secret. The *omertà* of the banks stands firm.

Those names, though, are documented in the many lists compiled by Lynn's office as he set about busily borrowing tens of millions before absconding. One such list, prepared in the autumn of 2006, charts the progress of a €10.3 million tranche of loan applications to five different banks. Lynn's statements of affairs and accounts for Kendar were dispatched by courier and registered post to support the finance requests. Follow-up calls to check progress were noted. Commission, no doubt, was dangled. Free holidays, perhaps, were mentioned, though not necessarily accepted. The money – and much more after that – was paid out. Commission or bonus payments were pocketed.

Properties against which the loans were to be secured were also listed – some of them pledged three and four times over to different banks. Eight of the most relied-on properties supporting the applications were pledged no less than twenty-six times to different banks. Sometimes the properties were listed in the same order, apparently cut and pasted from one application to the next. Lynn, the ultimate chancer, was clearly confident no one would realise until it was too late.

17

So Close

HE KNEW IT MIGHT HAPPEN AT any moment. But it still came as a shock.

Nothing about the morning of Tuesday, 11 August 2009 gave Michael Lynn any cause for concern as he strolled into the air-conditioned Váci ut branch of Budapest's FHB Bank at 9.15 a.m. The prospect of rain, with the sky darkening to a colour akin to the muddy hue of the city's Danube river, wasn't going to bother an Irishman. If anything, it would bring relief from the searing heat more typically associated with Budapest in August.

Just a few blocks over from Lynn's nearby apartment, the Váci ut FHB bank was one of many, throughout Europe and beyond, that Lynn continued to use after his Irish assets had been frozen eighteen months earlier. The bank's proximity to his Oktogon apartment made it an easy stroll through a safe, upmarket area of the city lined with boulevard cafés and designer outlets. In addition, Brid could shop in the West End shopping mall across the street while Lynn met his bankers by appointment.

This morning, however, things would be different. Lynn would leave the bank in handcuffs. He'd be led through the bank's front door, beneath the large green FHB letters above the entrance, by Captain Lóránd Jámbor from the International Criminal Cooperation Centre – the unit of the Hungarian police responsible for liaising with Interpol.

Bundled into a police car that had been tucked out of sight when he entered, Lynn's mind now swarmed with the fears he must have anticipated a thousand times – fears he'd dreamed of as he imagined what being arrested would really be like. Fears that – absurdly – may not have felt all that far from relief. This was, after all, a fate he had written for himself and one he couldn't outrun forever.

Finally, it seemed, the slow arm of the law was reaching out for him from Dublin. In its hand was arrest warrant number 32-15-3469-00-07, issued five months earlier by the International Criminal Cooperation Centre via Interpol.

Speeding through the busy streets of Budapest, the squad car carrying Lynn made towards police headquarters in Budapest's sixth district. Deafened from the sirens above his head and accompanied by armed police officers, Lynn felt the fuss was ridiculous.

Churning through what had just happened in his mind, Lynn realised two things. Firstly, he'd been set up. The police had been waiting for him and he'd sauntered into their trap. Secondly, there are certain unexpected disadvantages to being wealthy enough to bank by appointment.

Police headquarters in central Budapest is a drab six-storey building with an ugly facade of green and white tiles on Szinyei Merse Street. To the side of the door a soot-stained Hungarian flag hangs permanently alongside a tattered blue EU flag.

On arrival, Captain Jámbor abandoned his squad car outside and led Lynn upstairs to the Criminal Investigation Department's Economic Protection Subdivision. There, Lynn was handed over to Police Lieutenant Colonel Janos Juhaz, the man heading up investigation case number 01060-824/2008. The case – officially listed as an investigation into an 'unknown offender for the suspected offence of fraud of material value' under Section 318 of Hungary's Criminal Code – related to Lynn's former firms and development projects in Budapest.

Lieutenant Colonel Juhaz, a sharp, no-nonsense veteran who'd seen it all before, had wanted to question Lynn under caution for some time. Not knowing Lynn's location, he'd been unable to. 'Considering the fact that our authority did not know the address of the above person's place of stay in Hungary, the above-mentioned person could not be summoned to police headquarters,' reads the official police file.

So, instead, Lieutenant Colonel Juhaz sent an official request to FHB bank – a bank he knew Lynn used. In response, the bank's lawyer, Dr Andras Imre, confirmed that Lynn 'regularly visits the branch office of FHB Bank located at No. 20 Váci Street, Budapest, and he is likely to visit the branch office on 11 August 2009'.

Bingo.

Upon arrival at police headquarters, Lynn was cautioned and, at 10 a.m., an official interpreter, Judit Fenyves, was appointed to translate for him. He was also allowed to make one call, which he used to summon his Budapest lawyer, Dr Attila Márton.

All formalities completed, Lynn's interrogation – carried out by Police Lieutenant István Balogh – began at midday. The questioning related mostly to Croi 61 Kft – a defunct firm of Lynn's that had planned to build on a Budapest site. But Balogh also grilled Lynn about Anthony Cantwell – aka Patrick James Holcomb – who had been extradited from Kyiv to the US six months earlier. The Hungarians now knew Cantwell had been a fraud.

'Do you know Anthony Cantwell?' Lynn was asked.

'Yes, I do know him. He used to work for Kendar Holdings Ltd in Dublin,' Lynn answered. 'He worked as a sales manager. I was the director and owner of Kendar Holdings Ltd. And there were two other managers besides me.'

'For how long have you known Anthony Cantwell?' the police asked.

Lynn said Cantwell had been hired by others in 'July or August 2007' and that he'd played no role in his recruitment.

'Have you ever seen any personal identification documents of Anthony Cantwell? What kind of relation did you have with him?'

'Yes, I met him. I did not see any of his papers,' Lynn answered, saying others had interviewed him. 'Anthony moved to Hungary from Dublin. I must have met him about three or four times.'

'Do you know Patrick James Holcomb?' Lynn was asked.

'I do not know him,' Lynn answered. Then he added a clarification. 'I wish to add that Zoltán Krisztián [a lawyer associated with the sale of Lynn's Croi 61 firm] informed me that Anthony Cantwell was not really Anthony Cantwell. This happened around March or April 2009. I myself did not employ Anthony in any form. When I sold my interest in Croi 61 Kft, this business relationship ceased to exist totally. He was actually an employee of Kendar Holdings, but he came to Hungary in October 2007. Kendar Holdings had some financial difficulties around 15 October 2007, that is why he came to Hungary. I do not remember exactly when his employment was terminated, because I had quite a lot of problems at that time.'

'Did you give any authorisation to Anthony Cantwell to act in full power for and on behalf of Croi 61 Kft?' Lynn was asked.

'Yes, it is possible. As I can recall, I did.'

Lynn was then shown the authorisation he had signed handing control over to Cantwell on 1 November 2007 and was asked to confirm his signature.

'Yes, this is my signature,' he confirmed.

He was then asked why he had signed two authorisations for Cantwell to act on behalf of Croi 61 Kft.

'The reason was that one of them was made in Dublin,' Lynn answered. 'And I was not sure if that document would be acceptable here, so we made another one in Budapest.'

After a few more questions, the interrogation drew to a close, but there was another shock in store for Lynn. The Hungarians wanted to extradite him to Ireland.

The Interpol duty officer at the International Liaison Building in police HQ in Dublin's Phoenix Park was dumbstruck. Across a secure line from Budapest's Interpol office, his Hungarian counterpart had informed him that wanted fugitive Michael Lynn was in custody and would be extradited imminently.

The news was greeted with disbelief by the handful of people informed in Dublin. The Irish authorities were nowhere near ready to arrest Lynn and he couldn't be legally extradited. The Irish police investigation into Lynn was still ongoing and they had not yet issued criminal charges or sought an international arrest warrant. Officially, Lynn should not have been arrested – at least not on foot of any request sent through Interpol from Dublin. What, they wondered, were the Hungarians at?

At the request of the police in Dublin, Lynn had been the subject of an Interpol blue notice for years. Unlike a red notice – which would have seen him arrested and extradited on sight – a blue notice meant Lynn's movements in foreign jurisdictions were simply noted and any information gathered passed on through Interpol to the authorities in Dublin.

The blue alert for Lynn had been triggered dozens of times since he'd absconded. His many movements through land border crossings in Europe and his name on passenger manifests to and from the US and elsewhere had all been logged. So, too, had any instances in which his name featured in criminal investigations abroad. But Lynn wasn't supposed to be arrested on foot of Interpol's blue notice, never mind extradited. Something strange was afoot.

According to the Hungarian police file, the arresting officers were told a warrant for Lynn's arrest and extradition had been issued through the International Criminal Cooperation Centre on 12 March 2009. Yet there was no valid warrant. Either someone had misunderstood and misinterpreted the Interpol blue notice, or there had been a more sinister, conspiratorial plot orchestrated against Lynn in Hungary.

With Lynn in custody and ready to be put on a plane home, the authorities in Dublin had to tell their Hungarian counterparts to let him go. At 5 p.m. on the day of his arrest, Lynn was released.

Justice Brian McGovern – like many of his peers in the High Court – was puzzled. For years now the courts had been dealing with application after application from banks seeking to repossess properties once owned by Lynn, but there was still no sign of the man being arrested. No sign at all.

This time Anglo Irish Bank was seeking an order to repossess Donegal investment properties bought jointly by Lynn and an associate in February 2007. The bank had lent Lynn and his associate €671,140 to fund the purchase. Not a single cent had ever been repaid.

The case was cut and dried and Judge McGovern granted the order without fuss. But something bothered him. It was 'difficult to believe', he said, that Lynn was still at large, and he queried 'whether an international arrest warrant had been served?'

'Can you tell me something?' he asked. 'Are there – have there been – any steps taken to have Mr Lynn charged?'

No one could answer. It was 16 March 2010 – seven months after Lynn's brief detention in Budapest. It would be another four years before he saw the inside of a police cell again.

18

Because I'm a Nice Boy?

ROBERT EAGAR FASTENED THE SWIVEL CATCH holding the table to the seat before him, tightened his seat belt in preparation for landing and gazed down at the glistening Algarve coastline stretched out below. It had just gone 2.10 p.m. local time on Monday, 6 September 2010 and flight FR7032 from Dublin to Faro was bang on time.

A criminal defence lawyer and an expert on extradition, Eagar would go on to be appointed a High Court judge in 2014. But today he had a meeting with one of his more intriguing clients, Michael Lynn.

More than a year since his Budapest arrest – and release – life for Lynn had settled down somewhat. He'd needed to take some time out, to step off the treadmill, to focus on his marriage and to keep sane. Long, brooding walks with his beloved and ever-loyal dogs on Tavira's windswept salt marshes brought some solace. So did chatting football in pigeon Portuguese with old-timers at the local bar. Playing music – his first passion – focused his mind on something other than his plight. And counselling with a psychiatrist helped too.

'I had to accept what I did, accept responsibility for it and get rid of my guilt,' he'd later tell me. 'It was eating me up. I couldn't actually take responsibility and do something about it, and that's where I'm at now. I know. It sounds terribly American.'

After our interview in Portugal and subsequent meeting in Budapest, Lynn had remained in contact. His calls – always on Skype from an undisclosed number at completely random hours of the day and night – continued until shortly after his Budapest arrest. Then they petered out completely. He'd been ignoring emails, too.

To the wider world and media Lynn was old news – for now. He had spun out of the news cycle. But his case was not closed – far from it – and I wanted to re-establish contact. In the meantime, Robert Eagar – Bobby as Lynn called him – was as busy as ever. Though he never went on record or represented him in court, Eagar had been dealing with Lynn for some time.

So, too, had Ray St John Murphy – a London-based solicitor and partner at the Merriman White law firm. But if Eagar was widely esteemed and beyond reproach, Murphy had had his difficulties. In 2007, Murphy had been fined £25,000 sterling by the British Solicitors Disciplinary Tribunal for mishandling clients' funds, bad accounting practices and other offences. Despite this, Lynn trusted Murphy, and both lawyers were on board to help if they could.

This presented certain problems, such as the fact that dealing with Lynn meant wading through considerable amounts of hyperbole.

'Lets [sic] be straight about this,' Lynn had written to Eagar and Murphy in October 2008. 'I will not be elegant or eloquent here but frankly I have a pain in my bollix with the spirit of taking it on the chin.'

The tone was typical of Lynn. So, too, were the scattergun instructions that followed.

'I want us to agree that we start media attacks – i.e. proceedings,' Lynn demanded. 'I want to pay a private investigator to do certain vital research work for us. I want us to cause legal chaos and show the key individuals involved in driving this against me that my days of rolling over are at an end.'

Inevitably Lynn would seek a cheesy way of ending his emails.

'Lets [sic] be clear guys,' he'd concluded in this instance. 'I'm no virgin but even a prostitute gets paid. Mmm, not my best metaphor ever,' he admitted.

Somewhere between fielding the wisecracks and keeping up with the roadrunner-on-a-treadmill-mind of Lynn, it was Eagar's role to advise, to counsel and to mediate with the authorities back in Dublin. In the absence of being able to arrest Lynn, Irish detectives were agreeable to questioning him outside the jurisdiction – something Lynn appeared amenable to. And it was through Eagar – who had once worked in the Irish government's Chief State Solicitor's office – that correspondence between Lynn and his would-be-prosecutors flowed.

I'd never met Eagar and had only recently become vaguely aware of his role. He'd not responded to a call from me two weeks previously. Hardly a surprise. Now – unbeknownst to us both – we were sitting just rows apart on the same plane as it prepared to descend to Faro. Both of us, I'd soon find out, were heading for a meeting with Lynn. Except Lynn had no idea I was coming.

'Jesus! How the hell are ya?' Lynn cheerily called out from the open ground-floor window of his Tavira villa.

This whole trip had been a punt – a complete gamble. Lynn had cut all contact more than a year earlier and I had no idea if he would look favourably on a fresh approach. I did, though, have a good reason to try.

Thanks to a grant from the EU fund for investigative journalism, I'd begun a collaboration with a team of Bulgarian journalists I'd first met while pursuing Lynn in Sofia. The project was investigating international property corruption and its possible links to criminal money laundering. That's where Lynn came in.

We had some intriguing and unlikely leads. For example, the office right next door to Lynn's Bulgarian HQ in Sofia's Bellissimo Building housed a legal firm that had been used by relatives of one-time IRA Chief of Staff Thomas Slab Murphy to invest in Black Sea properties. As many as twenty-one other individuals living close to Murphy had also bought Bulgarian properties via the same lawyer. Who knew where such avenues of inquiry could lead?

I'd disembarked quickly at Faro, grabbed a hire car and headed straight for the villa, half hoping to hit the beach if he was not home – something I'd yet to do despite more than half a dozen trips to this paradise.

I knew I'd struck lucky as soon as I pulled into his street forty minutes later and let the car slide quietly past the property. This was not the locked-up home of the hunted-down fugitive I'd staked out years before. Everything appeared normal again. The gate was open, as were all of the building's white wooden shutters. Lynn's Audi was openly parked beside a nearby kerb.

Parking around the corner, I doubled back on foot, my dictaphone silently recording in my pocket. From an open window at the front of the house Lynn's voice – wheeling and dealing – bounded out across the property's well-tended flowers towards the street. From the snatches of conversation that reached me, it seemed he was dealing with a business associate in Budapest. I waited until he'd rung off and called out.

'Sorry to surprise you like that,' I began as he scurried out to meet me. 'I had no way of knowing if you were here.'

'Michael, there's no problem,' he smiled. 'It's very coincidental you arriving, because Bobby Eagar – my lawyer – he arrived out on the plane just now. Did you arrive on the 2.10 plane?'

'Yes.'

'How long are you here for?'

'I have a flight Wednesday evening.'

Lynn did a double take, amazed at the coincidence.

'You're flying back the same flight and you fucking came out together. I swear on my fucking grave,' he chuckled. 'Do you know Bobby, do you?' he then asked.

'I tried to contact him about two weeks ago.'

'He wouldn't want to talk to you. Even if I asked him to, he wouldn't – with a journalist! You know. He's not that kind of fella. He's a criminal lawyer.'

Lynn, though, was more than happy to talk. The next morning, we met in a nearby café. It was mid-morning and amidst the froth and hiss of a busy cappuccino nozzle and clanking cups, most of the voices rising to the spinning ceiling fan were those of local pensioners.

Lynn was on the phone as he walked in. 'Okay – so I'll leave you to have the discussion. Is that okay?' he told whoever he was speaking to, gesturing to me that he'd be done in a second.

'Sound,' he continued into the handset, moving almost out of earshot, only the odd word and phrase now audible. 'Thanks a million. Cheers,' I heard him say as he rang off.

Always busy – ducking, diving, negotiating, plotting. Nothing stays still for long in the world of Michael Lynn. There are always several balls to juggle. Here he was meeting me in between talks with his lawyer and constant interruptions from other associates from different locations across the world as he continued to do business years after going on the run.

'So how are you?' I asked.

'Not so bad,' he said with an exaggerated merry Mayo lilt as he sat down, grinning.

'I've interrupted your day. Sorry about that.'

'You're all right. Don't worry.'

Small talk over, I got down to business. Lynn, it turned out, was happy to help with our EU-funded corruption investigation in Bulgaria and he provided some vital leads. Aside from that though, I was certain he had more to tell about his own story and, even if the press pack back home had lost interest, I wasn't about to stop digging. Plus, he'd long ago made a commitment to show me documents to back up some of his assertions about lenders being complicit in his deceptive dealings with the Irish banks. I wanted to see those records and knew they would reveal more truth than any amount of talking.

In the meantime, though, I was more than happy to listen. Increasingly I could not believe what I was being told.

'This guy got some cash – absolutely. I organised a direct debit.'

The words were clear. Nevertheless, my brain hit pause and replayed the sentence to itself to be sure. Was Lynn now admitting to bribery in return for loans? Loans he never repaid. Loans that were secured – on his word – against properties already pledged to other banks.

During our meeting I'd been pushing him about the possibility of turning State's evidence – trying to bargain what he knew about financiers in return for more lenient treatment. I'd hoped the move would illicit admissions about bribes and corruption, but I didn't expect it to work so well.

'Sorry,' I asked, 'he got a commission, is what you mean?'

'From me – he got paid cash,' Lynn corrected.

I was dumbfounded. This was a mammoth step up from what I'd heard him speak of before. Holiday offers and corporate entertainment for banking associates was one thing. Using commission as a carrot with brokers and lenders was another. But barefaced bribery was a different ball game altogether.

It quickly became evident that Lynn had considered the option of State's evidence, though he'd completely discounted the possibility. The case of Frank Dunlop – a renowned lobbyist who famously spilled the beans about Irish planning corruption – seemed his primary point of reference. Lynn was acutely aware that Dunlop, having turned State's evidence, was nevertheless sent to jail for corruption himself.

'You want some assurance that they're not going to just take you, use you, lock you up and throw away the key,' I summed up.

'That's correct. Exactly.'

'Do you have evidence of that?' I asked about the cash he says he handed over. 'It's your word against theirs.'

'I don't know. Yeah – maybe I can say look at my bank account. That cash was for him,' he trailed off, realising the likely inadequacy of such evidence.

'The bank records alone are going to show you withdrawing something – your bank statements. If he wasn't clever, the exact same amount is going to be lodged,' I thought out loud.

'That's correct,' Lynn answered. 'But then I think the most he'll have is tax problems because he'll say he got it from whoever.'

'For how many people could you demonstrate cash leaving your account and going potentially into the account of someone else?'

'In relation to him, three or four times. In relation to two other banks maybe four or five times. It's good enough for a journalist to ask questions about. It's not good enough for the cops. Sorry, it's good enough for them to ask questions.'

It was clear he did not feel any State's evidence he may be able to offer was sufficiently strong. But I pushed further. This was not a strand of conversation I wanted to let go of just yet.

'I don't know,' I responded. 'Imagine a case where they stand up and demonstrate ten examples of money leaving your account and on ten times – different people, different banks – the same amount of money within a day or so is put into other people's accounts and they are the people who gave you the loans.'

'But that would be hanging me,' he interjected. 'You're saying I deliberately set out to steal their money.'

I held my tongue. That's precisely what I was saying. That's precisely how those who lost out because of Lynn's actions would feel.

But Lynn's perspective was different. Irreconcilably so. Warped in fact. In his view, he didn't steal any money from anyone. He got loans he fully intended to repay but was unable to because of circumstances beyond his control. Bankers lent him more than they should have. Sure. They continued to lend to him even as he failed to honour previous loan commitments. Sure. But – Lynn would say – weren't they doing that with everyone?

In Lynn's mind that did not equate to fraud, even if he had offered cash to ensure a smooth loan application.

'That's not fraud. Absolutely, you accept that,' he told me. 'That's – that's civil liability.'

'I don't know the law, but it looks like you paying a bribe to get the money,' I responded, puzzled at his logic.

Lynn painted an example.

'If I owe you €10 and you lend me another four – we're now at €14 – and I'm meant to repay you four. I don't, and a year and a half later I come back to you. You say: "But Michael, you never paid me the four." Now what would you do? Give me more? Why would they do that? Because they liked me? Because I'm a nice boy?'

His meaning was clear. They did it because he made it worth their while. But did he really believe it was not fraud?

'There are two crimes there,' I began.

'There's mine,' he added.

'There's yours and there's his.'

'That's correct,' he agreed.

'What's more important to the banks or the cops at the moment,' I asked, thinking out loud about what leverage his evidence may have, 'bankers or Michael Lynn?'

'Well, bankers,' he began in a la-di-da mock tone. 'We don't want bankers dragged through the mire.'

This sentiment – born from a deep-seated resentment – is one that remains a bitter barb within Lynn's psyche. The bankers and lawyers who once enabled his corruption all pulled up their collars when the storm swept over and walked on without a backward glance, leaving Lynn to carry the can – and a warped sense of victimhood forevermore.

19

When a Camel Has Sex

YAHIYA MEGOMEDOVICH HASHIEV IS NOT THE kind of person you'd want to fall out with. He's not the kind of person you'd want to fall in with either. Michael Lynn managed to do both.

A notorious gangster and mafia lord in Bulgaria's Varna region, Hashiev has a penchant for chunky gold rings and head-to-toe white suits. It's a look he's been deprived of for much of the past decade as he's languished in jail for VAT fraud.

Hashiev's renown comes from his association with a vicious Black Sea-based criminal gang known to be involved in raising funds for terrorism, extortion and human trafficking. Hashiev's one-time leadership of the Black Sea Boxing Club does nothing to diminish his fearsome reputation. He once escaped a brutal assassination attempt – surviving only after two life-saving operations. Between jail terms, he's protected round the clock by five burly bodyguards, something Lynn found out when they first met.

'I went over to Bulgaria and I was greeted in Varna by him and his people – all of them carrying pieces. All with bulletproof vests,' Lynn had told me when we'd last met in Portugal in September 2010. 'I thought, mother of God what am I involved in here?'

What he was involved in was corruption and bribery at a considerable cost to others. I was about to stumble onto the proof.

Two weeks after renewing contact with Lynn in Portugal, I'd flown back to Bulgaria for the first time since we'd hunted him there in 2008. This time – thanks to the EU fund for investigative journalism – I'd partnered with local journalists and did not have to rely on an imaginative fixer.

This time if I wanted to meet the secret service – which I did – it would not involve an ominous note under my hotel-room door in the dead of night.

This time I would come home with a cache of documents that proved Lynn was completely aware of who he was dealing with when he went into business with Yahiya Hashiev. Lynn just didn't care, so long as there was a deal to be done and money to be made.

'At the time it was what can I get – and can I sell it?' Lynn had told me two weeks earlier in Portugal. 'My concern was sales,' he'd scoffed.

Then he'd added a phrase that struck me – not so much for its simple honesty, but for its callous indifference to the suffering he had caused. 'You know Michael,' he'd said, 'I cannot say that I was raped as an innocent.'

Osman Oktay could resolve pretty much any problem you might encounter in Bulgaria. In a world where corruption is simply an additional business tax that must be endured, the silver-haired, smooth-talking, one-time member of parliament is the ultimate troubleshooter.

Caught in a blackmail plot? No big deal. Being swindled by local mafia figures? No problem. Need access to a government minister or two? Sure. Being subjected to industrial espionage? Taken care of. Fed up being asked for bribes? Sorted. Need a private meeting with a police chief? No problem. Received a death threat? Don't worry, Osman Oktay is your man. For a fee. Naturally.

He'd been Lynn's fixer, too, once the Irishman began to encounter the more challenging aspects of doing deals in Bulgaria. If anyone knew of Michael Lynn's dealings in Bulgaria it was going to be Oktay. He was the reason I'd come back.

Oktay's pedigree is solid. Declassified intelligence files show he was an 'agent for State security' in Bulgaria from 1975 to 1983. Then, after the fall of the Soviet Union, he had been the deputy head of the Movement for Rights and Freedoms (DPS), an ethnic Turkish political party in Bulgaria. That role ceased abruptly in 2001 when a $350,000 cash donation – allegedly handed to Oktay but not delivered to party coffers – was revealed. Nevertheless, his tenure as a member of parliament, which had started in 1991, continued until 2005. For part of that time he served under party leader Ahmed Dogan, a former member of the Bulgarian Communist Secret Service, and he was also vice chairman of several parliamentary committees.

When Lynn met him, Oktay was running a Sofia-based consultancy called ARIS. On its now-deleted website the firm advertised some particularly unique services. These included 'signalling the competent authorities and institutions in the event of disloyal competition, heavy bureaucracy, or bribery and blackmailing attempts by the State and municipal authorities'.

It was the bribery bit in particular – and how it might relate to Michael Lynn – that I wanted to learn about.

We met at Oktay's headquarters – a corner third-floor apartment overlooking Sofia's Boulevard Gotse Delchev. From behind his desk Oktay listened intently as my colleagues translated my intentions and communicated his responses back to me in their broken English. With poor translation it was difficult to get a clear sense of anything. It was documents I needed, documents I'd come for.

As Oktay spoke I looked around. Though clearly designed as an apartment originally, the room was furnished like an office. Strangely there appeared to be no paperwork anywhere. Nothing on the conference table in the corner, nothing on Oktay's desk, nothing on the shelves, nothing on the glass coffee table in front of the leather couch.

'Tell him please that I will need proof of whatever he says about Lynn's activities,' I told my colleague.

Oktay nodded a reassurance and waved his hand as if to say, 'No problem. Don't worry.' I sensed he could easily speak to me in English if he chose to. But he didn't.

'He has everything. Don't worry,' I was reassured.

In between translations, I thought of Lynn sitting in this room seeking to avail of Oktay's services years earlier. Lynn had also come here for help after he went on the run. That much he'd told me himself.

'I met him in November/December 2007, when he offered to protect the investors by putting all the assets in his own name,' Lynn had guffawed, raising his eyes to heaven to indicate he hadn't fallen for that one.

'There's not many Bulgarians with an apartment in Monaco,' he'd continued. 'Have you seen his apartment in Monaco?'

Lynn was clearly unimpressed with Oktay.

'Osman Oktay absolutely fucked us,' he'd told me, though he conceded he'd signed up willingly for the consultant's unique services.

For Oktay, the feeling was mutual. Lynn owed him €1 million, he claimed, and had dishonoured their arrangement. After more than an hour, he finally brought out the files and gave me unrestricted access. The cache proved that Lynn – to coin his own phrase – had certainly not been raped as an innocent. Far from it.

Michael Lynn's foray into Bulgaria's seedy underworld was sealed the day after he'd given away one of his yet-to-be built Bansko apartments on *The Late Late Show*.

The *Sunday Business Post* Property Expo 2006 opened its doors at the Royal Dublin Society grounds on Saturday, 4 February 2006, at the very height of Ireland's property and credit bubble. 'This is a business proposition you cannot afford to ignore,' advertisements for the event urged. Thousands took heed and Lynn's sales force, dangling sun-kissed real estate dreams before credit-rich customers, clocked up sale after sale with ease.

But Lynn, too, was a target at this event, though the bait required to spark his interest – and detailed in Oktay's documents – was considerably larger. For months a Chechen national living in Ireland had been trying to sell a Black Sea development opportunity to Kendar. There'd been some initial stumbling blocks, but when Lynn and the Chechen met at the Property Expo, they hammered out an agreement to make it work.

Lynn would buy the land at Shkorpilovtsi for €1,629,000 on the understanding that the project could yield profits in excess of €37 million. This figure was more than sufficient to grab Lynn's attention. He was hooked.

But there was a catch. For starters, the deal was corrupt and it required that public officials be bribed. It would also bring Lynn directly into business with figures from the murky underworld of Varna.

Undeterred, he forged ahead. Two weeks after meeting Lynn, the Chechen emailed his invoice to Kendar. It listed a commission figure equal to 5 per cent of the purchase price (€81,450) to be paid as a finder's fee. So far, nothing unusual.

But there was something else – and it was far from usual. The invoice also listed a separate €30,000 fee for the Chechen described as 'assistance to get the contract for the project preparation with architect Saraliev'.

This was key.

Architect Saraliev was Liana Saraliev, the daughter of Simeon Saraliev – the chief architect of the local municipality responsible for the pristine Shkorpilovtsi area. Lynn was not just paying a finder's fee to someone who had brought him a lucrative deal. He was buying the cooperation of those who would be deciding upon zoning and planning decisions.

Brazenly, the corruption was written into every step of the deal right from the very beginning. It had even been referred to repeatedly and explicitly in the original brochure put together to sell the project to Lynn in the first place. 'Getting planning permission includes "a gift" to architect,' a note read.

Right from the beginning, Lynn knew he'd secure planning permission in the heart of an important nature reserve because the municipality's architect was being bought off with 'a gift' and the lucrative contract for designing Kendar's resort was going to the architect's daughter. Such is business in Bulgaria.

On 13 March 2006, one of Lynn's firms – Kendar Holdings – transferred €40,000 into an account at the College Green branch of Ulster Bank in Dublin in part payment to his Irish-based Chechen associate. The deal had been sealed. Lynn's dalliance with Bulgarian corruption had begun. It was about to bring him into contact with some very dangerous players.

Less than a month later – on 5 April 2006 – Kendar agreed to pay Yahiya Hashiev a €97,794 fee – half of which was paid that day. In return Hashiev would secure a change of land use designation for Lynn's Shkorpilovtsi lands. Lynn, the son of a farmer from small-town Ireland, was now officially linked with one of Bulgaria's most notorious crooks. More than that – he was paying him to ensure a treasured nature reserve would be rezoned to allow Kendar to build.

Worse still, Hashiev and a network of criminal associates had secured the land in the first place using their fearsome reputations to ensure local smallholders sold up en masse for a pittance. They then bundled the land together in an all-in-one package that included the necessary bribes and corrupt influence to secure rezoning and full planning permission. For many Irish people, such a land grab would be abhorrent, given Ireland's painful history of violent evictions under British rule. But Lynn didn't care. That was clear from his comments to me weeks earlier in Portugal.

'These farmers were under pressure to sell for €5 per square metre for something that costs €55 per square metre,' he'd chuckled, before checking himself. 'Okay – basically that's terrible. I don't want you quoting me, but in the Celtic Tiger it was what can I get? What can I sell it for? How's she cutting?'

What he got, in this instance, was a tranche of prime Black Sea development land that became the property of Kendar Bulgaria in August 2006, shortly after it had passed through the hands of Yahiya Hashiev and a couple of his underworld associates. Those associates included Cristo Danov, who was paid €250,000 by Kendar for a 3,473 square metre part of the site. Danov, the grandson of former Minister of Home Affairs and one-time Chairman of Bulgaria's Constitutional Court Hristo Danov, was a municipal councillor in Varna for the Bulgarian Party of Justice. He was also a crook, who'd been imprisoned, together with his father, Vaselin Danov, for running prostitution, money laundering and human trafficking rings.

In September 2006, still undeterred by these criminal links, Kendar agreed to pay a further €41,052 to Hashiev to secure necessary permits – bringing the cost of securing land use changes at Shkorpilovtsi to more than €138,000. After that it was time to ensure planning permission. Thanks to the Saraliev family, Lynn knew this wouldn't be an issue.

On 3 October 2006, the architecture firm owned by Liana Saraliev – DZZD Ecoconsult – was paid an initial fee of €40,000 by Kendar. Among the files provided by Oktay was the receipt the firm had issued in return for the money. Saraliev – thanks to her father's position in the council – was expecting to be paid €16 per square metre for designing Lynn's Black Sea resort – a total of €1.2 million according to her contract with Kendar.

But by February 2007 – a year after the Varna deal had begun – things were getting too much for Lynn. His mafia associates were becoming impatient for payments they believed they were owed. And they weren't afraid to say it.

'Kendar is showing disrespect. I don't allow this to anyone,' Yahiya Hashiev wrote to Lynn. He also contacted Lynn's manager in Bulgaria – a Turkish national called Haldun.

'When two camels have sex and there is a fly between them, it dies. You are no longer of interest to me,' Hashiev told Lynn's manager. 'I don't believe the Bulgarian State will mind if I fuck one Turkish arse.'

In response Lynn bravely defended his manager. 'Yahiya, please refrain from any further threats to Haldun. Please understand that if you threaten Haldun, you also threaten me.'

Hashiev remained unfazed and demanded a payment of €50,000 for 'moral damage'.

'I feel humiliated. I need to know who will give me that money. Kendar or Haldun,' he raged in an email to Lynn.

Lynn, meanwhile, had other problems. His empire was on the verge of imploding and he knew it. He would soon go on the run. When he did, in a desperate bid to resolve matters in Varna, he turned to Osman Oktay.

The move worked – for a while. Oktay quickly filed a criminal complaint against Yahiya Hashiev with State prosecutors for the explicit threats he had made. He also forced the architect, Saraliev, to resign from the Shkorpilovtsi municipality by threatening to expose his conflict of interest.

'We were ready to give the case to the prosecutor's office. It was a case of conflict of interests,' Oktay told me. He secured another architect to complete the design work for a quarter of the price Saraliev's daughter was charging.

In the meantime, though, Lynn – unbeknownst to Oktay – double-crossed his fixer and secretly took on other advisers to help him liquidate his Bulgarian assets completely – as I'd discovered years earlier.

'He should have paid me,' Oktay said. 'What they did for him, I could have done much better. There would have been no traces. If the Irish authorities or Interpol want the information from me, I will cooperate,' he told me.

In turning to Oktay to resolve his problems with Hashiev – as a popular Bulgarian proverb goes – Lynn had jumped from a thistle to a whitethorn.

20

Lynn Does a Ronnie Biggs

BRAZIL WAS ALWAYS AN OPTION. It's likely to have been the plan all along. One way or another – now that he was safely there – Michael Lynn was not being shy about it.

'Any1 [know] the name of a good pub in the São Paulo area of Brazil to watch the Mayo Cork match on Sunday,' he tweeted on 27 July 2011. 'A place with a singsong a bonus.'

The message was the very first communication from a new Twitter account in the name of Lynn created that day. Composing the blurb for the account, Lynn described himself in typically self-deprecating fashion: 'Fun loving musician with a love of travelling,' he wrote. 'Used to dabble in law and property but got out in time. Available for weddings in the greater São Paulo area.'

This was a new Lynn. A bolder, in-your-face, get-over-it, you-can't-catch-me-now Lynn. He said as much himself.

'To those who have been inappropriately wronged in the past, I say sorry. I wanted time to rescue the situation but was not afforded this,' he wrote. 'I hope everyone can move on, forgive and forget. Life is short and the next opportunity is round the corner.'

Many of those Lynn signed up to follow on social media were Irish media personalities and journalists. Some followed him back. Most must have thought the Twitter account was a fake. But the turn of phrase, the mannerisms, the inappropriate jokes and the identity of some of those he was privately messaging indicated the Lynn account was legitimate.

There was a reason for Lynn's brash move into the Twittersphere, even if he knew many would not believe the account to be genuine. Brid was about to give birth to their first son. Now he felt untouchable.

'Please wish my darling wife Brid luck this week as she prepares for the birth of our 1st child,' Lynn tweeted.

In case the benefits of having a child born in Brazil were not clear to anyone, Lynn was happy to explain.

'Any of you guys know where to get good, free straight no bullshit legal advice (preferably on the net) for the following scenario ... 2 non Brazilian parents applying for permanent Brazilian residency through their baby being born in Brazil ... Thank you, Sincerely.'

Then, within minutes, he was off again, unleashing a gleeful crescendo sure to infuriate the victims of his actions.

'Its [sic] f***ing melting here, a few notches up from the Algarve. Nice all the same. Backs of the legs got f***ing reddened lying out yesterday.'

'A few more weeks of this and I should be saying goodbye to the farmers [sic] tan. Arse to the grass & belly to the sun ... if the Queen doesn't pop!'

Over the course of the next year, Lynn took to his account on just four separate dates, typically firing off multiple messages in one sitting before lapsing back into silence for months. Meanwhile, back in Europe, the consequences of the financial tidal wave caused by his actions continued to wash ashore.

On Wednesday, 22 June 2011 – a month before his carefree Brazilian tweets began – Lynn's one-time Portuguese firm, Vantea, formally Kendar Portugal, was declared insolvent. Creditors who lost out included the Portuguese Commercial Bank, which was owed €6,230,403, and the Portuguese electricity service, which was due €537,740.

Four Portuguese construction companies also claimed they were owed more than €64 million between them. According to court documents they filed in Tavira as part of Vantea's insolvency, construction firm Bemposta was owed €16,646,482, L'Antic Colonial was owed €6,204,360 and Construções Marques was owed €37,289,137. A handful of private individuals also claimed to have lost over €7 million when Vantea went bust, with one – an Irish businessman – out of pocket to the tune of €4,641,800.

No wonder Lynn had left Portugal behind. It may have taken longer, but just as in Ireland, he'd burnt every bridge in sight in the Algarve, fleeing across them just as they collapsed. Now, from São Paulo, he appeared to be jeering at those he'd left behind.

'What is a good rent for a Manhattan apartment this weather,' he tweeted on 9 August 2011. 'Long-term tenants moving out … 3 bed spacious penthouse, concierge etc., etc. overlooking the Park.'

Slowly though – painfully slowly – the long arm of the law was beginning to flex. Soon it would reach out for Lynn.

At almost exactly the same time as Lynn was tweeting brashly about being a New York landlord from Brazil, Fraud Squad detectives in Ireland were finally submitting their investigation file to the DPP. After close to five years, the scales of justice were on the verge of tipping against Lynn. The detectives were confident they could prosecute him for theft and fraud. Soon the DPP would agree. Soon Lynn's past would catch up with him.

For now, though, Lynn, a new father after years of trying, felt safe. There was new meaning to his life. And he could move on. Nevertheless, he still indulged in one final game of cat and mouse with those pursuing him. He agreed – for the fourth time – to meet Fraud Squad detectives in Portugal.

The date set for the meeting was 24 October 2011. But Lynn had not been seen in Portugal for months and those pursuing him knew he was in Brazil. The truth was he had no intention of showing up – just like all the other times.

By then, Lynn didn't care about the authorities in Dublin. He was over Ireland. That was for sure. And, in his view, it was time for Ireland to get over him. The past was done and dusted – a bad debt written off. Who cared? So what if back home in Dublin the High Court – on application from the Office of the Director of Corporate Enforcement – had finally disqualified Lynn from acting as a company director on 10 October 2011, and banned him until 2023? As if he cared. His business interests lay elsewhere now. He was, he felt, way ahead of the game.

'São Paulo didn't quite work out for us,' he tweeted on 6 January 2012. 'But opportunities are presenting themselves to us, up North specifically. 2012 is filled with hope.'

'BTW, a lot gets put in perspective when you see your own eyes looking back at you, in that respect 2011 was tough but life-changing.'

Life-changing indeed. Not so long ago Lynn had been snapping up New York properties alongside the great and the good of the world. Now he'd joined a different list. One of ignominy. The most infamous name on that list was Great Train robber and prison escapee Ronnie Biggs, who lived as a fugitive in Brazil for decades before returning to Britain to serve out his time and die. One-time SS officer and Nazi war criminal Josef Rudolf Mengele – nicknamed the Angel of Death for his sadistic medical experiments – lived out his life in Brazil. Franz Stangl, the former Nazi commander of the Treblinka concentration camp in Poland, had also fled to Brazil before ultimately being extradited to face justice.

Mengele, Biggs ... Lynn. It takes some doing to get on a list like that. Lynn achieved it just the same.

The agenda for the meeting was clear. The date: Wednesday, 10 January 2007 – eleven months before Lynn would go on the run.

First, Michael Lynn wanted to know how to set up a company in Brazil. Then he needed to know how best to transfer money into it from abroad. Finally, he needed advice on how he and his wife could become Brazilian residents.

Sitting before him in their air-conditioned, downtown office, lawyers Cristina David and Simone Neri took Lynn through the requirements. After eight years in business, they knew the spiel by heart. That was the easy bit. Whether Lynn would hire them at the end of it was anyone's guess. But he seemed a good catch.

Glad of the respite from the searing heat outside, Lynn nodded as his assistant, Robert Lee, took notes. Outside, on Avenida Antônio Carlos Magalhães, the noise of Salvador's traffic throbbed like the beating heart of the city, vehicles pumping through its veins.

Known for its Portuguese colonial architecture, Salvador – with its historic heart of cobblestone alleyways and tropical coastline – is the teeming capital of the northeastern Brazilian state of Bahia. It was here that Lynn first came – just months before he'd go on the run – to begin setting in train his plans for Latin America. It was here a back-up plan began to take shape.

Business done, the meeting concluded with firm handshakes and a promise from the lawyers that they'd forward a written brief to Lynn. As he stood up, Lynn sucked in his belly and hiked up his trousers. Increasingly he was conscious of his spreading girth – the price of middle age and the high-octane luxury life he'd lived in recent years. It wouldn't be long, though, until he sorted that out, he told himself – thinking briefly of the books he'd picked up at the airport en route to Brazil: *Sly Moves: My Proven Program to Lose Weight, Build Strength, Gain Willpower and Live Your Dream* by actor Sylvester Stallone and *The Complete Book of Personal Training* by Douglas Brooks.

Lynn and Robert Lee – Kendar's Portugal manager – had set off for this exploratory trip to Brazil on 5 January 2007. During the two-week stay, Lynn stayed in a five-star lodge at the Costa do Sauípe resort. To cover everyday expenses, he'd withdrawn €5,000 in cash from an AIB bank in Maynooth, County Kildare, before leaving Ireland.

Content in his beachfront lodgings among a nature reserve near the Atlantic rainforest of Mata de São João, Lynn did what he always did. He made offers to buy property. He was thinking of buying a luxury condo off-plan in Quintas de Sauipe Grande Laguna – a beachfront development under construction near Salvador. Before leaving Brazil, he instructed his new lawyers to carry out due diligence on the deal.

Visiting Guarajuba, another beach town nearby, he'd popped into Bar Carlinos. Its owner, Carlos Canuto, was also a part-time realtor and the pair got talking. Before leaving – and on foot of nothing more than a casual acquaintance – Lynn made an offer of R$1 million (€300,000) for a beach-facing villa and offered a further R$900,000 (€285,000) for four vacant plots behind the beach. The deals never went through, but just a few months before he absconded from Ireland, Lynn was laying the groundwork for a life in Brazil.

On 12 November 2007 – just weeks before Lynn fled Dublin – his first Brazilian company was formed. Golina Empreendimentos Imobiliarios Ltda – translated as Golina Real Estate – was owned by Lynn and Brid. The firm was based in Fortaleza, another of the locations visited during Lynn's 2007 reconnaissance trip.

The call from was from a private number. I knew it was likely to be Lynn. Since moving to Brazil, he'd re-established contact and, over Christmas 2011, we'd discussed the prospect of a second interview. Provisionally we'd agreed to meet in the São Paulo region in March. I'd received my jabs, obtained Sebastian's approval to go and was waiting for confirmation to book flights. So Lynn's call – on Friday, 17 February 2012 – was not unexpected. The Lynn I spoke to that day was in good form, full of the joys of parenthood and inappropriate jokes about breastfeeding. As ever, he was keen to hear of developments back home.

A month earlier, on 16 January, Ireland's richest man, Sean Quinn, had declared himself bankrupt. Lynn could relate to the plight of the Quinn family. Like Lynn, their assets had been frozen by a High Court order. Like Lynn, they had sought to move them anyway, keeping them out of reach of creditors. And like Lynn, they would encounter the perils of the shadowy netherworld such decisions invite.

'I feel it's the [sic] appropriate to make a statement on the Sean Quinn affair as I was the first victim of the banks and I wont [sic] be the last,' Lynn would later tweet. 'I have a lot of sympathy for Sean and his family. Hard working people let down by the system. To Sean Jnr, head up you still have your dignity. Not many in that country can say that at this stage.'

Though no specific time or location had been finalised, our call ended with an agreement that he'd pose for photos – though not with his son – and that any interview would not reveal his location in Brazil. He also wanted to keep his job and employer – which he had refused to specify – secret.

The following morning news broke that the DPP had finally decided to formally lay criminal charges against Lynn. There would be no interview and I never heard from him again.

'We do not believe he is out of our reach,' a police source told the newspapers.

I didn't believe he was out of reach either. And now that he was officially accused of being a criminal, I resolved, once again, to track him down.

21

First Among Equals

MICHAEL LYNN TURNED OFF RUA ENGENHO Poeta and nosed his front bumper up to the red and white security barrier. The SUV's air conditioning heaved a powerful sigh as he slid down the window to let security see his face. Glancing up briefly from his hut, the guard saw Lynn was a gringo and raised the barrier swiftly. No one would ever dream of stopping a white man in a place like this.

This place was the Caxangá Golf and Country Club – one of Brazil's most exclusive establishments. Situated in the northeastern city of Recife, the club occupies a luscious, sixty-three-acre site on the banks of the slumbering Capibaribe river.

It was 29 March 2012 – a little over a month since the DPP had decided to lay criminal charges against him – and Lynn had come to join up. Located on the edge of Recife, the Caxangá Golf and Country Club is conveniently located for two important groups of individuals: the region's privileged land-owning elites who occupy vast country estates among the hills inland; and the influential business, legal and political classes who occupy the best of the city's shorefront and downtown real estate.

Here, the great and the good of Recife and its hinterland come to relax, to mingle, to play tennis, to watch their children showjumping, to enjoy a round of golf, to practise their target shooting and to be seen at the restaurant and bar by the pool. The club offered just what Lynn needed if he was to relaunch his real estate career in Brazil – access to the region's most influential and wealthy individuals. Once a member, Lynn would be moving in privileged circles. Back among bankers and financiers and property tycoons. His type of people.

Plus, Lynn's firstborn, now a bundle of blond-haired energy, had been delighted to see the horses when club members had first shown Lynn's family around as guests. And the grounds were safe for family walks – not something you could say about many areas of Recife.

Lynn swung into one of the shaded parking places before the clubhouse, gathered his papers and strolled to the nearby administration building – a small, picturesque chalet with pretty, deep-blue traditional wooden shutters and doors. Inside, the receptionist, dressed in a smart, crested club blazer, took him through the application process. Business done, she withdrew an embossed envelope from a cabinet in the corner and popped the documentation inside before handing it ceremoniously to Lynn – a business-like gesture all club staff are trained to observe. After all, when someone pays 95,000 Brazilian Real (approximately €30,000) for a lifetime membership, they deserve to be treated like royalty.

'*Obrigado*,' Lynn thanked her, accepting the package with a smile. He was in.

On the top left of the envelope in Lynn's hand was the club's blue and yellow coat of arms with its feathered helmet from a medieval suit of armour. Below that was the club's motto – *Primus Inter Pares* (First Among Equals).

Michael Lynn was back where he felt he belonged. For now.

The task was just like before – only infinitely more difficult.

When Lynn first absconded, there were hundreds of leads – he'd stayed primarily in Europe and, if spotted, could be reached within a day or so on budget airline flights with little expenditure of time or money. Brazil was another matter entirely.

Unlike most European nations, Brazil was an infrastructural and bureaucratic nightmare. Company reports and foundation documents in most Brazilian regions were not accessible online. It was the same with land ownership records. And much of Brazil could not be considered an entirely safe location to work from. With 200 million people in a landmass about the size of the United States, finding Lynn would be near impossible and far more expensive. Even if I knew exactly where to go, I couldn't get there quickly or cheaply. There'd be no punts taken on this one. Resources wouldn't allow it.

But I did have some leads. And, now that Lynn was facing prosecution, his story was back on the radar again. If anyone managed to track him down – especially after he'd played his last desperate card – it would be one hell of a scoop. I set about the challenge with relish.

If Lynn kept his own name – which he appeared to be doing – there would be clues to follow. There always are. Even if he took on a fake identity – a more difficult thing to do successfully than most assume – leads would still pop up. Few ever cut ties with their families and friends entirely, and Lynn was not one of those for sure. There would be communication going back and forward between them. There would be family visits. There would be tickets bought. There would be post and parcels sent and received. Sooner or later a postman or courier would note the sender's address on a package from Brazil. Perhaps a relative would let slip a telling detail in a pub conversation. Something would slip. Something would give. It always does.

Lynn was – at one point – widely assumed to be in São Paulo. He'd told me as much himself before cutting off contact. His tweets hinted at São Paulo too, though they'd recently indicated he'd moved on from there. That January 2012 tweet said, 'Opportunities are presenting themselves to us, up North specifically,' just before Lynn went to ground again.

Salvador was north of São Paulo. I knew Lynn had made offers on a beach villa there. He'd sought residency advice from local lawyers there too. Fortaleza was also north of São Paulo. And I knew Lynn's 2007 trip had seen him investigate business possibilities in the city. A month before going on the run, Golina Real Estate had also been formed there.

I ran through the possibilities. Salvador and Fortaleza lay 1,624 kilometres apart. Between them lay countless towns and tens of millions of people. Still, this would have to be the target area. He had to be here, somewhere between the two cities if not in one of them.

Almost equidistant between Salvador and Fortaleza, just an hour's flight from both, lay a third major city – Recife. If I'd drawn a bullseye on my target area, the very centre would have encircled Recife. But I had no way of knowing if Lynn was there. He'd been careful to keep his presence in Recife off the internet. Even if I knew he was there, he'd be one of more than four million inhabitants of the fourth largest metropolitan area in Brazil. I stood little chance – bar a stroke of luck or a mistake on his part – of finding him. No such good fortune would reveal his location before fate intervened.

In the absence of anything better, I began tracking down those Lynn had met in Salvador and Fortaleza years earlier. Helpfully, Robert Lee – Lynn's assistant on the 2007 trip – had compiled a detailed report of all their meetings and contacts. And I had it. But I was getting nowhere. And I knew that every time I cold-called someone who'd been an associate, I was running the risk of tipping off Lynn.

Everyone either refused to speak, feigned ignorance or said they knew nothing. Everyone, that is, until I called the reception desk of the five-star Quintas de Sauipe Grande Laguna development close to Salvador.

I knew, thanks to Robert Lee's report, that Lynn had expressed interest in buying an off-plan condo there in 2007. Situated on the coast a short drive north of Salvador, the project was now built and fully occupied. It was just the kind of place Lynn would want to live. And it had a concierge service.

'Can you put me through to the home of Michael Lynn?' I asked when a thick-accented employee answered the phone.

'Michael Lynn. No problem. One moment, sir,' came the answer.

I was dumbstruck. Could this really be it? Why not? It made sense. Lynn had asked his Salvador lawyers to carry out due diligence on the deal.

I was put through immediately. Too quickly. If Lynn was there, I didn't want to alert him to my call. I had planned to hang up. We would want to catch him by surprise.

I was too late. The call clicked through – to an answer machine.

'Hello, you've reached Michael Mullins,' said a distinctly uppercut British voice on the message. 'Please leave a message.'

Michael Mullins. Not Michael Lynn. Jesus. The two were virtually identical when spoken in a thick Brazilian accent across a bad international phone line with a fraction of a second time delay. Had I hung up on time – as I'd intended to – I'd have blown thousands getting on the next flight to expose Lynn's new beach hideaway and instead wound up at the home of an unfortunate British expat.

Recife, the capital of the state of Pernambuco, has some of the most beautiful beaches in the world. Named for the majestic coral reefs that stretch for miles along its shores, the city should be an idyllic swimmer's paradise. But no one goes in the water anymore. After more than sixty shark attacks in recent years, swimming is forbidden. The problem arose after Recife began building a new industrial port – Porto Suape – in the 1990s, displacing the natural breeding and hunting habitats of thriving bull and tiger shark populations. Now, stark warning signs every few paces warn of the danger.

Michael Lynn didn't mind, though. He had his own pool at home and access to another one at the Caxangá Club. He wasn't a jump-in-the-sea kind of guy anyway. If he went to the beach, it was only to walk his dogs in the breeze that kept the tropical temperatures here pleasant. As in Portugal, these walks gave him time to think. To brood over what was and what could have been. To delve fleetingly into the fractured angst of the past before resolving once again to make good the future.

Increasingly, Lynn was trying not to think of the past. Sure, it was always there and he would catch his mind almost subconsciously drifting back to it sometimes. But after more than half a decade of uncertainty, he now knew his future was here. He had no choice anymore. Now on Interpol's red wanted list, he was hemmed in. He'd be arrested almost anywhere else. But there were worse places to wind up. And the certainty, the finality of his circumstances grounded him. So, too, did fatherhood. If ever Lynn was going to settle down for good, it was going to be here. If he was allowed to.

Lynn was here for the same reason as the sharks – Porto Suape. Fast becoming one of Brazil's most important industrial ports, the facility was the engine room of an unprecedented economic boom, the benefits of which were spreading out across the entire state of Pernambuco. Michael Lynn did booms. And he had a little something up his sleeve for Recife – as I would later discover.

When they first moved from São Paulo, Brid and Lynn took up residence in one of the towering, beachfront skyscrapers favoured by many middle-class locals in Recife. With secure underground parking, these towers are generally safe compared to the calamity of the streets outside – especially after dark. Even during daylight hours, locals have learned not to drive with their windows open and to keep car doors locked to prevent would-be carjackers.

But Lynn, a free spirit weaned on acres of green fields, didn't like the high-rise. He was determined to find a villa – preferably with a pool and a garden for the family dogs and cats – even if it meant living in a more dangerous neighbourhood.

Candeias – a suburb half an hour south of downtown Recife – was the answer. Here, ten blocks from the beach on a rubbish-strewn, unpaved road called Rua Professor Mario Ramos, Lynn found a smart villa for rent. Though the pot-holed street outside, with no street lighting, was a no-go zone after dark, the villa came with a security compound and high walls topped with live electric wire. Inside, Lynn and his family were safe and enjoyed a life of luxury – though the sounds and stink of teeming poverty from nearby favelas was a constant reminder of a less fortunate and more dangerous world.

On 26 June 2012 – four months after learning he faced criminal prosecution in Ireland – Lynn got the news he'd been waiting for. On that day, the Official Journal of Brazil's Ministry for Justice listed the outcome of residency case number 08505.098618/2011–93 concerning Michael Thomas Lynn and Brid Christina Murphy. Thanks to their son – born the previous year in São Paulo – Brid and Lynn were now permanent citizens of Brazil.

Residency secured, Brid could finally take her son back home to her family in County Clare. The week-long trip, in November 2012, saw her stay in the Old Ground Hotel in Ennis. Wrapped in a colourful, stitched Brazilian blanket, the child was presented to doting friends and family. Everywhere he went he clutched a favoured toy – a stick attached to a furry horse's head, a reminder perhaps of the horses his father brought him to see at the Caxangá Golf and Country Club.

Though he had bigger plans for the future, Lynn sought some part-time work teaching English. The move was a way to improve his own faltering Portuguese and it created a social outlet for him too. There was, after all, only so much walking alone on the beach that a guy could do. And friends were hard to find behind the walls of his villa compound.

It was in this way that Lynn and Brid became friends with Mark Astle and his wife, Regina. The owner of the up-market Britanic chain of English and Spanish language schools, Mark was a British expat who'd settled in Candeias twelve years earlier. Unannounced, and with no teaching experience, Lynn had simply popped in to ask for a job.

'He was the definition of Irish charm,' Mark later recalled. 'But in any case, native speakers are a prized possession, so I took him on.'

Lynn – a fugitive once worth millions – was now earning 2,000 Real (about €600) a month in exchange for thirteen hours a week of tutoring. The wage wouldn't even come close to covering his rent. But it wasn't about the money for Lynn. He had other plans in that regard. Now that he was officially a permanent resident of Brazil, Lynn felt untouchable. He was coming out of the shadows. After years on the run, he finally felt safe enough to go on the books as an employee of a respected company. He was stepping back into normality. He was no longer hiding.

'Everything he had here was positive,' Mark Astle would later say. 'Maybe this was a redemption for him.'

It certainly looked like it. In photos from the time, Lynn, wearing lurid green trousers, looks relaxed and content as he celebrates St Patrick's Day with students. But working at Britanic gave Lynn something else too. It was

Astle, a longstanding member of the Caxangá Golf and Country Club, who vouched for Lynn when he became a member. The club's first among equals ethos means no one can join without being referred by a trusted sponsor who is already a member.

Teaching English at Britanic – Recife's most renowned private language school – also offered Lynn further access to elite circles. The school counts many prominent businessmen and figures among its graduates. Typically, only the well-off in Brazil learn English. Only the really well-off do it in a private school. The young adults Lynn tutored would soon be taking their place among the ranks of those who controlled Recife.

Michael Lynn knew precisely where he wanted to get to – and it wasn't a teaching career, that's for sure. There was a local property boom to be exploited in Recife and he wasn't going to sit idly by teaching English part-time while others made millions. He had plans. Big plans. Soon, I'd learn just how advanced those plans already were.

22

Case No. 1326

PERHAPS IT WAS KARMA. PERHAPS IT was fate. One way or another, Michael Lynn's timing stank. Just as he began to feel safe in Brazil, the authorities there had decided they'd had enough of their country being regarded as a safe haven for criminals. Protecting murderers, fraudsters, thieves and war criminals was not a reputation Brazil wanted anymore – especially as the nation prepared for the international spotlight that the 2014 World Cup and 2016 Olympics would bring.

Since the beginning of 2012, the change of attitude had been quietly noted by ambassadors in Rio and passed back through diplomatic channels to London, Rome, Wellington and Dublin – all capitals with prominent citizens accused of various crimes who had sought refuge in Brazil.

The message was clear. If you wanted to seek the extradition of one of your citizens for legitimate reasons, Brazil would not – as before – make it difficult. From now on they would cooperate, even if a fugitive had sired a child in Brazil. Brazil wanted to be seen as promoting law and order – even if the reality was different for many of the country's own citizens. And nothing grabbed negative international headlines more than a crook living it up in Rio with impunity.

London's Foreign Office was the first to move. It wanted to secure the arrest and extradition of Michael Misick – the former Premier of the Turks and Caicos Islands, a British-controlled territory 600 miles off the coast of Miami. Misick was precisely the kind of fugitive with which Brazil was tired of being associated and he attracted all the kinds of headlines the country wanted to eliminate.

Frequently photographed with celebrities such as Catherine Zeta Jones and Michael Douglas, Misick had turned his country's tropical islands into a party destination for the rich and famous. But in 2009 Britain accused him of corruption, bribery, profiting from the sale of Crown lands and money laundering on a massive scale. He had gone, prosecutors say, from being worth $50,000 in 2003, when he first became Premier, to an estimated $180 million by the time he resigned in disgrace in 2009.

Misick's ex-wife, LisaRaye McCoy, an American model and sitcom actress, had testified before a corruption inquiry about her $200,000-a-month clothing allowance. She also spoke of the $300,000 she'd been paid by the Turks and Caicos Islands tourism board – which also came under Misick's remit – to pose in a swimsuit for an advertising campaign. The marriage ultimately foundered, she said, after she discovered that a Rolls-Royce Phantom Misick had gifted her as a birthday present had been hired through her own company – and she was left liable for the rent.

Now Misick was living in a luxury apartment with a new girlfriend overlooking Rio de Janeiro's Ipanema beach, confident in the belief that he was safe. But the sands had shifted.

On 7 December 2012, Interpol officers arrested a surprised Misick at Rio's Santos Dumont Airport as he tried to leave for São Paulo. The arrest warrant had been issued by Brazil's Supreme Federal Court on 22 November, at the request of the UK government. To pave the way for the arrest, the UK and Brazil had quietly cooperated to close any loopholes previously in place. The authorities in Brazil watched with satisfaction as Misick's arrest was reported around the world. Their plan to rehabilitate the country's image was working.

'This arrest serves to discredit the idea that major international criminals can live peacefully and spend their dirty money in Rio,' said the city's Interpol chief, Orlando Nunes.

Meanwhile, as he exhausted all legal avenues, Misick was detained in Rio's Ary Franco prison, a place described by a United Nations report that recommended its closure as 'dark, dirty, steamy and cockroach-infested'.

Two years after his arrest in Rio, Michael Misick was deported back home to face trial.

Alan Shatter received the news of Michael Misick's arrest with satisfaction. This was a good omen. If he had his way, Michael Lynn would be next. But, for now, he could tell no one.

As Ireland's Minister for Justice, Shatter had already secured a top-secret cabinet decision to enter into extradition negotiations with Brazil. It was a decisive move that would ultimately seal the fate of Lynn. A solicitor himself, Shatter despised what Lynn represented. Before becoming minister, he'd publicly described Lynn's actions as 'appalling and indefensible' behaviour that had 'created substantial difficulties for many individuals and undermined public confidence in the legal profession'. Shatter's private opinions of Lynn were unprintable.

Now that he was in government – and Lynn was facing criminal charges – he had to keep his mouth shut about the case. But he could do something about it. And he did.

Cabinet sanction secured, Ireland's Department of Foreign Affairs instructed Frank Sheridan, the Irish Ambassador to Brazil, to open formal correspondence with the authorities in Brasilia, the country's federal capital. By the spring of 2013, it was clear to the handful of people who knew of the move that soon – very soon – Ireland would reach a landmark extradition understanding with Brazil. The deal would see both countries agree to enter talks on a formal extradition treaty. The first item agreed was that both would allow reciprocal extraditions even before a formal agreement was concluded. Such cooperation is permitted under a little-used section of the 1965 Extradition Act and it was now being utilised specifically with Lynn in mind.

The trap that would bring in Michael Lynn was set. In the meantime, it was vital that complete secrecy be maintained. Any leak could see him flee again.

TRUST ME, I'M A SOLICITOR: A fresh-faced and proud-as-punch Michael Lynn poses for a promotional photo outside his first office.

TROUBLED WATERS AHEAD: A carefree Michael Lynn enjoying a cruise on the River Shannon before it all went wrong.

SELLING THE DREAM: A promotional photo of Michael Lynn speaking at the launch of Costa de Cabanas in Portugal in 2004.

A FRESH START: Newly laid tarmac marks the beginning of the construction of Costa de Cabanas phase one in 2005. Early investors were lucky – stage two was never built and those who paid deposits lost their money.

WELL CONNECTED: Michael Lynn with former Taoiseach Albert Reynolds and Irish rugby international Shane Byrne at one of Kendar's early property exhibitions.

LYNN'S CABANAS HQ: The Kendar office at Costa de Cabanas as it was when Sean and I first began tracking Lynn. Overnight, the Kendar logo was removed and replaced with the new Vantea insignia as Lynn's assets were dispersed beyond the reach of creditors.

(© Sean Dwyer)

FOR BETTER OR WORSE: Michael Lynn with his ever loyal wife, Brid Murphy, pictured behind the High Court in December 2007. Within days, with €80 million unaccounted for, he had absconded. (© Paddy Cummins)

NOWHERE TO BE SEEN: A day after Lynn fled, gardaí were dispatched to his home in Dublin. When the authorities eventually gained entry just a portion of Lynn's wine collection and a damaged flat-screen TV remained. The wine was auctioned for €3,000.
(© Collins Photo Agency)

PAPER TRAIL: The torn and discarded paperwork from Lynn's Cabanas office in my hotel room as I pieced together the clues the documents held. (© Michael O'Farrell)

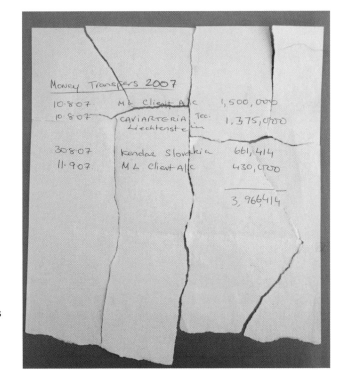

MOVING MILLIONS: This handwritten note from the cache showed transfers worth millions involving Michael Lynn's client account before he went on the run.
(© Michael O'Farrell)

LYNN'S LAIR: Michael Lynn's Algarve villa, overlooking Tavira. He spent Christmas and New Year here in the weeks after becoming a fugitive, placing calls to financial associates in New York, London, Kyiv and Dubai. (© Sean Dwyer)

NO ONE HOME: By the time we found his initial base in Portugal, Lynn had moved on. Following his trail, we continued to pursue him across Europe for the next twelve months. (© Sean Dwyer)

EMPTY PROMISE: Nothing was ever built at Lynn's Bankso site. When I visited in 2008 the site was vacant, with a fading Kendar billboard towering above the weeds.
(© Sean Dwyer)

NO JUSTICE: Kerry publican Sean O'Mahony is one of hundreds of small investors who together paid Lynn as much as €13 million for foreign apartments that were never built. The DPP decided not to prosecute these cases. (© Sean Dwyer)

RISKY BUSINESS: One of Lynn's more dangerous associates, Yahiya Hashiev, a notorious Bulgarian criminal who forced landowners to sell their valuable Black Sea land to Lynn at a fraction of its true value.

THE FIXER: Former Bulgarian politician Oktay Osman became a fixer for Michael Lynn in Bulgaria before falling out with him. Here he hands over Lynn's files to me in Sofia.
(© Michael O'Farrell)

Above: CHANCE
ENCOUNTER: Lynn is spotted
with his wife by a keen-eyed
tourist in Budapest in the
summer of 2008. This photo
was taken beside the apartment
Brid had renovated near the
theatre district.

Right: NO FEAR: Just days
before we caught up with
him in Portugal, Lynn is seen
enjoying a rugby international
on the other side of Europe, in
an Irish pub in Budapest.

IN OUR SIGHTS: Our first sighting of Lynn in almost a year as he exits the Vila Galé Hotel after a meeting to negotiate access to the pool at Costa de Cabanas.
(© Sean Dwyer)

FACE TO FACE: Out of breath, I catch up with Lynn on the morning of Saturday, 13 February 2009 and talk him into having a coffee. We had been hunting him down for more than a year. (© Sean Dwyer)

Right: DEFIANT: Wearing my shirt, Lynn poses for Sean in the basement car park of the Vila Galé Hotel. Within hours this image, on the front page of the *Irish Mail on Sunday*, is rolling off the presses and being distributed to every newsagent in Ireland.
(© Sean Dwyer)

Below: BEATS WORKING: Sean and I arrive back into Dublin airport to see our work on the newsstands. It will be another three years before the authorities lay criminal theft and fraud charges against Lynn in February 2012, by which time he has fled to Brazil.
(© Sean Dwyer)

BRAZILIAN HIDEAWAY: This is the secure compound in which Lynn and Brid lived near Recife. Though the area is dangerous after dark, the property includes a private pool and is within a short walk of pristine beaches. (© Michael O'Farrell)

BACK IN BUSINESS: The site in Cabo de Santo Agostinho where Lynn and Brid planned to build 140 apartments. (© Michael O'Farrell)

DETAINED: A screen-grab of a police video of Lynn being escorted to prison in Brazil.

BEHIND BARS: The front gate of COTEL remand prison in Pernambuco State where Lynn was held for nearly five years as he battled extradition. (© Michael O'Farrell)

EXTRADITED: In cuffs, Lynn is escorted through Recife airport by Brazilian Federal Police and handed over to Detective Inspector Paddy Linehan, who will accompany him home.

COLD RECEPTION: As soon as they land, Detective Inspector Linehan (right) formally charges Lynn and accompanies him to Dublin Circuit Court where bail is denied. (© Paddy Cummins)

BAIL: After several months in Dublin's Cloverhill Prison, Lynn is released on bail and is collected by his wife, Brid. (© Paddy Cummins)

FAKE SIGNATURES: Liz Doyle was Lynn's PA and a legal executive at his firm. In both trials she admits repeatedly forging signatures on loan applications and following Lynn's instructions to divert the money elsewhere. (© Sean Dwyer)

WOULD-BE PARTNER: In negotiations to be a partner of Lynn's solicitor's practice, Fiona McAleenan signed the legal paperwork for various Lynn loans. She testifies that she signed blindly, without looking at the documents. (© Sean Dwyer)

ON TRIAL: Lynn poses outside court towards the end of his first trial. (© Sean Dwyer)

STRONGER TOGETHER: Lynn and Brid Murphy exit court together as the the retrial nears a conclusion. (© Sean Dwyer)

PRE-DAWN SEARCH: With Lynn awaiting sentencing in prison, detectives following new money-trail leads swoop on his home. (© Sean Dwyer)

David Elio Malocco was having something of a busy start to 2013. Famously, the one-time libel lawyer and demi-celebrity had been jailed for forgery and fraud in the 1990s before reinventing himself as a filmmaker and writer. Now, in his latest reincarnation, he'd decided to become a magazine publisher.

Malocco's magazine – *Dublin's Best* – would not survive for more than a few issues. But as springtime loomed, Malocco was giving it his all. He just needed to find a corker of a story for the front page of the launch edition, due to hit the news-stands at the beginning of March 2013 – something that would cause a stir, make headlines and create publicity.

That's when Michael Lynn called from Brazil.

According to Malocco, the pair had spoken before during chance encounters at Faro airport and, six years earlier, Malocco had given Lynn his number. There was another link too – Malocco had worked in an administrative capacity in the offices of Merriman White alongside one of Lynn's solicitors, Ray Murphy.

Lynn's interview with Malocco saw him virtually taunt the authorities back home, so secure did he feel in Brazil. 'In one weekend I raised €10m on the strength of a letter,' it read. 'The feeling was one of euphoria. It was better than sex. Property development was the ultimate high.'

Lynn went on to justify his actions and branded the Law Society disciplinary hearing that had barred him from acting as a solicitor and fined him €2 million 'a kangaroo court'. According to the article, Lynn felt he'd never get a fair hearing in Ireland.

'There's not a chance in hell I would get a fair trial,' he was quoted as saying. 'I am already a condemned man.'

But the article contained something else. Lynn felt he was untouchable, beyond the reach of the law.

'Brazilian government papers seen by *Dublin's Best* confirm that the first child of Michael and Brid Lynn who was born in Brazil was given a permanent visa on June 26 last year,' the interview read. 'Therefore the parents are also entitled to permanent visas. Michael Lynn was never charged with a criminal offence. Even if there was a bilateral agreement between Brazil [*sic*], which there isn't, there would be no question of Michael Lynn ever being extradited to Ireland simply because the High Court issued a summons for him to attend before it.'

You can't touch me now, Lynn was saying to those intent on prosecuting him.

A few select individuals knew otherwise. But they couldn't say it yet.

Extradition case number 1326 landed on the desk of Supreme Court Judge Marco Aurélio on Friday, 30 July 2013. Michael Lynn knew nothing about it.

On Monday 2 August, lawyers representing the Irish government petitioned the court with documentation relating to the Lynn investigation and the charges he was facing. Lynn still knew nothing about it.

On Tuesday 20 August, Judge Aurélio approved the extradition request and ordered Lynn's detention. Lynn remained blissfully unaware. The process had been kept so secret that even the Fraud Squad detectives who had prepared the case against Lynn knew nothing.

On Thursday 22 August, Interpol's National Crime Bureau in Brazil was informed of the court's decision and issued with an arrest warrant for Lynn. Brazil's Federal Police chief, the Minister for Justice and the Minister for External Affairs were also brought into the loop.

Lynn was oblivious to it all. He was, by then, under permanent surveillance, trailed by a team of undercover detectives from Pernambuco's Federal Police headquarters. They watched as he walked his dog, went to and from work at the language school, and shopped in nearby malls with Brid and the son he doted on. As surveillance goes, this was as easy as it got.

On Sunday 25 August, the detectives staking out Lynn's home were bemused by the delighted roars and hollering coming from within. Never one to miss a match, Lynn had stayed at home to watch Mayo trounce Tyrone in the All-Ireland semi-final.

On Friday 30 August, they made their move. Michael Lynn offered no resistance. He would miss the All-Ireland final, where his beloved Mayo would lose by just one point to rivals Dublin.

23

Behind Bars

I WALKED UP TO THE GREEN iron gates of the prison and knocked. A gaggle of people sitting around on the kerb outside looked on, baffled.

The Centro de Observação e Triagem Professor Everaldo Luna – known as COTEL – is one of Brazil's most notorious detention facilities. Everyone arrested in Pernambuco state is detained there pending trial or transfer to another prison – or in Lynn's case, extradition. No one wants to be here. Not everyone makes it out alive. People – especially like me – don't usually pitch up asking to be let in.

The place was more like the entrance to a cattle mart than a prison. It was rough. And it stank. Raw sewage trickled through the earthen car park from open, unplumbed toilets used by families waiting to visit inmates. In the street outside, rubbish was strewn everywhere, picked at by birds, dogs and rats.

A heavy set of keys jangled and a uniformed guard opened a side door to the left.

'We'd like to see the governor,' Larissa Brainer, my translator and fixer, explained.

The guard listened impatiently. I noted the weapon holstered around his waist and strapped tightly to his upper thigh. Behind him I could see a second gate. Beyond its bars, three prisoners glanced in our direction as they passed, a guard marching behind them. On one side of the security zone between the inner and outer gates, two guards sat at a rickety desk. Behind them, handheld metal detectors rested on a shelf. Facing them on the other wall a flat-screen TV flashed colour images into the dimly lit entrance.

'Wait here,' said the guard, wrenching the heavy door closed.

Beneath the searing midday sun, I sucked from a bottle of mineral water and waited, sweat soaking through my shirt. A prison van with a large gold crest on its jet-black bonnet – a lion sitting atop an ornate key – roared into the car park and sounded its siren as a signal to open the gates. Inside the vehicle, two officers in shades and with chunky gold chains around their necks stared us down.

'You wanted to see me?' João Fernandes stepped out of the gate. I shook his hand and thanked him for coming out. His grip was firm but friendly.

We asked about Lynn.

'Sure,' he said, 'Michael Lynn is here. He's fine. Everything is okay. That's all I can say.'

'Can we visit him?'

'I can't give permission for that,' he replied. 'You will have to petition the Supreme Court for permission. There is an open case.'

'No problem, I'll do that. But perhaps you could allow us to visit the prison facilities – without meeting Michael Lynn. Give us a tour so we can report the true conditions about your prison.'

'For me it's no problem,' he shrugged. 'But the State authorities would have to authorise that. I cannot give permission myself.'

He glanced at his watch. It was clear we were getting nowhere. Then he offered something.

'I can bring in a note to Michael Lynn. I will give it to him personally. Leave your number. If he wants, he may be able to contact you.'

I scribbled a note on my notepad asking Lynn for an interview and handed it over. Twenty minutes later the governor called. Lynn didn't want to talk.

On the very day Lynn was arrested in Brazil, I was driving across Spain from an assignment in Marbella to begin working on a new story in Portugal, accompanied by photographer Michael Chester. The route took me directly past Tavira. As Lynn was being transferred to COTEL prison halfway around the world, I was pulling up outside his old hideaway – now repossessed by the banks.

Boarded up and empty, the once-sublime garden was a mess. Dry leaves crunched underfoot as I pushed through an overgrown path to the rear. The floor of the pool, empty of water, was layered with stinking vegetation and algae. The pool-house door lay open, its rusting water pump and filter mechanisms silent. On the floor lay some old Kendar brochures and a DVD of a 2006 TV3 news report about Lynn's firm. Hints of one-time achievements. There was a basketball too and a Jeffrey Archer novel – remnants of a life left behind. Fragments of the past.

A disposable camera lay covered in leaves, exposed to the elements. It appeared beyond recovery but would later offer up visual clues to a life Michael Lynn had long since abandoned. A simpler life. A life lost to greed.

The snaps showed a very young-looking and carefree Lynn captaining a cruiser on the River Shannon and drinking cans of beer on a tatty couch in a run-down Irish cottage with friends. This was another Michael Lynn. From another time – before it all went wrong.

Beneath the cool dawn fog that often envelops COTEL at sunrise, a tide of sorrow is played out each Sunday. Approaching the prison – an hour's drive inland from Recife – the road begins to resemble a refugee camp, with hundreds of women and children sleeping rough beneath plastic sheets.

Sunday is visiting day at COTEL. Each week as many as 3,000 desperate family members begin to queue up the night before to see their children, brothers, husbands and fathers. Some camp out against the perimeter walls from Friday to be first in the queue on Sunday morning – something that ensures more visiting time inside.

There are only two wretched huts outside the gate that serve as open toilets. Often ankle deep in human excrement seeping from within, they are so repugnant that most prefer to risk the snakes and rats in the adjoining forest. The stench of sewage and rotting rubbish hangs permanently in the air mixing with the smoke of cooking fires and stoves.

Twice a week, through this heaving mass of humanity, Brid arrives in her blacked-out Hyundai Santa Fe jeep, seven months pregnant with Lynn's second child. This is a long way from what she signed up for when she married Lynn in five-star splendour in 2006. In the months and years he will languish in prison, she will prove her loyalty and love by showing up each Sunday – and for conjugal visits on Wednesdays – to keep her husband's spirit strong.

There's a burgeoning hidden economy outside the walls of COTEL, one that Brid will soon become familiar with. The shacks that spring up to sell coffee, drinks, food and other necessities are obvious. So, too, the hawkers who pile wheelbarrows full of fruit or other goods to wheel along the queues. Not so obvious are the fees charged for special services – such as standing in line for someone, minding their possessions while they use the forest, or smuggling in contraband. Each week there are those who show up early just to make money from selling their place in the queue on Sunday morning.

At 5 a.m. the guards open the outside gates, allowing the women into a corralled area beneath a corrugated iron roof. There they wait, hemmed in like cattle at a mart, clutching plastic bags of clothes and food, until 8 a.m. when visiting begins. Often they must endure hours more frustration as each visitor is searched and bags are put through X-ray machines. Sometimes the machines work, sometimes they don't. Delays are routine. Not everyone gets in. Tempers flare. Emotions run high. Some faint in the heat.

Inside COTEL things are worse. As a remand prison, inmates are supposed to be there temporarily, pending trial or transfer. But the reality of Brazil's creaking and over-burdened justice system means a trip to COTEL will typically last years. Innocent or guilty you'll serve time either way.

Hopelessly overcrowded, rife with smuggled drugs and weapons, and crawling with illness and disease, the jail is a seething cauldron frequently close to boiling point. Every now and again, when the pressure erupts, someone's father, son or husband leaves in a body bag. Cases documented by Human Rights Watch include a prisoner being gang-raped at knifepoint by ten men and forced to have anal and oral sex. The attackers refused to use condoms and threw semen in his face.

'I cried for help and the men were shouting and singing. Nobody came,' he said. When he did inform a guard about the incident, the answer was almost as devastating as the attack itself.

'Prisoners have to suffer,' he was told.

As a graduate and a professional, Michael Lynn was detained separately in COTEL, among others of similar qualifications. Funny how even a denounced law degree has its benefits. In the right circumstances it can save your life.

Mark Astle sipped his gin and tonic and shrugged. Who was he to judge Michael Lynn?

'I know Michael in Brazil and he's a top man in every possible way,' he told me. 'As a father, as a husband, as a bloke to drink with.'

It was to Astle's home that a distressed Brid had retreated in the days following her husband's arrest. I'd come to speak to him – and to request an interview with Brid.

'He's very down-to-earth,' Astle continued, describing the Lynn he knew. 'And not knowing what went on previously in his life, I'd describe him as a model human being.'

Sitting in the Dorisol Recife Grand Hotel across the street from his language school, Astle was both weary and a little wary. All week he'd been fielding calls from journalists struggling to find anyone else who could speak of Lynn in English. In the absence of Lynn or Brid, he was as close as anyone could get. And he wasn't going to dwell on whatever Lynn had done. For him Lynn was a friend. Simple as that.

'He'd walk the dogs on the beach every day. He loved that,' Astle recalled. 'He had a piano at home and he told me he'd begun working on new material with a recording studio somewhere. My children described him as the coolest person ever, and he was a great dad. He loved to spend time with his kid. He'd bring him up to the country club to see the horses. They loved spending time together.'

The only slightly negative comment related to drink. 'Michael does like to drink. The problem can be getting him to stop sometimes. He did give up for three months when Brid became pregnant.'

But for someone protecting Brid – and apparently determined to stand by his friend – Astle was strangely open about Lynn's business plans. Lynn planned to build apartment blocks and had bought a plot in the hills beyond the Caxangá Golf and Country Club, where he was building a villa for his family.

I knew where I was going next. It was time to do some digging. That would prove a little more difficult than back home.

24

The Brazilian Money Trail

MONEY ALWAYS LEAVES A TRAIL. Some countries just make it more difficult to follow.

The database of the Commercial Registry of the State of Pernambuco could be put online in an instant. But that would be too easy. That would not be Brazil. That would not have allowed Michael Lynn to keep his affairs secret.

Instead, at 7.30 in the morning, an orderly queue forms outside the registry office on Rua Imperial in Recife. Getting there – even from just a few kilometres away – involves an hour stuck in the city's abominable traffic chaos.

When the doors open at 8 a.m., everyone takes a ticket and queues again inside, watching the electronic screens until their number comes up. Then a clerk will slowly type the name of the company you are searching for into a terminal and turn the screen to show you. All the information is there in a neat PDF – Michael Lynn's name and that of Brid included.

But you can't have it yet. Instead, the clerk will issue you with a bill – one you can't pay in the registry office. You must, once again, endure an hour of traffic to get to and from the Central Bank – the only location where registry office payments can be made. At the bank you must queue again to be told that payments must be in cash – a visa card is no good – before driving around for a further hour to find one of the few ATMs that's not broken. Back at the Central Bank, after queuing again, you must obtain stamped proof of payment and bring it back to the Commercial Registry, where you must take a new number and stand in a different queue. You must pray the line reaches your number before lunch – when the office closes for the rest of the day.

This is how, minutes before closing and after nearly seven hours of frustration, I found out about Quantum Assessoria E Empreendimentos Ltda – Lynn's new property company in Recife. It was worth the effort.

Ushered out by security as they closed the doors for the day behind me, I flicked through the company's registration documents beneath a palm tree in the car park. The firm – jointly owned by Lynn and his wife – had been established on 27 October 2011. That date rang a bell. It was two days after Lynn had failed to show up for his final scheduled meeting with Fraud Squad detectives in Portugal. Had he been leading the authorities on a merry dance to the very last, all the while implementing secret plans to go back into business, this time in Recife?

Cabo de Santo Agostinho was mad. It was like Calcutta shrink-wrapped and dropped into a new location where virtually nothing had been before.

Located 35 kilometres from Recife, Cabo is a new residential town for the tens of thousands of workers flooding in to work at the new port of Suape. So successful is the port that the area surrounding it has mushroomed into a vast, industrial complex creating jobs so fast they can't be filled quickly enough.

Struggling to get through the streets in my battered rental car, it felt like I was in the middle of a gold-rush town. And I was. There was commerce in every square inch of the place doing a roaring trade supplying the needs of newly middle-class workers. Everything you could imagine was for sale everywhere. Household items and hardware stock spilled from beneath plastic and sheet-metal lean-tos right beside glass-fronted dealerships selling Mercedes jeeps and brand spanking new earthmoving equipment. Live cattle and chickens were hemmed in between the glistening façades of new banks and real estate dealers. Above it all giant billboards advertised luxury apartment schemes.

And that was where Michael Lynn came in.

Now that we had the name of Lynn's local firm, we could check the cartório in Cabo – the property register – to see what land the firm owned. Thankfully the registry office, a modern air-conditioned building, was just about the only thing that worked smoothly. It had to. Without proper land-ownership records in a place like this there'd be war.

Those records showed that Lynn and Brid's new Recife firm – Quantum – had bought a 4,182-square-metre site in Cabo in December 2011 for just over €253,000. Just one month later, the site was officially valued for tax purposes by the local municipality at over €1 million. The increase in value is likely explained by Lynn's plans to build apartments on the large plot.

'He told me he got approval for 140 flats one to three months ago and he's been trying to sell them to port workers,' Mark Astle had told us.

Within months of his former Portuguese firm being liquidated – leaving tens of millions in claimed debt behind – Lynn had gone back into business in Brazil with a €1 million development plot to his name.

Standing at Lynn's site, I took it all in. The place was nothing more than waste ground, cattle meandering between vines and thick shrubs. But right next door, on a similar-sized plot, a long, three-storey apartment complex of perhaps sixty units was close to completion. Inside, workers were finishing off tiling jobs and installing beds – two bunk beds per tiny room.

'These are for workers,' they told me. 'One company bought all of the apartments for its employees even before they were built. The whole lot. There's huge demand. We can't build fast enough.'

Michael Lynn stood in the corner of the prison yard, arms folded, in a pair of knee-length shorts and flip-flops. This religion stuff wasn't his cup of tea. But it was Christmas after all – and he hadn't been given a choice.

All prisoners from COTEL's C Block had to attend and be on their best behaviour.

Dressed in a blood-red robe, adorned with golden crosses, Dom Fernando Saburido – the archbishop of Olinda and Recife – read a sermon about the meaning of freedom, fraternity and hope. It was 26 December 2014 – Lynn's second Christmas in jail. Just weeks earlier, Brazil's Supreme Court had finally cleared the way for Lynn's extradition. He had exhausted almost all appeals and legal arguments. But still he resisted.

At one point during 2014, Lynn had sought permission to be treated for TB in a private hospital in Recife. His lawyers claimed he was suffering from 'chronic respiratory disease and had manifested symptoms of cough and secretion with blood'. But the claim of an urgent medical emergency requiring hospitalisation – backed by reports from private doctors who had visited Lynn in prison – was rejected by COTEL's governor, whose own doctor and psychiatrist believed he was fine. Tests for TB showed he did not have the disease.

By 2015 Lynn had just one legal avenue left. He could ask for a review of the case – and he did. By now Lynn had been in COTEL for close to three years. Yet he still hung on.

As he remained in prison, another noted criminal being extradited to Europe from Recife would come and go from Lynn's quarters in COTEL. In May 2015 Italian mobster Pasquale Scotti joined Lynn among the ranks of the more privileged COTEL prisoners. Like Lynn, he'd chosen to flee from his past to Recife. Unlike Lynn, the Italian's past was exceedingly violent. Wanted by the Italian authorities since 1991, Scotti was a notorious member of the Camorra Neapolitan mafia and had been sentenced to life for twenty-six murders and other crimes. After ten months in COTEL, Scotti was extradited to Rome.

In April 2016 Lynn's case review concluded and rubber-stamped the court's original decision to deport him. He would be extradited. Mark Astle, who stood by his friend throughout, told newspapers that Lynn was now 'keen to get the extradition process over and done with'.

'In the beginning, Michael thought his extradition was worth challenging because he believed he could fight the case brought by the Irish government in Brazil on a series of technicalities,' Astle said. 'But over the last year and a half he's realised the result was inevitable and he now wants to get back to Ireland and to move on.'

Brid was busy as her husband languished in jail. Her second child was born shortly after Lynn was detained in 2013. A third was born in the summer of 2015. Although Brid had help – a nanny and a housekeeper – she was virtually a single mother, alone in a foreign land, besieged in a lonely villa. But she was tough and got used to taking the kids to see their dad in prison. Two of them had never seen him anywhere else.

There were also other matters to attend to – business. With Lynn facing prosecution, the couple's finances had to be protected. Once Lynn was arrested, Brid stepped to the fore. First the shares in Quantum – the couple's Recife real estate firm – were rearranged to make Brid the controlling shareholder. At the same time 32 per cent of Lynn's stake in the couple's firm was transferred to another Brazilian firm controlled by associates from Tavira.

Then, in February 2016, Brid put the company's Cabo development up for sale with an asking price of R\$3 million – the equivalent of €667,886. Asked about the price, the agent selling the site was quick to say they would accept as little as R\$1.8 million, or €400,000.

Eventually Lynn would face trial at home in Ireland. And one thing was for sure – he was not going to roll over and plead guilty. A defence would have to be funded.

Despite Mark Astle's prediction that Lynn wanted to get back to Ireland, he continued to deploy every delaying tactic possible. Time and time again his lawyers filed new arguments – each time delaying matters further. In doing so, he even missed his mother Angela's funeral.

With conjugal visits allowed weekly at COTEL prison, Lynn and Brid's fourth child was born in October 2016. And in the summer of 2017, his lawyers asked for a new review of the extradition case based on Lynn's parentage of four Brazilian-born children. A decade on from his desperate dash from Ireland in December 2007, Lynn would spend his fifth Christmas behind bars in Brazil. It was to be his last there.

25

Homeward Bound

HANDCUFFED AND BUNDLED UNCOMFORTABLY INTO THE hatchback boot of a blacked-out Federal Police jeep, Michael Lynn struggled to find his balance. The cuffs binding his hands had been looped through his jeans belt, pinning his wrists to his waist. It was virtually impossible to maintain stability as the vehicle jolted around.

Lynn had resisted extradition to the very end but now, ten years and seventy-nine days since he'd first fled his homeland, he was finally being sent home as Ireland's most notorious fugitive. As recently as a week previously, his lawyers in Dublin had tried and failed to head off the extradition. Now Lynn's time in Brazil was over. Soon he'd be on a flight home.

With every bump, brake, twist and turn on the rough roads between COTEL and Recife International Airport, Lynn was reminded of how he used to ferry his dogs about in the boot like this – minus the handcuffs. As a bone-crunching jolt from a pothole smacked his head against the metal grill separating him from the accompanying federal agents in the rear seats, he remembered how Brid used to give out to him for driving too fast with the family pets in the back and thought, *That's Our Lord coming back to taunt me. Now I know how the dogs felt.*

But soon enough this final trip would be done. Soon the bursts of jumbled Portuguese from the police radio up front would be no more. As the green, iron gates of COTEL prison had closed behind him, the most physically demanding chapter of Lynn's life had come to a close. Now a different challenge lay ahead.

Sweeping into the airport concourse, lights flashing and siren blaring, the prison vehicle drew to a halt beneath the sheltered drop-off concourse outside departures zone A1. There, press photographers and local TV crews were waiting, poised to capture Lynn for that day's headlines. Their glaring camera lights and flashes lit up the shadows of the concrete underpass as a federal agent gripped Lynn tightly by the elbow and led him inside. From white taxis lined up beneath the concourse, drivers and tourists laden down with baggage gawked as Lynn was directed inside the terminal.

The backtracking news crews advanced in front of Lynn, microphones thrust like sabres at his tightly closed lips. Their footage of Lynn, fitter-looking than ever and dressed in jeans and a purple, skull-print T-shirt, would make the morning papers in Ireland even as Lynn's flight home was still airborne.

Inside the airport, Detective Inspector Paddy Linehan formally took possession of Lynn just after 18.00 local time on 28 February 2018. Originally a Fraud Squad officer, but now a member of the Garda National Immigration Bureau, Linehan had led the Lynn case from the very beginning in 2007. He was always going to be the one to see it through. After ten years pursuing his quarry, Detective Inspector Linehan knew every detail of the Lynn case by heart. For him, this would be the biggest case of his career. And that's saying something.

A no-nonsense, by-the-book cop with an enviable track record, Linehan had already seen corrupt stockbrokers and even members of parliament successfully prosecuted for fraud. He'd also investigated and brought to justice District Court Judge Heather Perrin, who, as a solicitor, had fleeced her clients to enrich herself before being elevated to the bench. Michael Lynn, though, was different. He'd been the one who got away – until now. Now, with Lynn in his custody, Detective Inspector Linehan knew what he wanted to say.

'The best thing for you to do now when you go home is to plead guilty,' he urged his prisoner.

Lynn, in chains and still sore from the rough trip in the police boot, was more intent on feeling sorry for himself. 'He came up to me to say that and I'm there shackled – you can imagine it's a pretty difficult time for me at that juncture,' he would later tell me.

Besides, Lynn knew he was never going to plead guilty. As if. That would avoid a trial and an opportunity to expose others he felt were just as responsible as he was for what had gone on. To plead guilty would mean he was a thief, that everything had been his doing and no one else's. That was something Lynn would never accept.

The sun dips quickly and early in Recife. The city's proximity to the equator sees to that. So, when Condor airline's flight DE2343 took off with Lynn on board at 18.40, a heavy veil of darkness had already drawn in for the night. Lifting into the air, the Boeing 767 climbed sharply and banked north-eastwards over the Southern Atlantic towards Frankfurt and an onward connection to Dublin. Far below, the back-to-back, rush-hour traffic of Recife trailed white headlights and red tail lights through the smog of its hopelessly clogged urban arteries.

Somewhere down there, amid the fading pinpricks of light being quickly left behind, lay the remnants of more than half a decade of Lynn's life. This was the place where he'd first become a father and where he had tried to start again. It was here he had gone from poolside to prison. And it was here that ten years of furtive exile had just come to an end.

Soon, as Lynn's flight chased the faint glow of the sun dipping beyond the earth's curvature, there was nothing left to see. Just time to think. About coming home. About family. About what might have been. About giving up or continuing the fight. About justice and injustice. About guilt and innocence. Wrong and right.

The same topics were on the minds of his minders – two officers from the Extradition Unit, one from the Fraud Squad, and Detective Inspector Linehan, who remained with the case even though he'd been transferred.

'Look Michael, you seem like a nice fella,' they'd say periodically during the flight. 'The best thing for you to do is to plead guilty when you get home.'

Lynn just ignored them.

The officers chuckled to themselves as they realised that the in-flight entertainment menu offered *Home Again* as one of the movie choices. Jokes aside, however, they took their job seriously. They'd been hunting Lynn for as long as he'd been on the run and, even though he wasn't deemed a threat on board, it would not do for something to go amiss. So they took it in turns to doze during the long-haul leg to Germany, and the only time Lynn was alone was when he was in the bathroom – even then, they waited for him just outside the door.

Anne Jordan struggled to see through the windscreen as she approached the outskirts of Dublin in near blizzard conditions. It was 1 March 2018, a day after Lynn's departure from Brazil and he was expected home by midday. It was strange hearing her brother's name repeatedly mentioned on the radio as hourly news reports cited his imminent return. But she'd get used to it and she was there for him, no matter what.

In recent weeks the Lynn siblings had been busy, organising a home in which Brid and Lynn's children could live. Anne also made arrangements to have €100,000 in cash available to offer as an independent surety in case Lynn was granted bail.

Meanwhile, aboard flight EI651 from Frankfurt, Michael Lynn's emotions were racing. A vicious winter storm was whipping up the Irish Sea and driving snow at gale-force speeds across the Irish capital. Most scheduled flights in and out of Dublin Airport had already been cancelled. Initially, Lynn's flight from Frankfurt was not going to take off, but the authorities were unsure of the legality of holding Lynn on German soil, so they ensured Dublin Airport remained open for Lynn's arrival.

Already an hour late, the flight captain saw the tiniest of breaks in the surging storm clouds and lined up his final approach north of Howth peninsula – the location of Glenlion, Lynn and Brid's supposed dream home. Low-lying cloud and driving snow made Glenlion impossible to see, but it must have been in Lynn's thoughts as he flew over its location. Soon the property would feature prominently in the case against him.

At 13.21 Lynn's flight touched down. It was the last one to make it in or out of Dublin that day – as soon as he landed the airport was closed to all other flights. But not even the 'Beast from the East', as the news writers dubbed the storm, could prevent Lynn's return.

When Lynn had first made a run for it in 2007, Twitter had barely been conceived. Upon his return it was the platform through which many people received the news and shared their views. Now the keyboard warriors competed with themselves to outdo each other as Lynn's return was marked. One quick-witted user greeted Lynn as the 'Pest from the West', a cheap pun on the storm accompanying his return. 'Wonder will he get a frosty reception?' another chimed in, as the brief Twitter frenzy gained momentum.

But for Michael Lynn – and those whose lives he had affected – this was no laughing matter. The next chapter of a truly extraordinary saga was about to begin.

26

Back to Square One

'IF YOU DON'T CHANGE DIRECTION YOU'RE going to end up where you're going,' says a wise old Chinese proverb.

Since he'd jumped into that taxi on the morning he fled Dublin, Michael Lynn had never looked back. But he'd never escaped what he was running from either. Now it had finally caught up with him. At the airport in Dublin, he'd been formally arrested on Irish soil by Detective Inspector Linehan. Then he'd been whisked away under armed police guard through strangely empty and snow-covered streets.

Transiting through the suburbs towards Ballymun Garda Station, Linehan leaned into the back seat for a word in Lynn's ear. 'Do you know, Michael, your wife and their children, they deserve their father at home now,' he said, seeking to drive home a message already repeatedly delivered. 'The best thing you can do is plead guilty.'

Lynn just nodded. He was used to this by now.

Inside the station house, Lynn was formally charged with twenty-one counts of theft involving almost €30 million stolen from seven banks. To each charge Lynn made no reply. There'd be plenty of time to say what he wanted later.

All courts had been closed due to the snowstorm, but that evening a special sitting of the Dublin District Court was hastily arranged.

Before arriving at the court, Detective Inspector Linehan tried one more time to coax Lynn. 'You know, you're not going to get bail Michael. I don't think they'll ever give you bail. You should plead guilty and get it over with.'

Fuck you, thought Lynn.

On the frozen pavement outside the court, TV and newspaper crime correspondents were waiting, their lenses polished and microphones ready. Among them was Paddy Cummins, a freelance court photographer who has photographed virtually everyone entering or leaving this building for fifteen years.

'Anything to say Mr Lynn?' a TV reporter shouted as Lynn was accompanied inside by Linehan and Detective Superintendent Gerard Walsh.

Lynn did not even flinch in response. From now on – and until the conclusion of his trial – the public would hear Lynn's story only through the formal and restricted reporting of court proceedings. The real story – and its corrupt, twisted details – would have to wait.

Once inside, Lynn brazenly asked the court for bail.

'I am here to answer for the charges,' he said as if he'd come home voluntarily. 'I have no intention of leaving the jurisdiction. I need to face these charges and I need to face up to these charges and get this aspect of my life over. I have never been a fugitive from Ireland and I'm prepared to abide by any conditions. The day of Ronnie Biggs is over.'

Judge Gerard Jones – after hearing Detective Inspector Linehan's view that Lynn was a flight risk – denied bail but granted legal aid. The cost of Lynn's defence – like his debts – would now be borne by others.

Watching the RTÉ news that night in his new accommodation – a remand cell in Cloverhill Prison on the edge of Dublin – Lynn marvelled at the fuss the Irish can make over a little bit of snow. He watched mockingly as regional correspondents – some in areas with no snow in sight – spoke about conditions deteriorating rapidly and the amount of gritting salt stockpiled by local councils. How small-minded it all seemed. How Irish. Still, though, this was his homeland and there were constant sounds, sights and smells – even in jail – that resonated in the fabric of his being.

Lying beneath his prison blanket that night, Lynn listened to the unfamiliar sounds of his new surroundings and mulled things over in his mind. For him, much of this first day home had been a blur. Now the TV news, echoing from the cells around him, reminded him of every minute. His future – his innocence or guilt – rested on the contents of the case against him.

Every detail of the prosecution's case had been carefully detailed in a 500-page book of evidence compiled by the Fraud Squad. Detailed though it was, it hardly touched the surface. Regardless of the trial's outcome, Michael Lynn could be accused of far more than he'd ever be held to account for.

Now, pending any trial, he just wanted one thing: to get out on bail. While it wasn't as bad as COTEL, there was nothing appealing about Dublin's Cloverhill Prison. 'Jesus, the things that go on in prison here,' he'd later tell me. 'Someone really should have a look at that. They even steal your clothes.'

With an initial trial date set for January 2020, Lynn was facing more than twenty months behind bars in Ireland before his trial – having already served four and a half years in Brazil. He wasted little time trying to put that right as he set about seeking bail, at the same time settling down to a prison job of working at reception, where he was responsible for welcoming incoming prisoners, showing them the ropes and issuing their jail garb.

A month after his deportation, on 6 April 2018, Lynn made a second bid for bail – this time to the High Court. The application was once again knocked back, this time by Judge Una Ni Raifeartaigh.

Lynn, represented by his then lawyer Michael O'Higgins, subsequently appealed to the Court of Appeal and threw everything at the effort. On 21 June 2018 the three-judge appeal court delivered its decision. Lynn could go free. For now. Justifying their reasoning, the judges said the 'disturbing' delay in a trial date – and the amount of time Lynn had already spent in custody – were important factors.

The move was stridently opposed by the DPP on the basis that the State still believed Lynn to be a flight risk. But Judges John Hedigan, Alan Mahon and John Edwards decided the risk of him leaving the country before his trial was now 'much diminished'. It was not possible to find that there was no flight risk, the judges said, but Lynn now had a family of four young children, the youngest of whom was about to start school, and there was almost nowhere to which he could flee that he could not be retrieved from and jailed again.

As Lynn's lawyer, O'Higgins, had put it, the 'Ronnie Biggs scenario' was no longer workable.

Moving testimony from Brid, who told of the tragic situation the family found themselves in and how they longed for Lynn's presence at home, was also considered. Important, too, was a €100,000 surety. This was provided by Lillian Lynn, a sister-in law of Lynn's, who had taken over this responsibility from Lynn's sister, Anne. The court warned these funds, which had to remain frozen pending the conclusion of the trial, would be 'very much at peril' if Lynn did another runner.

Lynn, now able to live with a young family that hardly knew him, stayed put this time. His bail conditions included stipulations that he reside only at an address in Maynooth and sign on at the nearby Leixlip Garda Station daily. His passport, and those of Brid and the children, were surrendered, and Lynn was forbidden from applying for a new one. He was also ordered to stay away from all ports and not to leave the jurisdiction. A strict curfew forbade him from leaving home between the hours of 9 p.m. and 6 a.m., and he had to be available to gardaí on a given mobile number twenty-four hours a day.

'When I tell the wife I'm only going out for a pint,' Lynn would soon be quipping, 'I'm the only man in Ireland who's guaranteed to be back on time.'

On 21 June 2018, sporting a smart, open-necked grey shirt and dark shades, Michael Lynn was collected from Cloverhill Prison by Brid and driven home to his insta-family. His first time out of custody since his arrest in August 2013 came just in time to enjoy the longest day of the year. Now aged forty-nine, Lynn had been on the run – or behind bars – for more than a third of his entire adult life.

But his extraordinary story wasn't over yet. Not even nearly.

27

Counting Time

Inside the lobby of Leixlip Garda Station, Michael Lynn is sitting in the corner with his back to the window. He is waiting to sign on, a daily requirement of his bail conditions. Hunched over, with his elbows resting on his knees and head hanging low, he is wearing a white TK baseball cap, Ray-Ban shades, a T-shirt, red shorts and trainers.

Outside, Brid and the couple's four children wait in their blue Ford Galaxy with the engine ticking over and Brid at the wheel. Already, just two weeks after his release on bail, Daddy's daily trip to the police station is part of the Lynn family routine. It is something to be slotted in between school runs, kids' activities, walking the dog and the weekly shop.

It is 5 July 2018, and I had not spoken to or heard from Lynn since his last call from Brazil on 17 February 2012 – the day before he'd been formally charged with the theft of millions and suddenly cut all contact. Now, six years later, it was time to re-establish contact.

I had no idea if he would speak willingly or send me packing. But I suspected he'd play the game, as before. And I was right. Spotting me approach, his tone is welcoming.

'Do me a favour,' he says under his breath. 'I'll talk to you, but just wait outside and let me get this done.'

I wait in the double doorway as his turn to approach the counter comes up.

'Michael Lynn, here to sign on,' I hear him say as he gives his address to the desk sergeant. Then he bounds out and switches to schmooze mode. It's as if we've just met at a rugby game or in the pub – or at a property expo where he wants to sell me a condo with a smile.

'You're looking well,' he says, beaming.

'There's no one taking photos is there?' he then enquires, looking around in a theatrical, paranoid fashion, before explaining, 'There were muppets here from *The Sun* the other day. They were all jittery. I said, "Lads calm down – I'll stand for you. You can even take a picture of my penis."'

So this is it. This is how it will be. He hasn't changed a bit. He exudes bonhomie, revels in childish humour and still has an ego big enough to halt the passing double-decker bus in its tracks.

'Do you think I'm guilty – do you think I'll be found guilty?' he asks, fixing me with his intense blue eyes. He is watching for a tell. Trying to take a read.

'I don't know,' I hedge. 'Sometimes I think so and sometimes not. I haven't seen the book of evidence.'

'I'll give it to you,' he promises emptily.

I don't believe for a moment he ever will. He never does.

'So you've written a book,' he says, having picked up on some press reports of the project. 'Sure why wouldn't you?'

I jest that, given his reputation, he'd probably be difficult to libel at this point.

'Wait until I'm found innocent,' he smirks. 'Then you're in trouble with your libel. There'll be lots I could come after.'

He is though, perfectly happy to concede he did wrong.

'I was morally wrong. I did wrong. I was greedy,' he admits. 'Like many,' he quickly adds.

Then he speaks of other boom-time developers who broke from the intense pressure. Some committed suicide. Not all had the reserves of strength or stubbornness Lynn drew on to keep going.

'I'm still here, thank God,' he says, casting a look at his children's heads bobbing up and down in the car next to us, where Brid, in dark sunglasses, is chatting on her mobile phone.

Though he appears to have mellowed somewhat, the large persecution complex that he has carried for more than a decade now has not been discarded.

'How many times do you think the Embassy visited me in Brazil?' he asks with an accusatory tone. 'They only came three times in five years and it was life and death. I needed it. Now how often do you think they visited Pat Hickey?' he asks, folding his arms dramatically and nodding like a gossiping fishmonger. 'Every fucking day.'

Famously, Hickey – the then seventy-one-year-old head of the Olympic Council of Ireland – had been seized from his hotel room, arrested and detained for eleven days during the Rio de Janeiro Olympics in 2016. The Brazilian authorities had accused him of theft, tax evasion, money-laundering and criminal association relating to ticket-touting allegations. The matter, which was reported globally, caused something of a diplomatic crisis, though Hickey was ultimately cleared of any wrongdoing. But to Lynn, watching from his prison cell in COTEL, it was proof that there was a conspiracy against him.

'I'm entitled to be treated with respect, you know,' he'd lament. 'The State has an obligation to assist Irish citizens.'

'If I am guilty of those crimes which they allege, at what stage in your view, did I stop becoming human?' he'd later ask me. 'When the State closes in on you, may God help you.'

In the absence of help from the Irish State, Lynn had to adapt, something he's proved extraordinarily capable of doing. He did so by using his charms to gain allies in prison. Some taught him how to survive, while others imparted valuable advice.

It's 4 a.m. during a warm and sticky October night in 2017 and a furtive phone call is received in Michael Lynn's prison cell in Brazil. The timing of the call is planned to minimise the risk of the illegal mobile phone being seized or stolen.

Lying in his bunk, Lynn listens as his cellmate, Raymond, speaks quietly to a journalist from his hometown of Heemskerk in North Holland.

'Seeking adventure has always defined my life. Sailing into the jungle, doing something that others say is impossible, I think it's wonderful. I've always had that,' Raymond is saying. 'When I'm standing on the boat and I see our plane unload bales of cocaine into the sea, I know I'm alive.'

A one-time mechanic, Raymond turned car thief and was caught and jailed in the Netherlands, where he was introduced to smugglers. Later, a €20,000 gambling debt saw him blackmailed into transporting – and being caught with – a 598-kilo shipment of cocaine in French waters in 2007, for which he was again jailed.

Raymond joined Lynn in his cell in COTEL after he was arrested once again – this time off the Brazilian coast in 2015 with 613 kilos of cocaine on board his yacht. The pair had become good friends in prison and got on well. At one point Raymond had even contacted the Dutch Embassy to ask that they contact the Irish Ambassador when Lynn was in fear of his life.

'I'm lucky to be in a section with more normal people – like lawyers and ex-cops who have been up to something,' Raymond tells the Dutch newspaper.

The call is taking place because Raymond has used his mobile phone to type out a book, and some pre-publication publicity is required back home. *KAPITEIN COKE: Waargebeurde avonturen van een Nederlandse cocainesmokkelaar* (Captain Coke: The sailing adventures of a Dutch cocaine smuggler) is a fascinating read and a nice little earner for the imprisoned author, who protects his identity by simply referring to himself as Raymond K.

For Lynn, Raymond was a reliable ally. The pair even partnered to purchase bricks and build a security wall to protect themselves from the less privileged detainees in the general prison population. Using his skills as a mechanic, Raymond earned privileges with the prison governor, who ran a car business on the outside.

'I respected him because you know, you knew where he stood,' Lynn later told me. 'He was a good ally to an extent in prison,' he added. 'He minded his own business and he wasn't looking to create any drama.'

Raymond's book was also a source of inspiration for Lynn.

'I've a book in me, too,' he'd told me upon his return to Ireland. 'Three books: the stuff here, the stuff away and the stuff in Brazil is a book in itself. Never mind a book,' he enthused. 'I'll probably get a movie deal.'

You never forget those you've spent time with in prison and Michael Lynn never forgot Paul Lange. Now out of COTEL, and fond of posting Facebook photos with his beautiful Brazilian wife from the beaches of Recife, Lange was once another of Lynn's fellow inmates.

Lange began life as apprentice painter in his native Germany. But, fed up earning a pittance for tough physical work, he turned to small-time internet fraud in 2011 and quickly earned a small fortune.

In the beginning, Lange advertised mobile phones and laptops on sites such as eBay at ridiculously low prices. Having pocketed the money of unsuspecting shoppers who thought they'd bagged the deal of a lifetime, Lange delivered a cruel joke. Instead of the electronics they'd paid for, he sent each victim a DHL package containing nothing but bag of flour or sugar. The ruse saw him nicknamed the Mehltüten-Betrüger – the flour-bag scammer – in the German media.

From there he fled to Brazil and graduated to an online Trojan horse investment company that duped hundreds of thousands from clients on foot of glossy brochures promising handsome returns. While living in a neighbouring suburb to Brid and Lynn's onetime Recife home, Lange was finally caught in September 2015 and imprisoned in COTEL. After fourteen months, he was extradited and put on trial in Germany where, in May 2017, he received a sentence of six years and two months at the Dresden Regional Court.

Lynn kept a close eye on the case. In particular, he noted one vital point. There was a value to each day spent in prison in Brazil – a value he could utilise himself. When sentencing Lange, the German court ruled that each day in COTEL was worth two and half days in a German prison. 'Such conditions are a violation of human rights,' defender Ina Becherer told the court as she described the murders Lange had witnessed and the beatings and blackmail he had suffered in jail.

Lange's six-year sentence was consequently reduced to three. Today he is back in Recife, living openly, and has established a successful internet firm. It is a remarkable fact that much of Paul Lange's criminal career, his period on the run, his detention in Brazil, his extradition and his trial all took place as Lynn languished in COTEL resisting his extradition.

In the meantime, Lynn was doing his sums. If the Irish courts were to apply the same rules in his case as the Germans had with Lange, they would have to sentence him to more than twelve years in order for him to serve any time at all in an Irish prison.

'I can now officially confirm that the wheels on the bus go round and round.'

Settling into the routine of life with a young family, Lynn is in a jovial mood as he places one of his occasional WhatsApp calls to me. It is clear that having children has changed his approach to life.

'Look, man, I was four and a half years in a Brazilian prison,' he says. 'I'm at home now with my wife and children. I couldn't think of anything more valuable to me. So, you know, my sense of what's important has severely adjusted for the better.'

So, too, he tells me, has his sense of wrong and right.

'It's very important for me to be able to say to my children: "Look guys – and this is the truth – don't ever do what I did and don't ever be enabled or fooled by those who can give you the gold."'

But he still refuses to let go of his battle with the authorities. He remains obsessed with various court attempts to challenge the legality of his deportation and head off his trial. Failing that, he is content to delay things as much as possible. He is certainly not willing to walk into court, plead guilty and accept his punishment. Nor is he in any rush to facilitate a quick hearing.

'Sure, the trial might not be for two years,' he'd told me immediately after his release on bail.

'That long?' I'd responded.

'Yeah, we'll delay things – let's see.'

This heel-dragging – on the part of someone who supposedly admits he's guilty of wrongdoing – smacks of self-serving delusion to me. And I have seen it before. It is something Lynn shares with many of the corporate crooks I've pursued in my career.

Those content to break the rules before they are caught tend to think they can remain above the law afterwards, too. They never really think of themselves as criminals. Deep down, they just don't accept the system is entitled to put them away. They feel they are entitled to a get-out clause, as if life is a sales contract with small print designed to their advantage. Then, when they realise this privileged safety net has been whipped away, they seek to drag others down with them, as if a bank robber is any less guilty for having had an accomplice. Lynn is no different.

'My message would be really, if I'm the guy facing criminal charges, then why aren't there some bankers in here and perhaps one or two other people?' he asks in one of his calls.

'The garda investigation has been incredibly biased,' he says during another call. 'I benefited from the money, largely speaking. But they have totally, totally focused their attention on me, whereas other people actually in our proceedings, they admitted to committing crimes.'

Having been the one caught out, he feels offended that others have not been subjected to the same fate.

'Do you know there are two judges with double mortgages,' he tells me on several occasions. 'I'll give you their names.'

He never does.

28

An Ominous Sign

THE DECISION WAS QUIETLY PLACED ON the back end of the Central Bank's website, just before close of business on Friday, 22 December 2019 – as the country shut down for Christmas. Despite being a bombshell development, the Central Bank made no fanfare at all when its inquiry into Michael Fingleton was dropped. There was no public announcement. No press release. Instead, the matter was to be quietly buried – except that a source tipped me off.

For years the Central Bank had been pursuing an official inquiry into the former Irish Nationwide boss – who had also been one of Michael Lynn's biggest lenders. Now, Fingleton would never be held to account for his role as the boss of Ireland's most toxic boom-time bank.

When public hearings first commenced in December 2017, Fingleton attended only to make an opening statement, in which he accused the inquiry of being 'an artificially trumped-up case' aimed at deflecting blame for the economic crash away from the authorities. Thereafter, he snubbed the inquiry completely, sending in a steady stream of doctor's sick notes. As a result, the inquiry floundered and was forced repeatedly to postpone its questioning of the man who had walked away from Irish Nationwide with a €30 million pension pot as taxpayers bailed the bank out to the tune of €5.4 billion.

Fingleton had been one of the reckless boom-time bankers whose assets I'd been tasked with tracking down by *The Irish Mail on Sunday* as the Celtic Tiger imploded a decade previously. The job had taken me from the heart of London's financial district to the Balkans and beyond. His main asset – a planned €70 million hotel resort – was located along the rugged coastline of Montenegro at the foot of a majestic fjord on the Adriatic. Hotel Fjord – in the medieval town of Kotor – had lain derelict for years, and its redevelopment was to be Fingleton's crowning glory. His cash cow in retirement. He had ploughed €5.5 million into the purchase of the site in 2006 before a row with a fellow investor got ugly, sparking allegations of fraud and police complaints.

Eventually, by the end of 2017, Fingleton had managed to move beyond the legal quagmire and had secured a buyer willing to pay €10 million. There was just one problem. The sale was scheduled to go through in January 2018 – the same time Fingleton was due to be questioned for the first time by the Central Bank inquiry.

The solution was simple – and typically brazen. For Fingleton there was only one priority – money. He provided a certified sick note saying he was too sick to attend, and instead travelled to Montenegro to sign the sales contract and pocket €10 million. Thanks to contacts long established from earlier assignments in Montenegro, I was able to expose this hypocrisy in *The Irish Mail on Sunday*. Otherwise, the Central Bank may never have known of Fingleton's duplicity.

Now, two years later, Fingleton was legitimately sick. He had suffered a catastrophic 'medical event' in May 2018 that had rendered him unfit to testify or even understand the proceedings. He would bring his secrets to the grave. Writing this news for a Christmas 2019 edition of the newspaper, I felt little satisfaction at securing the scoop – not even when *The Irish Times* and the *Irish Independent* scrambled to catch up the following day. Fingleton would now never be brought to task. He wouldn't even be questioned publicly.

Michael Lynn, though, had a different perspective when he called a few days after Christmas.

'How is he by the way?' he inquired of Fingleton, so casually that I initially missed the leading intent behind the query.

'I don't actually have a true answer to that,' I admitted, since the nature of Fingleton's illness was being withheld for privacy reasons. 'But it's clear he's very, very, very sick.'

'Well, he's an important witness for Irish Nationwide,' Lynn chortled, almost gleefully. 'And they're eleven of the twenty-one charges.'

My mind somersaulted as the implications of one of the most important prosecution witnesses against Lynn being indisposed filtered through my brain. Could this be a blow to the impending trial? Might more than half of the charges now be dropped – and what would that mean for the remainder of the case? It didn't bear thinking about.

'Nice man, Mr Fingleton,' Lynn was prattling on. 'Bit of a bollix in his own way – but a nice fella.'

I had no way of knowing it then, but Michael Fingleton would not be the only important one of Lynn's bankers to be absent when his trial commenced.

The first week of January is usually a barren period in the news-gathering business. It is a time when little happens, newspaper sales are slow and news desks are manned only by skeleton crews. To counter the news deficit, correspondents have annual go-to holiday stories they prepare in advance before clocking off for the festive season. The 'year that was' and 'the year ahead' articles are classic examples of this trade craft.

On 4 January 2020, *The Irish Times* rolled out one such filler: '2020 THE MAJOR COURT CASES' by Courts Correspondent Mary Carolan. The article, accompanied by a photo of Detective Inspector Linehan escorting Lynn back from Brazil in handcuffs, reported that the Lynn trial was set to begin on 13 January 2020.

Then Covid happened.

A year later – on 2 January 2021 – *The Irish Times* once again rolled out its holiday holding story. Nothing had changed. Once again, the Lynn trial featured, this time reported as imminent, on 11 January. However, due to the ongoing coronavirus pandemic, this trial date was also shunted to a later date. Several subsequent dates also had to be moved forward. It would not be until February 2022 – four years after his extradition – that Lynn's trial would finally be able to proceed.

In the intervening years, Lynn took the opportunity to make every effort to stop his prosecution. He fought court battles on other fronts, too. One early court face-off involved his attempt to claim disability benefit from the government. Alleging that he was unable to work due to the severe mental trauma he'd suffered in COTEL, Lynn told the courts of experiencing death threats and extortion there. He spoke of having witnessed another prisoner being stabbed and of how he'd developed an ongoing lung issue while imprisoned in Brazil. This, he argued, continued to affect his health. The State initially denied his claim, though he was granted an unemployment allowance.

Most of his court appearances, though, were aimed at avoiding a trial – just as he had fought tooth and nail to avoid extradition in the first place. After being brought back to Ireland in 2018, he had launched a judicial review aimed at halting his prosecution.

During its top-secret diplomatic extradition negotiations with Brazil, the Irish State had guaranteed that, if convicted, Lynn would not serve more than thirty years in prison. The extradition deal with Brazil also saw the number of charges Lynn would face reduced. When originally charged in 2012, Lynn faced being prosecuted for twenty-one counts of theft, six counts of forgery and another six counts of using a false instrument to commit fraud – thirty-three counts in all. Since the forgery and false instrument charges do not correspond to any similar offences in Brazilian law, they had to be dropped. Now Lynn, whose deceptive and deceitful loan applications had gained him millions, would only face the simple theft charges – just like a shoplifter or burglar.

Furthermore, under the extradition terms, he could not be prosecuted for any other offence committed in Ireland prior to his return that may come to light afterwards. This in effect was a free pass for Lynn. If he could beat the theft charges, the State could never prosecute him for anything else relating to his crooked dealings with the banks.

Once home, Lynn claimed that in agreeing to not jail him for more than thirty years, the minister for foreign affairs, the attorney general and the

DPP had overstepped the separation of powers that the constitution dictates must be maintained between the judiciary and the executive. Deciding on sentencing, Lynn argued, was exclusively a matter for the judiciary, and the government should not have intervened to influence this.

The courts disagreed, largely on the basis that the maximum jail term for a single count of theft is ten years and virtually no one here has ever been imprisoned for more than thirty years for anything. Lynn lost his judicial review in the High Court, as well as a subsequent appeal ruled upon by the Court of Appeal president, Judge George Birmingham.

In the summer of 2019, Lynn sought permission to challenge this decision in the Supreme Court. He claimed the Court of Appeal had erred in law and that the issue at stake was a significant matter of public importance. The Supreme Court disagreed. It rejected his arguments outright and refused to grant leave for the case to be heard.

Following this, Lynn went through several new legal teams as his lawyers spent the years between the rejection of his case by the Supreme Court and the start of his trial for theft seeking discovery of documents and computer servers from the DPP and gardaí, which he required to fight the charges against him. Then, at almost the very last moment – with the case set to proceed in the second week of February 2022 – he went back to court on 22 January. This time he argued that his new legal team – his fourth in three years – had only been appointed in December and had not had enough time to review all the case documents. Judge Martin Nolan, who had case-managed Lynn's case in the Dublin Circuit Criminal Court since his return from Brazil, did not agree. He refused the request.

Finally, with the trial set to commence on Monday 7 February, Lynn's new team went to the High Court on the preceding Friday to seek a judicial review quashing Judge Nolan's decision to proceed with the trial. Appearing before High Court Judge Charles Meenan, Lynn's new Senior Counsel, Feargal Kavanagh, argued again that the new defence team needed more time and better funding to deal with the voluminous amount of discovery documents that had been generated. Together with witness statements and other documentary exhibits, the case now involved just under a million documents.

'We are entitled to be paid for work we have to do which the prosecution doesn't have to do,' Kavanagh argued. He told the court that Lynn's lawyers had been limited to reviewing paperwork for four hours daily under the legal aid scheme payments available. Lynn's team had even written to Justice Minister Helen McEntee over Christmas to seek more legal aid funding but had been 'stonewalled', Kavanagh told the court. He argued that 'essential work necessary for the case' could not be done and warned that Lynn's fair trial rights would be infringed if the case proceeded as planned.

The DPP's Senior Counsel, Patrick McGrath, countered that while 'somewhat difficult', the case was not 'exceptionally complicated'. He pointed to the fact that Lynn's previous solicitors had twice indicated they were ready for trial.

Ultimately Lynn's final throw of the dice failed. Judge Meenan ruled his trial could proceed on Monday and should not be delayed until the issue of fees was resolved.

'If that was the case, criminal trials would be endlessly delayed, which undoubtedly would not be in the public interest,' he said.

Michael Lynn had run out of options. It was time to face the music.

PART THREE

JUSTICE?

29

Game On

THE CRIMINAL COURTS OF JUSTICE BUILDING resembles the drum of a tumble dryer or washing machine perched on its side by the entrance to Dublin's Phoenix Park. Inside the round, modern concourse, courtrooms on four floors around the circumference bear witness to all forms of human drama spinning through the turbulent cycles of justice. Few – especially those accused of crimes – ever leave this place cleaner than they came in, even if they are ultimately found innocent.

After a foolhardy odyssey, which had by that point lasted fifteen years, Lynn finally takes his place in the dock of Court 7 on the second floor on Monday, 7 February 2022.

I'd like to think I could pick his face out of a busy crowd anywhere. Yet, at first, I don't recognise the man sitting passively to the right of the courtroom. The black face mask and blue, woollen peaked cap don't help, but, for sure, he has changed. Heavier than when I last met him at Leixlip Garda Station, he is dressed in plain trousers, black leather shoes and a navy-blue jumper. His hair has whitened, thinned and lengthened from the closely cropped bristles of old. The toughened, square-jawed physique brought on by imprisonment in Brazil has mellowed back into a more comfortable form. But the eyes, piercing blue, are still alight beneath thick eyebrows and furrowed brow. There's plenty of fight left in this man yet. And he's waited a long time for a stage like this.

'How do you plead?' Lynn is asked after a single sample charge is formally read out to get proceedings underway.

'Not guilty,' he responds, defiantly.

Game on.

Up to this point Lynn could have pleaded guilty and avoided a trial. Now, for sure, there will be a hearing. This is a man, it seems, who is determined to fight.

Standing just feet away, towards the back of the court, is Detective Inspector Paddy Linehan, the only policeman on the early list of seventy witnesses to be called by the prosecution. There's nothing about this case Linehan doesn't know. After a long and noteworthy career, he'd like this one to be one of his last.

'What have you got left?' a police colleague whispers a little too loudly to him, as a pool of fifty jurors are siphoned through in groups of eight to be whittled down to those who will decide the case.

'Seventy weeks,' he replies.

Detective Inspector Linehan has less than a year and a half to retirement, should he choose to go.

'It would be nice to get this done and done with,' the colleague nods towards Lynn.

The Detective Inspector draws a deep breath and hikes up his trouser belt. 'Absolutely.'

Fiat justitia ruat caelum – let justice be done though the heavens fall – is the motto on the website of Lynn's Senior Counsel, Feargal Pirais Kavanagh. The maxim – signifying the belief that justice must be realised regardless of the consequences – is an apt one for a defence lawyer.

At sixty-three, Kavanagh – though a smoker – appears fit and slim, with a distinguished, silver beard and slicked-back, curling grey hair. If this were the movies he'd be cast as a country aristocrat atop a hunting mare, amidst an excited pack of foxhounds. With his crisp, white shirt and flowing barrister's robe, cufflinks and metal spectacles pocketed in his buttoned waistcoat, he could just as easily play the role of a windswept frigate commander in the mid-1800s.

Unusually for a barrister, Kavanagh, a passionate beekeeper and one-time Irish Army captain, is not a member of the Law Library. But he has defended all sorts in a varied career and has a fearsome reputation around the courts. Murderers, terrorists, members of organised crime groups, sex offenders, soldiers on court martial – he has seen it all. In 1994, at the United Nations International Criminal Tribunal for Rwanda, he even defended Eliézer Niyitegeka, a former minister of information for the Rwandan government that was found guilty of genocide, murder, extermination and other inhumane crimes against humanity.

Kavanagh's counterpart for the prosecution side is Patrick McGrath, a barrister with thirty-seven years' experience to his name. If Kavanagh is something of an outsider at the Law Library, where working relationships are forged beneath the traditional cloth lampshades above each desk, McGrath is the opposite. He has been chairman of the Professional Practices Committee of the Bar Council and it is not unusual to see him near the top of the list of lawyers paid most by the Chief State Solicitor's Office and the DPP.

Having successfully prosecuted rapists, killers, fraudsters and all manner of crooks and criminals, McGrath has the cynical air of someone who has seen it all before, heard it all before and believed none of it. Ambling through the courts building in his billowing black robe, McGrath could be mistaken for a homely grandfather from afar. But to underestimate him would be a grave error. Though seemingly dormant for much of the time as he soaks up what's happening in court, he can pounce with the agility of a panther and the ruthlessness of an assassin. He is also a master at gamesmanship and not afraid to deliver a timely blow below the belt when things get down and dirty. To watch him do so with utter civility and feigned innocence is a joy to behold.

McGrath's prosecution team is being assisted by barristers John Berry, a one-time engineer and IT consultant, and Karl Finnegan. Assisting the defence with the overwhelming number of documents involved in Lynn's trial are barristers Dermot Mara, Amy Nix and Paul Comiskey O'Keeffe – all funded by the legal aid afforded to their client.

Affable and diligent, seventy-two-year-old Mara has been a Junior Counsel since 1993. He is the only member of the team to have been with Lynn since his extradition in February 2018. Lynn refers to him as 'the library'. This will be Mara's last trial before retirement. It has also been his favourite – and perhaps his most lucrative – job.

Nix has been a Junior Counsel since 2019 and before that worked with concert firm Aiken Promotions. Comiskey O'Keeffe – who will outshine his more senior colleagues during Lynn's trial as he takes the lead in the cross-examination of witnesses – has been a Junior Counsel since 2006. Aged forty-two, he once ran for election to Dublin City Council in his native Ballyfermot for the Labour Party. From 2015 he was also a volunteer director of the Phoenix Project – a charity that provided financial, legal and emotional advice to those at risk of losing their homes because of debt. The entity lost its charitable status and ceased operating amidst funding – and now-resolved Revenue problems. But for Lynn, Comiskey O'Keeffe's association with the project is still attractive. Perversely, he sees himself as a victim of the Celtic Tiger rather than an insider whose actions contributed to the financial apocalypse that befell Ireland.

One of the original founders of the Phoenix Project was Lynn's trial solicitor, John P. O'Donohue from Waterford. Each day he comes to court with a different matching necktie and pocket square. In the Irish legal system only a solicitor can instruct a barrister, so officially O'Donohue is the point man for Lynn's wider team. Throughout the trial he sits in the front row, with his back to the judge's bench, facing the courtroom. From there, he acts like a manager in the dugout, following the action closely. But everyone knows that Lynn, sitting in the dock to his solicitor's right, is the team owner. He will call the shots from the stand. And only he will pay the price of a loss.

On the prosecution side the DPP's solicitor, the State's man in the dugout, is John Birmingham. Though a young man, he sports a shock of white hair and has a deep booming voice. Refereeing these two formidable and expensive legal teams is Judge Martin Nolan, a white-haired, no-nonsense individual prone to chuckling at his own quips. Admired by many for his instinctive cunning, Judge Nolan dealt with a number of the marathon trials relating to the collapse of Anglo Irish Bank, including that of late CEO Seán FitzPatrick, who was ultimately acquitted. A garda for a decade, in the 1980s he left the force to become a barrister, practising for fifteen years in the south-eastern court circuit before being elevated to the bench.

There are few defences Judge Nolan has not been presented with during his time as a policeman, a barrister and a judge. He has just about heard it all. Michael Lynn, though, is about to come up with something new – a defence no one could have imagined or expected – and one Judge Nolan has certainly never heard before.

Michael Lynn stands up in the dock, flexes his shoulders and, with an earnest expression, faces the jury across the courtroom. It is the morning of Wednesday 9 February and the trial is about to begin in earnest. He doesn't have to plead to each charge against him, since sample pleas have already been conducted on each of the two preceding days as an extended jury of fifteen was being selected. But now that the prosecution is commencing proper, with a jury in place for the first time, he insists on doing so.

Standing up, the court clerk reads each charge individually. The jury members' eyes widen as they begin to realise the astonishing thefts of which he is accused. According to the charges read out, Lynn is accused of stealing:

- €3.6 million from Ulster Bank on 20 October 2006
- €215,000 from Irish Nationwide on 23 October 2006 and further sums relating to separate loans of €256,000 and €224,000 from the same bank on the same date
- €439,000 from Irish Nationwide on 22 November 2006 and further sums of €264,000 and €300,000 from the same bank on the same date

- €250,000 from Irish Nationwide on 7 December 2006
- €2.7 million from Bank of Ireland on 13 December 2006
- €460,000 from Irish Nationwide on 15 January 2007 and further sums of €508,000 and €436,000 from the same bank on the same date
- €220,000 from Bank of Scotland on 8 March 2007
- €1.3 million from Danske Bank (NIB) on 16 March 2007
- €406,000 from Bank of Scotland on 29 March 2007 and a second equal amount from the same bank on the same date
- €4.1 million from Irish Nationwide on 4 April 2007
- €3.7 million from ACC Bank on 12 April 2007
- €3.8 million from Bank of Scotland on 19 April 2007
- €256,000 from Bank of Scotland on 20 April 2007
- €3.7 million from Irish Life and Permanent TSB on 12 June 2007

To each charge Lynn replies with a solemn and earnest 'not guilty' before retaking his seat in the dock. In all, he stands accused of stealing more than €27 million.

If they had not known who Michael Lynn was beforehand, the members of the jury are about to find out in forensic detail. Soon these fifteen citizens, most of whom will likely only ever secure one mortgage in their lifetime – if even that – will be responsible for the fate of a man who once obtained multiple multimillion-euro loans monthly without a second thought.

Now it is time for the prosecution's opening submission to the jury, but Lynn's lead, Feargal Kavanagh, wants to make a legal point to the judge in advance, which requires the jury to leave the court. Kavanagh is concerned that the jury may be given the impression that Lynn 'somehow got hold of €27 million and ran off with it'. This is a case which can only be heard 'in relation to theft', he says, adding that there is no allegation of fraud or dishonesty.

'We don't want the jury to commence this case thinking theft is fraud,' he argues earnestly. 'We'll be objecting to any reference to fraud or deception.'

Judge Nolan listens, nods and swiftly dismisses the concern, saying he 'won't interfere in any way' with the opening statement of the defence.

The jury is brought back in and the trial begins. 'You have become now judges in this case,' prosecuting Senior Counsel Patrick McGrath tells them as he begins his opening statement. 'You will decide if the accused is guilty or not guilty.'

McGrath explains that the DPP must prove its case. Lynn, he says, 'has nothing to prove' and 'could choose not to take part at all'. He explains that the offence of theft in Irish law occurs when someone 'dishonestly appropriates property belonging to another without the other's consent' and with the intention of 'depriving the owner of that property'.

'Dishonesty is at the core of that offence,' he adds, rejecting the argument Lynn's team have just made in private.

Moving on, McGrath quickly hits all his marks. He tells the jury that Lynn was responsible for 'a web of deceit'. 'He was stealing this money,' he says. He was doing this 'dishonestly and repeatedly and deceitfully'. McGrath outlines the structure of Lynn's fraudulent scheme, saying he was obtaining 'multiple loans on the same properties and in that way defrauding the banks'. He introduces the three loans secured by Lynn on Glenlion – Lynn's would-be family home – as an example. ACC Bank gave €3.78 million, he says. Bank of Scotland gave €3.85 million. Irish Nationwide gave €4.125 million. The value to Lynn of the loans was €11.75 million.

'You will begin to see the same properties coming up again and again,' McGrath explains, before listing the many other properties double- and triple-mortgaged with different banks. By the time the trial is over, the jury will know these addresses – many of which are near the court in the centre of Dublin – by heart.

The jury is told how Lynn's banks relied on the truthfulness of details provided in documents such as statements of affairs and solicitor's undertakings, which backed loan applications. McGrath tells them they will hear from vital witnesses, such as Fiona McAleenan – the solicitor who first reported Lynn to the authorities – and Lynn's PA, Liz Doyle. He explains how letters of undertaking – a critically important document in the context of a sale – were often forgeries.

When McGrath has concluded, Lynn's team immediately wants to address Judge Nolan and the jury are once more asked to leave. Taking to his feet, spectacles in hand, Feargal Kavanagh objects to the repeated references to his client as having 'stolen large sums of money'. He objects to the use of words such as 'fraud, deceit, dishonesty and misled'.

As Kavanagh speaks, Judge Nolan's smile grows. He sits back, scratches his head, leans forward again, places his chin on his hands and looks for all the world like a father who has decided to simply enjoy the sheer impetuousness of his two-year-old for a few moments.

Continuing, Kavanagh complains of not having been provided with materials relating to Lynn's Kendar business. These would, he claims, have facilitated Lynn's defence by showing he had the potential means to repay the banks. The court has been 'wrong-footed' by the prosecution, he suggests, and the defence has 'had one hand tied behind our back'. Concluding, Kavanagh asks for the jury to be discharged so the trial can start again 'with a clean sheet'.

Judge Nolan's response is short and swift. 'This will be a very long trial,' he says, adding that it will be 'totally fact dependent' and that 'I suspect very strongly that opening will be quickly forgotten.'

The trial will proceed, but Lynn's team have set down a marker. They will try everything and anything, at every opportunity, to see the case dismissed. That is their job. They will test Judge Nolan to breaking point. Once they know where that point is, they will pull back half a step, but they will keep nibbling away. All they need is to introduce a reasonable doubt into the minds of at least three jurors to achieve a hung jury.

'How are ya – how are the children – all well?' Lynn greets me enthusiastically as we meet for the first time in nearly three years.

Court has broken for the day and Lynn is in schmooze mode again as we file out of the courtroom.

'Listen, I know we were to talk, but we will have that coffee soon,' he assures me. 'I know we mentioned it before, but we should talk about Netflix. I will do a Netflix show with you, Michael, I will.'

Outside Detective Inspector Linehan is chatting to a colleague.

'Paddy, nice to see you again,' Lynn gushes, holding out his hand. 'How're you doing?'

Linehan hesitates for a split second. Covid restrictions still apply and everyone is still bound by law to wear face masks inside. No one shakes hands these days, whatever about an elbow bump. Plus, as the officer in charge of the case against Lynn, he is conscious of appearances. Nevertheless, he reciprocates the gesture and shakes Lynn's hand as he passes.

'Everybody's friend – huh?' Linehan mutters beneath his breath to his colleague after Lynn has passed. His colleague simply shakes his head at Lynn's audacity.

30

A Way of Saving Money

SITTING ON THE CURVED MARBLE BENCH built into the wall beside Court 19, Michael Lynn is awaiting the second full day of his trial. Because of Covid, the trial has been moved to the top floor where the courtrooms are bigger. Beneath his navy-blue Paul Costello overcoat, he is dressed in slacks and a blue v-necked jumper, with an open-necked shirt underneath. Beneath the shirt a white, slightly stained vest is visible.

As ever, he wants to talk. I sit down to his left and turn sideways to listen, tucking my right leg under my left. First, he asks about the book.

'I have a wife and children,' he begins. 'My only request to you is be kind to my wife and children.'

Then he speaks of the case.

'I will take the stand,' he tells me. 'I'll be a lamb to the slaughter, but I was always going to do it.'

His legal team has advised against it, but Lynn doesn't care. 'This is my fourth legal team,' he says. 'I might sack them still and do it all myself.'

Once again, he asks if I think he will be found guilty – if I think he is a thief.

'You were a chancer,' I tell him. 'And you gambled–'

'I was a chancer,' he agrees, interrupting me. 'Absolutely – not a thief.'

I hesitate but let him go on.

'Is that theft?' he asks. 'It was deception – not theft,' he reassures himself.

He brings up the case of Thomas Byrne, a solicitor whose theft of €52 million saw him convicted of theft and jailed for twelve years in 2013. 'The difference between Byrne and me is I didn't steal anyone's money,' he says. In Lynn's mind he borrowed money but always intended to pay it back. Until he couldn't.

As he speaks, he swings his left foot up onto the bench, places an elbow on that knee and leans back on the other elbow. It is the kind of position someone sitting on a beach towel or propping themselves up on a bunk would adopt.

'You're positively horizontal there,' Feargal Kavanagh remarks as he approaches.

Lynn collects himself and heads into conference with his lawyer.

For a brief moment in time, Michael O'Malley could have stopped his employer from losing €1.3 million to Michael Lynn. It all came down to just two phone calls. Had those calls gone differently, O'Malley – who was three years from retirement at National Irish Bank (NIB) when he took them in February 2007 – would never have been compelled to appear as a witness in Lynn's trial. But the decisions he made as he listened to the reassuring and confident voice of Lynn down the line changed that forever.

Now, ten years into retirement, O'Malley – a thin man with a greying beard and hair – is a witness for the prosecution. Dressed in an open-necked blue-and-white-squared shirt, with grey slacks and a blue jacket, he is the fourteenth of thirty-eight current and former banking employees who will appear at the trial. His story reveals a lot about how banks were run in boom-time Ireland. It also provides new insight into how easy it was for Lynn to raise finance almost from thin air thanks to his misuse of solicitors' undertakings.

In 2007 O'Malley was NIB's senior corporate lawyer and it was to him that a lender came when she had a concern about a loan application from Michael Lynn. That lender was Orla Deignan – an assistant to Lynn's usual NIB banker, Noel McCole, who was on holiday at the time. McCole knew Lynn personally from his time as the branch manager in Blanchardstown, after which he had moved up the ranks, eventually becoming NIB's Business Banking Manager, based in Tallaght.

In the absence of her boss, Orla was left dealing with what became 'pressing calls and emails' from Liz Doyle about the progress of Lynn's loan. Orla knew that the undertaking of an independent solicitor was always part of the security arrangements the bank sought before any funds were advanced. But in Lynn's case, it seemed a fellow partner in his firm – Fiona McAleenan – was proposing to sign the undertaking. Orla had an email to say so.

'I confirm that I am a partner in the practice of Michael Lynn & Co. and as such will be acting independently and at arms [sic] length from my client,' the 7 February 2007 email from McAleenan's address read. But Orla wasn't sure this was arm's length enough, so she forwarded the email to Michael O'Malley in the legal department.

'I have just received this in,' she'd written. 'I have not spoken to her in relation to this matter. Is this something we would do?'

After he'd received the query, O'Malley arranged a call with Lynn. He would sort this man to man, solicitor to solicitor.

'He said he understood a solicitor couldn't undertake his own warranty,' O'Malley testifies about the call with Lynn. 'He understood and I understood.'

'What solution was made?' prosecution lead Patrick McGrath asks.

In response, O'Malley recalls how Lynn spoke of being entirely focused on being a developer and that 'his former junior solicitor had now taken over the business and was now principal partner in the firm'. Ringing off, the pair had agreed that Fiona McAleenan should call O'Malley to verify this.

Soon afterwards O'Malley had received a call from a woman. 'I was told it was Fiona McAleenan,' he tells the court. 'We had a long conversation in which I set out the concerns the bank had. She fully understood them. She's a solicitor,' he says, adding that the woman had agreed that 'a man can't give an undertaking over his own borrowings'.

'I'm now principal of the firm,' he recalls being told by the woman purporting to be Fiona McAleenan. 'Michael Lynn is only a consultant with minimal involvement.'

'After that conversation you were satisfied she had the necessary independence?' McGrath asks.

'Yes,' O'Malley replies.

'Did she make explicit statements that she was the principal in the firm?' McGrath follows up.

'Yes,' O'Malley answers.

Satisfied, O'Malley had emailed Orla back to say the lending could proceed. 'I have spoken to both Michael Lynn and Fiona McAleenan,' he had written. 'They both confirm emphatically there will be no conflict of interest in her working for him.'

With this reassurance in hand, Orla had drawn up the letter of offer and had posted it to Lynn's office. When it was received on 21 February 2007, it was accepted, signed in Lynn's name and couriered back to NIB that same day.

Lynn was delighted with the efficiency of NIB when Orla called him to tell him the loan had been approved. 'I'll happily give your bank more business,' he enthused in a grateful email.

On 16 March, using bank details provided by Liz Doyle, NIB made an electronic transfer of €1,333,160 to AIB account number 28020545 – the client account of Lynn's law firm. The whole transaction had relied on the undertaking in the name of Fiona McAleenan, two phone calls with Michael O'Malley and an email from McAleenan's account. But the undertaking in McAleenan's name had been faked by Doyle, the email from McAleenan's account had not been sent by her and an imposter had impersonated her on the phone.

During his evidence, O'Malley explains why the process of solicitors' undertakings were streamlined into a standard Law Society-approved form introduced in 1999. Prior to that, banks had to engage their own solicitor to ensure their loan would be registered on the folio of the property they were lending against. The new system, which relied entirely on trust, was intended to cut out this cost for the banks.

'It was a way of saving money, rather than us paying a solicitor,' O'Malley tells the court.

Other bankers also tell the court of the importance lenders attached to solicitors' undertakings.

'It was the be all and end all of the process,' Permanent TSB's Group Chief Legal Officer Cathal McCarthy testifies.

Documents from Lynn's lending files in that bank show its lenders were aware of the problems with a solicitor signing his own undertakings.

'I think that a different firm of solicitors should act,' Permanent TSB's Commercial Lending Manager John O'Brien had written to a colleague on 3 May 2007 when one loan was being processed.

He had repeated this warning again the following month. 'I presume a different firm of solicitors will act on behalf of Mr Lynn,' he'd written in a June email to Ciaran Farrell, Lynn's local branch manager in Blanchardstown.

In response, Farrell – who had prepared Lynn's loan applications – had reassured the bank's legal department that Fiona McAleenan was acting independently of Lynn. At this point Lynn had also rebranded his law firm as Capel Law to reflect his ever-decreasing involvement in its legal work.

'Mr Lynn has contacted me and explained his partner in Capel Law is independent from him,' Farrell assured his bank's legal department by email. 'He would have no party to these dealings.' The email had added that Lynn did not want to 'incur additional costs by utilising a solicitor from a different firm'. This logic had been accepted without further question by the bank. They were, after all, trying to save money the very same way.

The only lender not to have lost out in this fashion to Lynn was Anglo Irish Bank, which had not trusted solicitors' undertakings. Instead, it insisted on using its own solicitors to ensure its security was tight. It had not tried to cut costs – and had, as a result, saved its money.

31

The Elaborate Squiggle

JUST PAST THE SECURITY SCANNERS, to the left of the main door of the Central Criminal Court building, a guide has assembled a group of visiting teenage school-goers in a semi-circle around her.

'The lower the court, the lower the offence,' she explains, gesturing to the courtroom numbers running clockwise from the building's entrance around the perimeter.

'The higher up you go, the higher the offence,' she continues, pointing towards the circular, inward-facing balconies of the upper floors looped around the interior of the building.

On the very top floor, outside Court 19, Liz Doyle and her husband, Paul Davis, are not sure what to do. Dressed in a white, knee-length overcoat over a black silk top, Doyle alternates between pacing up and down and sitting on the edge of the arched marble benches between courtroom doors. Glancing around as every passer-by approaches, she speaks in hushed tones to her husband.

It's 11.15 a.m. on Tuesday 22 March 2022 and Doyle's time has come to testify. She has the demeanour of a shocked relative waiting for the operating theatre doors to swing open with bad news from the surgeon. It is clear she would rather not be here.

Crossing paths with Lynn has sucked Doyle into a whirlwind that picked up her life, tore it to dizzying shreds and left it a scattered and smouldering ruin. She may have freely jumped on board the Lynn express as it sped through Celtic Tiger Ireland, but she couldn't have known how long and perilous that journey would end up being.

Even now, more than two decades after she first went to work for Lynn, his forcefield still draws her in and tears her asunder again and again. He is the gravity pinning her down to a fate she cannot escape. Today that fate means she must testify against her former boss about a time she'd rather forget. It soon turns out she's already forgotten much of it.

Inside the courtroom, Detective Inspector Paddy Linehan is sitting in the back left corner beside a small round table set aside for the investigation team. Each day they lock the soft cushions they are sitting on into the evidence room at the back of the court, together with all the case files and exhibits. Unlike the public and the press, they do not have to endure the hard, varnished, church-like benches in the courtroom.

It's been four years since Linehan first walked Lynn into this building in handcuffs, having escorted him home from Brazil. During the Covid pandemic he had grown a thick black beard, a distinguishing feature he kept during the first weeks of the trial. But today the beard is gone. He wants a clean face to mark the occasion, one Doyle will recognise.

Linehan greets his witness warmly when she walks in. He does his best to put her at ease. Today will be important. Doyle is a vital witness for the prosecution. She could tip the balance either way.

Taking the stand, Doyle removes her face mask and swears in. From the back of the court, seated on the last bench, her husband, dressed in a blue Dublin GAA jersey beneath his jacket, looks on intently. On the bench beside him lies the Jack Reacher thriller he is reading.

On the stand, Doyle clasps her hands in front of her and relentlessly rubs her right forefinger across the base of her left thumb as she delivers her evidence. Patrick McGrath takes her through her background, introducing her to the jury. She is his witness and he is gentle and soothing, but she's visibly and audibly nervous nonetheless.

Just the length of a small car away, to her right and three steps below her, Lynn watches intently from the dock, peering over the top of his black face mask through black-framed glasses. To Doyle's left, the same distance away but three steps up, Judge Nolan swivels his chair around to face her, peering down through the reflections of the protective glass screens between them.

Led by McGrath, Doyle confirms the outline of her career. Straight out of school at seventeen, she became a legal secretary with Good & Murray Smith in Dublin's Dawson Street, followed by stints at John Flynn & Co. Solicitors in Parliament Street and Tony Shiel Solicitors in Charles Street West. In these firms, for a period of seventeen years, she dealt with conveyancing, litigation and debt collection.

In 1997 her eldest child, Ciara, was born, followed by a son, Sean, the following year. By then Doyle, who was living in Maynooth – forty-five minutes from the capital – wanted an easier commute. The result was a new job with Michael Lynn & Co. In this way her fate had been sealed.

Nothing in her nearly two decades of prior legal experience had prepared her for the demands and pressures of working for Lynn in boom-time Ireland. Doyle could not have known it then, but she had been bound to a fuse that was already alight and snaking towards a powder keg around the corner.

Asked to describe Lynn's law office, Doyle tells the court the pace was 'hectic'. 'It was all quick, quick. We didn't have a chance to think. It was busy, busy, busy the whole time.'

Things were so tough, in fact, that Doyle had left Lynn's practice for a few months, together with another exhausted colleague. However, she had returned before getting married in 2000, when Lynn had invited her back and promised better working hours. Liz needed money for her wedding and Lynn had, as always, been utterly convincing.

In 2003 Doyle, now with three children, had become Lynn's PA. He had already burnt through four or five other PAs in less than that many years, but that had not fazed Doyle. The financial rewards made the pressure worth it and soon Lynn – who was abroad more often than not – had trusted her with everything.

'When you see me coming, you see Michael Lynn coming.'

According to Fiona McAleenan, this was how Liz Doyle had expressed her importance within Lynn's office. And it was no exaggeration. Doyle had not been just Lynn's eyes and ears. She had been his fingers too – and those fingers had held the pen that had forged his name on countless occasions.

'The elaborate squiggle, is that your handwriting or Michael Lynn's?' asks McGrath as he walks the court through hundreds of documents Doyle signed as Lynn.

'That's my handwriting,' she replies time and time again.

'Who instructed you to do this?'

'Michael Lynn.'

There is little that Doyle did not sign. Her version of Lynn's signature is on loan requests and applications, direct debit mandates, transfer instructions to banks, statements of affairs from Lynn's accountants and life cover declarations. Whatever was needed, she signed without question.

'If he was not there and a document needed to be signed, you would sign it?' McGrath asks.

'That's correct.'

'Did others know in the office?' he follows up.

'Others knew if he wasn't in the office, I could sign stuff.'

'On his instructions?'

'On his instructions – yes,' she replies.

Doyle, though, had also forged the names of others, including that of Lynn's wife, Brid Murphy, his accountants, Kinsella Mitchell & Associates, and his associate solicitor, Fiona McAleenan.

'That's my signature,' she confirms when McGrath displays one of numerous undertakings to lenders purportedly signed by McAleenan.

'You signed the undertaking as Fiona McAleenan?'

'I did.'

'Who directed you to do that?'

'Michael Lynn.'

'He instructed you to sign the undertaking in Fiona McAleenan's name?'

'He did.'

Doyle – in her capacity as Lynn's eyes – had also kept close tabs on the incoming funds from these loans.

'Do you recall cheques being received for these properties?' McGrath asks, referring to a tranche of loans from Irish Nationwide.

'I do.'

'Was Mr Lynn informed?'

'He was.'

'Was he always informed – was that a rule – that he had to be?'

'It was, yes.'

Doyle had also distributed these loan funds as Lynn required, rather than using them to purchase the properties they had been lent for.

'Were you asked to do anything with this money?' McGrath asks, as he displays an Ulster Bank loan offer.

'I would have been asked to transfer it to various accounts,' Doyle answers.

'To where?' McGrath probes.

'I can't recall – Kendar.'

'Once or more than once?'

'More than once,' she confirms.

'Did this happen frequently?'

'I can't recall.'

'On whose instructions was this done?'

'Michael's – always.'

'Did anyone query this movement of funds at the request of Mr Lynn?'

'No.'

When McGrath asks her why she didn't query the transfers, Doyle says, 'Because I was afraid to. It was just a hectic office – you know – and there was a fear there.'

She also confirms she had been aware that loan applications were being made to multiple banks for the same properties. McGrath demonstrates one such instance by displaying a Bank of Scotland (Ireland) loan application.

'Do you recall noting anything about the properties set out?' he asks.

'Yeah, they were properties that were on other applications,' Doyle answers.

'You noticed that at the time?'

'I did.'

McGrath then asks if Doyle 'raised any issues' with Lynn about this.

'I did,' she confirms.

McGrath pushes for details.

'What did you say?' he begins.

But instead of answering directly, something in Doyle breaks. Her composure collapses completely. She turns to Judge Nolan.

'Can I say something?'

'You can answer any way you want,' he assures her, then adds, 'until you're stopped,' displaying his authority.

'Can I explain that in late 2006 my husband's business had failed,' she begins. 'I had come home one evening to a suicide note and this was all happening and my mind was all over the place when I had to return to work to try to cope with what was going on.'

The courtroom is stunned.

'Sorry, I did not mean to ...' McGrath pauses to search for an appropriate word and gives up. 'You were under pressure,' he concludes.

'I was under extreme pressure,' Doyle responds.

McGrath moves on and soon wraps up his evidence with Doyle. His question about how precisely she challenged Lynn when she realised the same properties were being used for multiple loans remains unanswered. But the personal toll of the decisions Doyle made while working for Michael Lynn are devastatingly clear.

32

Bloodbath

SURROUNDED BY THE REMNANTS OF FRIED breakfasts for three, Michael Lynn has just finished an early morning meeting in the Ashling Hotel, a short stroll away from the court building. Each day throughout the trial, he arrives here early to prepare for the day ahead. Today, Liz Doyle – who has finished giving direct evidence for the prosecution and will now be cross-examined by his team – will be the sole focus of his efforts. Soon she will bear the full force of his venom.

Amongst the toast crumbs and case files on the crisp, white tablecloth, Lynn's phone vibrates. 'Brid' is the name that flashes up.

'Brid, love, how are you?' he answers in a soothing voice.

After a short conversation, the couple sign off.

'Love you.'

'Love you, too.'

As a couple, Brid and Lynn have been through a lot together and it hasn't broken them. He is not about to allow this trial or anyone involved to tear them apart again by sending him back to prison. Not without a dogfight at least – one in which he will pull no punches.

Briefed by Lynn, Paul Comiskey O'Keeffe is aggressive in his approach to Doyle when he commences his cross-examination. Early on, he asks what her salary was.

'It would have been fairly decent,' she answers.

'Was it €95,000?'

'No, it was not €95,000,' she answers.

'Was it €90,000?' Comiskey O'Keeffe probes.

Doyle can't recall – a response she frequently gives as Comiskey O'Keeffe delves deeper and deeper into her life.

'Did you buy property yourself, aside from your home?' he asks.

'We had one investment property.'

'Did you ever have two?'

'Sorry, we had two investment properties,' she clarifies.

Soon Doyle confirms that in addition to the Irish investments, she and her husband had put deposits on apartments in Budapest and Portugal. They had also moved into an €800,000 dream home in the Kildare countryside. This was financed by a loan from ACC Bank in Ballina, where Billy Loftus – a childhood friend of Lynn's – was relationship manager.

Comiskey O'Keeffe puts it to Doyle that, in addition to a car each, she and Paul had a Land Rover jeep just for weekend use.

'I don't recall,' she says.

He returns to Doyle's salary, asking if she got a bonus of €50,000 a year on top of her €95,000 wage.

'That's not correct,' she responds adamantly.

'But you don't remember what your salary was?'

'I don't, no.'

Comiskey O'Keeffe switches topic, reverting to Doyle's previous assertion that she was in fear of Lynn.

'Yes, I was in fear of him,' she insists. 'There were times I was in fear of him.'

'Did you ask Mr Lynn to sing at your wedding?'

'That's correct,' she confirms.

Next he rolls out a list to demonstrate Doyle's close relationship with Lynn, stopping after each point for her to confirm. His aim is to show she did not act like she was afraid of her boss.

She enjoyed social functions with Lynn and invited him to her child's communion. Tick.

Two of her sisters worked for him. So, too, did a brother-in-law and a nephew. Tick.

Lynn provided the seed capital for – and was a director of – her husband's engineering firm. Tick.

Lynn helped the couple relocate to Portugal after this business failed. Tick.

Lynn graciously allowed Doyle to holiday in Australia for two months on full pay. Tick.

Though forced to confirm each point, Doyle still insists there was a dark side to her former employer. 'Can I just clarify that Michael would have been a nice guy,' she says. 'But there was another side to Michael Lynn. There would have been a fear factor.'

Switching topics, Comiskey O'Keeffe, produces a power of attorney agreement. It is undated and unsigned. He asserts that the document gave Doyle full authorisation to sign as Michael Lynn.

'He did authorise you to use his signature but expected it to be done in the normal way by indicating you were doing so on his behalf,' he says.

'That's incorrect,' Doyle answers, adding that she had never been aware of this document.

Comiskey O'Keeffe now switches tack to go after Doyle's reliability as a witness. Soon he has her tied up hopelessly in knots.

'Could you be mistaken?' he asks, showing her a couple of the many signatures she had identified under oath for the prosecution as ones she had falsified.

'I could be mistaken,' she concedes.

Slowly, under creeping pressure from Comiskey O'Keeffe, her testimony becomes a farce.

'Can I just say I'm getting totally confused,' she says when her answers begin to contradict each other completely.

'She's accepting everything you put to her – even though it's contradictory,' remarks Judge Nolan. 'You must be a very good barrister.'

'They've got to get her off the stand. She's no good to anyone like that.'

During one of the frequent breaks Doyle requires for medical reasons, Detective Garda Ivor Scully is voicing a mounting concern among the prosecution team.

Doyle, oblivious to all but the torture she is being put through, walks slowly arm in arm with her husband in a continuous circle around the top-floor balcony. After a few minutes she braces herself and re-enters Court 19 through its heavy double doors. Gingerly walking across the room's deep red carpet for her final stint in the witness box, she might as well be wading through her own blood, spilt from the injuries Lynn's team is inflicting.

But there is one more wound Lynn wants to open. He is not done with Liz Doyle yet.

Comiskey O'Keeffe displays the details of a €245,000 loan from Permanent TSB that Doyle and her husband received in January 2006. The loan, secured on 45 Annamoe Park, Cabra, Dublin 7, had two strict conditions. Firstly, an existing AIB loan, already secured on the property, was to be paid off. Secondly, once paid off, the old AIB loan was to be replaced with a mortgage charge in favour of Permanent TSB.

This is not what happened. Instead, on 19 January 2006, the loan cheque from Permanent TSB had been issued and the proceeds had been diverted elsewhere by Doyle and her husband.

Displaying a list of the withdrawals from the funds, Comiskey O'Keeffe turns to Doyle. 'This should have been used to redeem the previous mortgage on the property,' he states. 'Instead, we have a number of payments out and you accept that you – or your husband – received the benefit of all of these payments.'

Doyle acknowledges this as the jury is presented with evidence of various electronic transfers that had been made directly from the funds supposed to have been used to redeem the previous loan on the property. The day after the loan money had been received, €15,000 was transferred to Zimways Ltd, the firm Doyle's husband shared with Lynn. It is one of numerous payments to the firm from the loan funds.

Funds were also distributed to others. A payment of €1,000 had gone to Doyle's sister Mary, €15,000 had gone to Doyle's husband Paul – though his Irish name was used – and two deposits of €5,000 each had been put on apartments in Budapest. By the time these transfers had ceased, there was a deficit on the account. There was nothing left to repay the previous AIB loan as promised and Permanent TSB had not received its security.

In other words, Doyle appeared to have been a mini-Lynn in this instance. She seemed to have mimicked her boss's deceptive behaviour faultlessly.

'You told the bank you had cleared the previous charge on Annamoe, but that wasn't the case,' Comiskey O'Keeffe says.

'That's correct.'

'You received the benefit of the monies between you and your husband and Zimways.'

'That's correct.'

Comiskey O'Keeffe is not finished. Mercilessly, he draws back, preparing to thrust the sword deeper. This will be the final blow.

He turns to a second loan application from Doyle and her husband to Permanent TSB in August 2007. This time the bank advanced €601,000 on condition that it be secured against the original family home in Maynooth and on 45 Annamoe Park, Cabra. In a statement of affairs presented to the bank, Doyle and her husband had told their lenders that no one other than Permanent TSB had any interest in the Annamoe Park property. Agreeing the loan, they also undertook to redeem an existing Bank of Scotland (Ireland) mortgage on their Maynooth home.

But these undertakings had been falsehoods, just like Lynn's. In reality, the AIB loan on Annamoe Park was still in place. Meanwhile, the Permanent TSB facility for Annamoe Park had never been secured on the property at all and the money had been siphoned away. Furthermore, the Bank of Scotland (Ireland) loan on Doyle's original family home in Maynooth had not been redeemed, and €101,000 from the proceeds supposed to do so had been redirected to her husband.

After Lynn absconded, Doyle and her husband had been accused of fraud, but they subsequently rectified their financial affairs to the satisfaction of all their lenders. Now this dirty laundry was being exposed for all to see and Lynn had made his point. If he had had multiple loans secured on the same properties, he wasn't alone. Liz Doyle – a vital witness for the prosecution – had, for a time, done so, too.

After four days on the stand Doyle is almost free to go – once the prosecution has had a chance to question her again. Rising to his feet, Patrick McGrath keeps it short. There is little need to address much of what has been heard as Doyle was cross-examined. Most of the damage inflicted on her by Lynn's team is tangential to the accusation he actually faces. McGrath simply steers the jury back to the pertinent facts – the loan money stolen and received by Lynn via fraudulent loan applications.

'You were told by Mr Lynn to sign those.'

'That's correct.'

'And you were told what to include in the loan applications.'

'That's correct.'

'It was always under his instruction?'

'Yes.'

Finally, he clarifies with Doyle that it was Lynn who instructed her to forge other signatures, such as those of his wife and Fiona McAleenan.

'That's correct,' she says.

And with that, Liz Doyle's time on the stand is over.

'You are free to go now,' Judge Nolan says. 'Best of luck.'

She could do with some.

33

Hear No Evil, See No Evil

Fiona McAleenan takes pride in her appearance. That much is clear from her smart dress sense and dignified, upright poise as she alights from the LUAS tram outside Heuston Station. Her neatly styled, long blonde hair, tucked behind her right ear, falls sideways over the other. On her right shoulder hangs a bright-red, patent-leather handbag, offset by a light pink three-quarter-length overcoat. A large diamond wedding ring is one of two on her right hand, and she also wears a large, oval ruby pendant set into an elaborate silver neck chain. Above a cross-over, black and white top, she wears a below-the-knee patterned black skirt.

It is Monday, 28 March 2022 and McAleenan will soon be giving evidence in the Central Criminal Court a couple of hundred metres away on the other side of the River Liffey. At the pedestrian lights on Parkgate Street, the rhythmic, beeping drumbeat of the aural cue to cross mixes with the squawks of swooping seagulls and the bell of a passing tram as she crosses the road purposefully with a smartly dressed female companion.

McAleenan, though, notices none of these cityscape sounds. She has other things on her mind. Approaching the court building, she pauses briefly outside the Guilty Bean Café on Parkgate Street to pull on a pink face mask and dark shades. This point marks the spot beyond which the press cameras outside the court building will be able to intrude.

Once past the media gauntlet and through security, she crosses the lobby and takes the plate glass lift to the top floor. There is just one more thing to do. Inside the ladies' bathroom, McAleenan removes the comfortable purple trainers she has been wearing, replacing them with a smart pair of leather ankle boots. Now she is ready. Taking her place on the curved marble bench to the left of Court 19, she waits to be called.

Suddenly, the door swings open and Michael Lynn, a blur of grey hair and sky-blue jumper, emerges and turns right. He has not seen her.

'Is that him?' McAleenan's companion whispers. She nods in answer as they watch Lynn's back disappear into the men's bathroom.

As an apprentice solicitor, Fiona McAleenan first worked with Paul Kelly Solicitors in Leixlip, Co. Kildare. Then, after qualifying in 1992, she became an assistant in the law department of Dublin Corporation where, until 1994, she helped defend that organisation against personal injury actions.

Following this she crossed sides, from defence to plaintiff, and began work with Synnott Lawline & Co., one of the country's leading personal injury and medical negligence firms. After six years there, she moved to City Gate Law and then to P.C. Moore & Co., spending two years at each practice. Finally, in 2004, she answered an advertisement for a position as a litigation solicitor with Michael Lynn & Co. After an interview with Lynn and his practice manager, Claire Cooper, McAleenan agreed to take up the position. Her salary of €76,000 was to rise to €81,000 after six months' probation, and after two years she would be entitled to a 10 per cent profit share. On 21 November 2004 she began her new job.

She quickly learned the basics of life at Michael Lynn & Co.: Carol Lynch was in accounts, Liz Doyle was Lynn's PA, Cooper was practice manager and Susan, Katie, Peter and Kerry were the apprentice solicitors. Kendar and Lynn's office was on one side of the stairs, while the law firm offices were on the other. Red files were for commercial cases and brown files were for conveyancing cases involving client property transactions. Primarily though, McAleenan was occupied with the office's blue files – the colour reserved for litigation cases. Though she had agreed, when taking the job, to do some conveyancing when required, McAleenan had not actually completed any conveyancing work since her time as an apprentice in the early 1990s.

A mother of seven children aged between two and eighteen when she started in Lynn's practice, McAleenan was busy in all aspects of her life. Too busy, perhaps, to notice everything. But she had no way of knowing that the distorted madness of Lynn's affairs at this time was hurtling towards a towering cliff edge. If there were warning signs, she didn't see them. It didn't help that, not being computer proficient at the time, McAleenan dictated her letters to staff and trusted others to type and send her emails for her. Then there was the fact that others collected and sorted her post before she arrived into the office after 10 a.m. each morning. Also not ideal was the way McAleenan signed anything Liz Doyle brought to her without question. These signatures, particularly those from the firm's brown conveyancing files, were ultimately responsible for McAleenan having to testify. In those strokes of hastily scrawled blue biro, penned without a thought for the consequences, she had signed up to a fate she never could have imagined.

In previous episodes during her long career McAleenan had managed to avoid being played for a fool. In 2002, for example, when a client's son pretended his mother was still alive in order to continue a personal injury action against a hairdresser, she was alive to the ruse. She was even commended by the judge in the case for her alertness and integrity in bringing the matter to the court's attention. With Lynn though, McAleenan – who was in the midst of negotiating a partnership deal for his legal practice when it imploded – was blind until it was far too late; until he'd dragged her over the cliff with him and there was no turning back.

Walking up to the witness box to swear in, McAleenan turns to stare at Lynn as she passes. It is a defiant, deliberate action. Lynn does not flinch. No words are exchanged. Whatever emotion his face might betray is hidden behind his black face mask.

As Patrick McGrath begins to lead her through her witness statements, McAleenan's deep, self-assured voice contains an intonation of a northern heritage. Unlike Liz Doyle, she displays no sign of being nervous. She is ready for whatever is in store. She is not going to let Lynn see any sign of weakness. When McGrath errs in his early questions – by dating her commencement at Michael Lynn & Co. to February 2004 – she immediately corrects him.

'It was November 2004,' she interjects, almost sternly, within a split second.

Listening to the exchange, I wonder whether McGrath has done this deliberately to signal her reliability to the jury. Soon McAleenan is being run through the many solicitors' undertakings, letters and loan documents on which Doyle has admitted to faking her signature.

'So, am I to take it that someone has forged your signature there?' McGrath asks each time.

'That is correct.'

'Do you know who forged your signature?'

'Yes – Liz Doyle. That is Liz Doyle's handwriting.'

Fiona answers this question time and time again for each forged document, each time barely restraining her apparent contempt every time she mouths the name of her former colleague.

'Did you authorise or give permission to Liz Doyle or anybody else to have your name forged on that document?'

'No, I did not.'

'You never gave any permission?'

'No, certainly not.'

McAleenan also has an explanation of the undertakings she did actually sign, some of which resulted in banks losing millions.

'She [Doyle] came into my office with the undertakings and had the undertakings open at the page that required the signature,' she explains. 'She would then turn over the page to the next section – that's the way it was done.'

'Were they already completed or not?' McGrath asks.

'Oh yes, they were all completed, everything was completed on the form when she brought it in,' she confirms. 'None of the undertakings were ever left with me on the desk – they were always taken away.'

McAleenan's undertakings, in other words, were worthless – even those containing her real signature. She had given them without looking at the documents. And as to actually making sure the undertakings were carried out – that loans had been secured in favour of the lender on properties and that funds lent had actually been used to purchase them – she presumed others would do this and never checked. Conveyancing wasn't her job, she tells the court repeatedly. She did litigation, dictating her correspondence for a PA to type. Conveyancing, it seems, was beneath her.

Listening to this attitude, I am reminded of a lawyerly in-joke made earlier in the trial by Cathal MacCarthy, the Group Chief Legal Officer to Permanent TSB. 'If you want conveyancing, get a bus,' he replied, when asked by the defence if he'd done property work at his private practice prior to joining the bank. MacCarthy, like McAleenan, did litigation.

It is clear McAleenan is intent, at every juncture, to distance herself from Lynn's lending. But what of the emails she sent to banks about Lynn's loan applications?

She has a ready explanation for this: Doyle had access to everyone's email accounts and computers were not password protected. 'If I was in court or at lunch or away from the desk, the computer was left on and anyone could have access to it,' she tells the court.

McGrath then leads McAleenan through other deceptions that fooled the banks, bringing one such instance up on the screen for the jurors to examine. Correspondence on 5 March 2007 to Bank of Scotland's Andrew Snow relates to Lynn's €3,850,000 loan application from that bank for Glenlion House. 'I confirm that I am a partner in the firm of Michael Lynn & Co.,' McAleenan's letter reads. 'I wish to advise that I am acting independently of Michael Lynn in this matter.'

But the letter and McAleenan's signature on it were both faked by Liz Doyle, who also signed the loan offer forms in McAleenan's name when the loan was ready to be issued.

'Is that your signature?' McGrath asks McAleenan, displaying the 18 April 2007 loan offer.

'No, it's not,' she answers.

Then McGrath displays exhibit no AJS43, an electronic funds request, dated 19 April, asking Bank of Scotland to send the €3,850,000 for Glenlion to Lynn's client account in AIB. It too bears a Fiona McAleenan signature.

'Is that your signature?'

'No, it is not.'

'Whose handwriting is that?'

'That's Liz Doyle's handwriting.'

'Did you give Liz Doyle permission to forge your signature?'

'No, I did not.'

McGrath then asks if she ever had anything to do with this €3,850,000 Bank of Scotland loan to Michael Lynn and Brid Murphy. The answer is the same one McAleenan gives repeatedly, day after day, document after document. By now some of the jurors are so familiar with the routine they practically mouth the answer together with her as she speaks.

'No, I did not.'

34

Hunting in Long Grass

IT HAD ARRIVED JUST LIKE ANY other fax, whirring mechanically as the message printed and delivered itself from within. But the contents of this communiqué – sent from Ulster Bank's lawyers, McKeever Rowan Solicitors, on 5 September 2007 – had changed Fiona McAleenan's life forever.

The bank, having lent €7 million to Michael Lynn, was enquiring about the loan undertakings. Looking at the list of properties involved, McAleenan realised she had already seen the same list somewhere before – in a similar fax from another bank a month earlier.

Until that moment McAleenan had trusted Lynn and Doyle completely. Now she was about to learn the horrifying truth.

After consulting with a solicitor and a friend, McAleenan had approached the Law Society. They had advised her to leave Lynn's practice immediately. On 10 September she had composed a handwritten resignation letter for Lynn. She and Lynn were now at war, both in a fight for their personal survival.

Early on the morning of 11 September McAleenan entered the offices of the firm from which she'd just resigned. At 8.01 a.m. she accessed her work email and forwarded a memo to her private Hotmail account. The memo, composed by Liz Doyle on 31 March 2007, had been sent to all staff and had been marked 'high importance'. To McAleenan it had represented evidence that Doyle ruled the Lynn roost. If something dodgy had gone on, McAleenan needed to distance herself from it quickly and prove that Doyle had really been in control of things.

'If any post comes in for Michael Lynn, or any phone calls through reception concerning matters pertaining to Michael Lynn, Liz Doyle will deal solely with these matters,' the memo reads. 'If couriers are ordered by Liz for Michael Lynn, please ensure ... the package comes back to Liz and not anybody else,' it continues. 'Liz will deal solely with all calls for Michael Lynn and Liz only.'

Similarly, Lynn had been digging for evidential weapons to use against McAleenan in the inevitable head-to-head that was to come. As soon as she'd resigned, he had ordered Doyle to retrieve all of her emails. Ever since then, he'd diligently taken note of anything else that emerged about McAleenan for future use against her. With her testifying in a court of law against him, the time had now come to deploy everything this arsenal held.

Paul Comiskey O'Keeffe begins his cross-examination of Fiona McAleenan slowly and deliberately. It will be six days before he finishes with her – a whole working week and more in which he steadfastly pursues his prey through the tangled forest of Lynn's affairs. His hunting trail through the million pages of documents in this case is marked by multi-coloured index flags protruding from the edges of thick folders spread around him. Each day these files and papers are hauled in and out of court in wheeled suitcases and in plastic containers on hand trolleys, which are parked alongside Lynn in the dock.

Navigating carefully, Comiskey O'Keeffe leads McAleenan down his hunting trail setting fresh traps as he goes.

'Were you ever an authorised signatory on cheques?' he asks her.

Trap set.

'I cannot remember.'

Bait taken.

Now, knowing his quarry can't escape, he moves on, marking the spot to return to later.

'Were you an authorised name on electronic transfers?'

'I don't know.'

Again he moves on, after whispering a quick instruction to Mara and Nix, the two document barristers behind him. They delve into their files to seek what he needs as Comiskey O'Keeffe returns to his pursuit.

'Did she ask you to transfer money?' he asks, referring to Liz Doyle.

'I don't recall that she ever did.'

In his own time, Comiskey O'Keeffe circles back to these issues, displaying an email or document to undermine the evidence McAleenan has previously given.

'Were you ever an authorised signatory on cheques?' he asks again, the following day, having now shown the documentary evidence that she was.

'I think I was.'

'You remember now, do you?'

'Yes.'

She has little choice but to agree. The evidence that she was is displayed for all to see on the court screens.

McAleenan would like to be seen as nothing more than an employee of Lynn's, someone who played no role in overseeing the firm and was certainly not aware of his property dealings and borrowings. But the truth, drawn out slowly by Comiskey O'Keeffe, is not so black and white. Inch by inch, her credibility is called into question.

'When I gave the answer yesterday, I had forgotten I had the authorisation to do so,' she explains when presented with evidence of her involvement in signing cheques and authorising bank transfers for Lynn's law firm.

Comiskey O'Keeffe chalks up each one of these dents to McAleenan's credibility as his pursuit delves deeper into the role she played. His aim is to wear her down, step by step, hour after hour, until she is exhausted and cornered with nowhere left to run.

The biggest prize for Lynn – reserved for the gaping, saw-toothed, bear trap in his arsenal – would be to prove that McAleenan was a partner in the firm.

If that were the case, she would have been responsible for what happened there at a time when he was largely absent abroad and so must have known how the banks were being conned. This would surely lead the jury to wonder whether she could have been part of the ruse. If it can't be proved that she was a partner, the best Lynn can hope for is that they see her as negligent, irresponsible and reckless in her duties as a solicitor.

'You were a partner?' Comiskey O'Keeffe asks repeatedly throughout her five days on the stand.

'No, I was never a partner in the firm,' she answers each time.

Comiskey O'Keeffe asks the question every which way. It is put forcefully and directly, slipped in almost as if an afterthought, dropped in suddenly amidst another topic. But the answer never changes. McAleenan insists she was not a partner.

Once again, though, the truth is a little less clear than that. If she wasn't a partner, it wasn't for the lack of trying. McAleenan did, in fact, actively hold herself out to be a partner. She was even announced as such to staff in a memo from Lynn in October 2006. To hammer this point home Lynn's team display the memo: 'Fiona has full authority to direct all members of staff with regards to their range of responsibilities and duties within the practice.'

The defence team also shows emails in which McAleenan herself suggested to Lynn that this very phrase be used in the memo announcing her partnership.

Confronted with the material, the witness has a simple answer.

'I don't recall it. It's as simple as that,' she says. 'I can't deny it. I can't recall it.'

She gives similar responses when confronted with her own request to staff that she be named as a partner on business cards and the firm's headed paper.

'I don't recall that and I was not a partner in the practice,' she repeats.

There is a lot McAleenan does not remember. She has no recollection of being involved in finances or fee matters at Michael Lynn & Co. No memory of being aware of any Kendar or Overseas Property Law matters. No memory of doing any conveyancing work. No memory of being involved in staff management. No memory of ever seeing client accounts. No memory of being in receipt of weekly management reports. She also has no memory of a 26 February 2007 meeting with Lynn and others at which all these issues – and many more management concerns – were discussed.

'I don't recall the meeting,' she says when asked.

'It was attended by a stenographer from Gwen Malone Stenography Services Ltd. Does that assist your memory?' Comiskey O'Keeffe retorts dryly.

'No, it doesn't,' McAleenan answers.

Now she is pinned down, as Comiskey O'Keeffe walks her through the transcript in which many matters she has no memory of are confirmed: 'I will hand over to you, Fiona, as a partner – what do you see?' the transcript reads, as Lynn had asked about an underperforming apprentice during the meeting.

'If somebody is not producing the results, unfortunately, they have to go,' she had replied. 'They have to be replaced.'

This, Comiskey O'Keeffe insists, must be evidence that McAleenan was a partner. But her answer does not falter.

The court then sees evidence that McAleenan notified the Law Society of her partnership status in June 2005. But this was a misrepresentation, she says, done at the request of Lynn to allow her to oversee apprentices at the firm. There are documents to show she told the firm's insurers that she was a partner. But these insurers later went to court to invalidate the policy on the basis that she was not – and won. There are umpteen examples of letters in which McAleenan tells the banks and their solicitors that she is a partner. There is even a partnership agreement. But it is a draft one and was never signed. However McAleenan may have portrayed herself – however much she may have wanted to be a partner – she never actually was.

The gaping bear trap Lynn hoped Comiskey O'Keeffe might bring her down with may have been triggered, but it has snapped shut without Fiona McAleenan in it. So there's only one thing left to do: inflict as much damage as possible. It is time for the gloves to come off.

'Did Michael Lynn give you €50,000 towards the purchase?'

It is day five of McAleenan's cross-examination and Comiskey O'Keeffe is asking about the purchase of her family home. Digging deep into Lynn's arsenal, he is no longer engaged in a stealthy pursuit. The hunting trail through the undergrowth has been abandoned. Now the entire forest is to be carpet-bombed.

'€50,000 – I don't recall,' stutters a stunned McAleenan.

'Michael Lynn will give evidence he contributed €50,000 to that house purchase in relation to a profit-share agreement,' Comiskey O'Keeffe continues.

McAleenan regains her composure. 'I do not recall that at all and I am completely taken aback by that.'

If Lynn needs evidence that this tactic could hurt McAleenan personally, it comes as soon as Isabel Hayes, the seasoned reporter from the CCC Nuacht court agency, files her daily story. 'Solicitor does not recall getting €50,000 from Michael Lynn for house purchase,' the headline, run by virtually every news outlet in the country, reads.

There is more to come. The next day – McAleenan's sixth in the box – sees Comiskey O'Keeffe overtly suggest she was complicit with Lynn and knew of the double and triple undertakings behind the loan documents bearing her name.

'Most certainly not and I am just horrified by that suggestion. Absolutely horrified and disgusted that you would put something like that to me,' she replies forcefully.

Once again, it is the suggestion of complicity and her denial of this that makes all the headlines the next day.

Now, Comiskey O'Keeffe has one weapon remaining – McAleenan's own emails and personal text messages, downloaded from the Blackberry phone she was using in 2007. The hope is that these will show just how complicit she may have been in fraudulent activities.

Among the messages is a series of urgent texts from Liz Doyle about a July 2007 loan drawdown cheque from one of Lynn's lenders: 'Pls arrange to have the chq collected by direct courier and lodged immediately to client account,' a message, dated 26 July at 12.20, reads.

Two hours later, at 14.34, Doyle followed up. 'Fiona, I need 2 get an urgent bank transfer done. Can you ring me. Tks.'

The money from the loan – which had been lent specifically to buy a house in Shelbourne Park, Dublin – was apparently needed for something other than its intended purpose.

The next message from Doyle, at 8.15 a.m. the next day, shows just where the money was to go.

'Hi Fiona, Did the chq for shelbourne cme in ysday eve. I need to get it lodged first thing and do a transfer 2 kendar b4 10 tis morn. Can you let me know pos re chq. Tks.'

Doyle had followed up again half an hour later, at 8.46 a.m.

'Fiona, can you make sure tat the chq is collected first ting this morn. I need 2 get it lodged urgently.'

Less than half an hour later, she had texted again.

'Hi fiona, can you get karen to type up an urgent transfer to the bank same as today only change the figure to the sum of 258,000 to be lodged to kendar. U can use the blank headed paper I left with my signature on it. Tsk again.'

Displaying the messages, Comiskey O'Keeffe puts it to McAleenan that they 'seem to contradict' her lack of knowledge and involvement in loans being funnelled away from their intended purpose and instead being sent to Kendar abroad.

'You had knowledge in relation to drawdown of funds,' he says.

Despite the evidence to the contrary, her denials remain steadfast and broad.

'I didn't pay any attention to the details,' she says.

Finally, Comiskey O'Keeffe raises the issue of the undertakings McAleenan signed for the Permanent TSB loans Liz Doyle and her husband Paul Davis had obtained. McAleenan had signed the first undertaking for the Doyles – relating to 45 Annamoe Park – in January 2006. However, she had not completed the conveyancing in favour of the bank and the Doyles had siphoned the money away from its intended purpose.

Having set the background, Comiskey O'Keeffe points to another of McAleenan's Blackberry texts. It came from Liz Doyle on 2 August 2007 and in it she asks McAleenan to transfer money from the loan funds to an account in her name and that of her husband.

'Hi Fiona, can you do up a transfer to our account for 3k,' the text reads. 'Would you mind doing this asap. Many thanks.'

The message adds that McAleenan should ensure the funds in the 45 Annamoe Park account are used to make this transfer.

This, Comiskey O'Keeffe suggests to McAleenan, is direct documentary evidence of her awareness of the 6 January undertaking she signed being breached. It is, in fact, evidence she may have helped siphon some of the money away. Yet, a month after this text, McAleenan had signed a second undertaking for Doyle relating to the same property.

'I didn't realise I had made a prior undertaking for that property,' McAleenan responds.

'You had the facts,' Comiskey O'Keeffe counters, pointing to the text. 'You had the facts a month before you gave the second undertaking.'

'I did not dwell on that,' McAleenan answers. 'I did not focus on it. I did what was asked because I did not suspect there was any reason not to do so.'

Instead of representing the lender's interest, as she had undertaken to do, McAleenan had been signing undertakings while blindly trusting others to take care of the details.

'This is a situation where you give a second undertaking when you knew the first is not complied with,' Comiskey O'Keeffe tells her. Her response is that it was 'common practice' for solicitors at the time to sign undertakings blindly.

'I can't recall signing either of these undertakings or noticing the properties to which they related,' she says.

McAleenan, it seems, saw no evil and heard no evil while working for Lynn. Yet, as Lynn's defence team has just shown the jury, there was a cacophony of it all around her.

35

Down the Rabbit Hole

IT IS 10.30 A.M. ON WEDNESDAY 13 April – the thirty-fifth day of his trial – and Michael Lynn is in jolly mode.

'Would you mind just taking my place for the day?' he asks me from the box as court prepares for a day of legal argument from his defence team.

It is a typical moment of levity from Lynn who finds humour everywhere, even when in the dock. Occasionally, throughout the trial, I can hear him humming to himself as he works his way through the day's material. He is happy when busy, too intense to sit still.

'Sure, no problem,' I say, playing along with the joke 'For the right price. Everyone has a price.'

Lynn bursts into laughter behind his mask and steps over to the press bench. We both know what I mean. I am referring to his bribery of bankers.

'It's not easy,' he says, referring to being in the box and tapping his head as if to demonstrate the mental difficulty his position involves. 'Have you ever done it?'

'No,' I say. 'I can imagine the psychology of it must be tough.'

'Do you know that box is three times the size of the space I had when I first went to prison in Brazil,' he responds. 'It's amazing what you can get used to.'

Then he switches mindset. 'I suppose you'll be doing all sorts of stories in the paper before the book is out?' he asks.

I confirm that I will.

'Will you do *The Late Late*?'

'They'd never have me,' I respond. 'I don't think they'd care.'

'Really? Well, we'll have to do an interview. It's in my interest to get my side of the story out.'

I tell him we can do one in advance of the trial concluding, for publication afterwards. He nods his approval, then switches mode again, turning his attention to his document barrister, Dermot Mara, who is sitting in his usual spot just in front of me.

'Dermot, you must be fed up with this lad breathing on your ears.'

'No, I don't notice,' Mara shrugs.

'I certainly know a lot about the hair of these two,' I say gesturing at Mara and Amy Nix, the other document junior beside him, 'but I'd struggle to describe their faces.'

Mara turns around and pulls a goofy face.

Lynn switches topic again.

'Will you write my defence?' he asks, nodding at my laptop screen.

'I'm not sure what you mean,' I say.

'If you had to write it now, what would it be?'

I dodge the question. But it sure as hell wouldn't have been what comes next.

'What precisely is alleged to have been stolen?'

Lynn's lead barrister, Feargal Kavanagh, begins a legal submission, without the jury present, to have the case dismissed. After five weeks of prosecution evidence, this is the opening salvo of the defence case.

Jumping through a series of theoretical hoops, Kavanagh concludes that what is alleged to have been stolen is not actually money at all. The only thing that's gone missing is 'an equitable interest arising from the existence of a charge'. No money has been stolen, he argues, just a bank's interest in the value of a legal instrument.

Judge Nolan, who alternates between bewilderment and impatience at the approach, sees things in a more straightforward fashion.

'The indictment says you stole almost €27 million,' he interjects matter-of-factly. 'You applied for money to buy houses and the State says you had no intention to buy houses,' he continues with a there-you-go gesture of his hands.

'But what did we steal?' Kavanagh asks slowly, as if the question was one of complex metaphysical science.

On the prosecution bench, Patrick McGrath snaps his chin up with a jerk, pulls an absurd face and cocks his head sideways like a chicken to examine his counterpart from the corner of his eyes. The look resembles an emoji personified and is one he uses to perfection throughout the day. It's a masterful technique that succeeds in drawing the attention of the judge and signalling his bewildered disagreement to the jury without the knowledge of the opposition.

'They say the money was transferred to you – you stole it,' Judge Nolan continues patiently, more amused than exasperated at this point.

'I think you are trying to create confusion – a huge amount of confusion when there is no confusion – you are very good at it,' he adds later.

'With respect,' Kavanagh replies, 'the confusion arises from the way the case has been presented.'

'All I know, from the evidence, is monies came from lending institutions and went someplace else,' Judge Nolan says. 'It's not as if law is a form of Einsteinium super science,' he adds. 'Most of us would not be able to do law if it was that difficult.'

Kavanagh, though, continues until Judge Nolan interrupts again.

'Mr Kavanagh, you simply try to overburden this court with complication,' he complains.

It is complicated, Kavanagh protests. 'What is the amount?' he asks as if the answer was a mystery.

Judge Nolan fumbles to find the charge sheet.

'If the jury finds your client hoodwinked the banks, €2.74 million is the amount for the first one,' he says, reading the first charge relating to Bank of Ireland.

'You can only steal an amount if it's something,' Kavanagh carries on.

'The amount went from Bank of Ireland to your client,' the judge snaps.

'But in what form?' Kavanagh continues. 'It's an intangible,' he theorises. 'We are not charged with the theft of money.'

The legal argument that a financial instrument – such as a cheque or an electronic transfer – is not property itself – stems from a 1996 House of Lords decision in a famous case known as 'R v Preddy'. In the Preddy case the House of Lords allowed an appeal by alleged mortgage fraudsters on the basis that they had not gained 'property belonging to another' when an electronic transfer passed between two banks.

'You can't steal an electronic funds transfer,' Mr Kavanagh persists, despite increasing signs of exasperation from Judge Nolan, who is clearly unimpressed.

'The House of Lords might be overthinking everything, like yourself,' Judge Nolan observes. 'You might do well in the House of Lords, Mr Kavanagh.'

Later Judge Nolan puts it even more succinctly. 'Basically, the English Supreme Court have made a bags of it,' he surmises.

But still Kavanagh proceeds with his arguments, prompting further criticism from Judge Nolan. 'I'm afraid if I follow you, I will be heading down to Alice in Wonderland,' he interjects. 'I have to use a lot of imagination to keep up with you.' The fairy-tale reference is used several times by Judge Nolan throughout this phase of the trial.

Lynn's team also seeks to have the case thrown out on the basis that after all the State's evidence had been heard, the court granted an application from the prosecution to amend the wording of the charges against Lynn. The granted amendment changed the wording of each charge so that the specific date of each theft accusation was removed and replaced with the words 'on or about'. The State sought this change after Lynn's team began to question whether the thefts had occurred on the day of drawdown, the day of loan approval, the day the money was transferred abroad by Lynn and so on.

Having nudged the prosecution into making the change, Lynn's team then immediately applied to have the trial scrapped on the basis that this change was a breach of the conditions under which Lynn had been extradited from Brazil. Citing the principle of 'comity of nations', under which nations mutually recognise and respect each other's legal systems, Kavanagh raises the prospect of asking the Brazilian authorities if they would agree to Lynn being prosecuted here under the amended wording.

'We don't know whether or not they would grant that permission,' he argues.

Again, Judge Nolan is nonplussed. 'I suspect the Brazilian courts might be dumbstruck and unable to act by reason of surprise,' he smiles.

Even Lynn – who has likely come up with many of the tactics his team are deploying – laughs out loud.

'This is serious,' Kavanagh persists, querying if Lynn would have been extradited with the new wording of the charges. 'Then he would not have faced the trial at all.'

Suddenly, an alarm sounds throughout the building and a recorded male voice blares from the public address system: 'Attention please! Due to an incident, it may be necessary to evacuate the building.'

Judge Nolan spots an opportunity. 'I think somebody may be telling you something,' he tells Kavanagh, delighted with his own wit.

These exchanges mark a watershed in the stand-off between Kavanagh and Judge Nolan that ultimately leads Kavanagh to suggest he is being unfairly treated.

'If you keep barracking us, it's going to give the client the impression that you are completely biased against him,' Kavanagh objects. 'You're being aggressive. I'm not here to be taking abuse from a judge. You're not entitled to be aggressive to me,' he continues, adding that the judge's behaviour 'comes across as bullying'.

'I don't think anyone in the entire judiciary would be capable of bullying you,' Judge Nolan retorts.

Ultimately, after two days of these legal somersaults from Lynn's side, Judge Nolan gives his ruling and dismisses the defence's arguments. The trial can proceed with Lynn's defence proper.

They call it the 'pinkie' and it is the most important document in any trial for a defence lawyer representing a client on free legal aid. Nicknamed for its bright-pink colour, Criminal Legal Aid form CLA8 is sacred.

Each morning, the court clerk leaves the form on Lynn's defence team's bench and it is carefully passed around and signed by all members of the team as court begins. Their signatures on that page certify that they have been present at trial that day and they will get paid. It doesn't matter whether the court adjourns after ten minutes or sits all day – which typically means four and half hours. If your name is on the pinkie, you will get paid for the day.

This trial – with senior barristers on more than €2,000 a day and juniors on approximately half that – costs more than €10,000 daily in lawyers' fees to run. That cost remains even when nothing happens. There are times – such as on Monday 25 April – when the system could easily have known nothing was going to happen. Nevertheless, everyone attended to be told so. And to sign the pinkie.

'All good to go?' I'd asked Feargal Kavanagh as he'd alighted from the lift that day.

'Afraid not,' he'd responded, shaking his head. 'Covid.'

'A member of the jury?' I'd asked, since the trial had already been delayed by a juror's Covid diagnosis.

'No,' he'd frowned. 'My client.'

When all had assembled – and signed the pinkie – the court was told of the issue. It was supposed to be Lynn's first day on the stand – a pivotal point in the trial – but he'd tested positive for Covid, for the second time, over the weekend.

'It appears he is not, unfortunately, in a position to give evidence today,' Kavanagh tells the court. 'He is obliged under the guidelines to self-isolate.'

It may have been unfair to Lynn, but many wondered whether he was really sick at all as Judge Nolan adjourned for a week. After all, he'd done a runner before.

Nestled into a patchwork of lush grazing fields, dark pine forests and crops of bright yellow rapeseed in full bloom, the picturesque village of Redcross in County Wicklow is named after the meandering mountain river that flows through the town on its way to nearby Brittas Bay. A short stroll from the picnic tables and flower boxes outside Mickey Finn's pub, lies the entrance to Millbrook Court. This partially completed boom-time development of family homes adjacent to the River Valley Holiday Park is where Michael Lynn has moved to from his prior residence in Maynooth.

Inside the estate, all is quiet outside the Lynn household in the late spring sunshine. It is nearly midday – less than an hour and a half since the trial has been adjourned. Lynn's Ford Focus and Brid's Ford Galaxy people carrier are both parked up in the paved, sloped driveway. Two children's bicycles lean against the front wall of the house.

Around the corner, out of sight, Detective Ivor Scully waits and watches from his unmarked silver Toyota. Like everyone else he had listened earlier as the opinion of a doctor who had spoken to Lynn by phone following his positive PCR test was read out in court. According to the physician, Lynn reported breathlessness, nausea, severe headaches, brain fog and pain in the lungs.

Detective Scully, though, had wanted to make sure. Lynn's word held little currency anymore. His days of being allowed to make fools of the authorities had long passed. Yet this time Lynn really was sick. His time on the stand – the most anticipated moment of the trial – would have to wait.

36

Lynn's Truth

PAUL COMISKEY O'KEEFFE IS CIRCLING THE top floor of the court building engrossed in thought. Sometimes he holds his hands at elbow height, tapping the tips of his ten fingers together in rhythm with his footsteps and thoughts. Occasionally, as he completes his circuit, he rubs his cufflinks – fashioned from a shiny pair of 1980 pennies minted the year he was born. These habits help him focus and prepare for important trial moments. There is little doubt that what is coming will be key and Comiskey O'Keeffe must be on form.

Today, after a Covid delay of just under two weeks, Lynn will take the stand. The move is Michael Lynn down to a T, but it is virtually unprecedented. None of the vastly experienced policemen or lawyers in the courtroom have experienced a defendant taking the stand like this before. No one thinks it is a good idea. But Lynn was always going to do it.

For Lynn the move will be a purgative one that proves cathartic. He has been waiting a long time for this and there are things he wants to say. His fate will rest on whether or not the jury believes him. His downfall or redemption will be of his own making and his alone.

For Comiskey O'Keeffe, this testimony is going to be a hell of a ride and the horse he must bring home is untamed, highly strung and chomping at the bit. This will be a very different experience from cross-examining Liz Doyle and Fiona McAleenan. They were nervous and wary. Easy to spook, but predictable. Lynn is a different beast. This ride, over rough ground, will be wild. Fast. Dangerous. Unpredictable. It is not at all clear who will be in charge – or if anyone will win.

Lynn's evidence begins nervously. After swearing in, he removes his black face mask, sits down, blinks repeatedly as if he is disorientated, fidgets and shifts in his seat.

'When were you born?' Comiskey O'Keeffe begins, easing his client in slowly.

Answering, Lynn promptly knocks over his water bottle. He is jittery but eager. Like a waterfall ready to plunge down a cliff face, there'll be no holding back once he starts.

Soon he is in full flow, with Comiskey O'Keeffe focusing hard, hanging on as best he can. The jury, transfixed by the performance, concentrate on every word. Lynn races through his childhood on the family farm, his schooling, his days as an apprentice with famed solicitor Ivor Fitzpatrick, and his move to become an in-house solicitor with Budget Travel, where he worked closely with iconic businesswoman Gillian Bowler, who would later become chair of Irish Life and Permanent.

Then he tells how – with a borrowed deposit from his mother, a 95 per cent mortgage from Permanent TSB and a promise of guaranteed legal work from Budget Travel – he bought a house in Blanchardstown. There, Michael Lynn & Co. had been born, with Lynn using the ground floor as his office space and sleeping upstairs.

Doing his best to keep Lynn on track, Comiskey O'Keeffe must repeatedly pull on the reins to steer him back on course. Lynn is prone to go off on flurries of irrelevance. He likes the sound of his own voice and gains in confidence hearing it.

'He just can't stop talking,' Detective Sergeant Ger Coomey, the Fraud Squad's witness manager, whispers during a break in proceedings. 'This guy is a classic narcissist. We saw it straight away.'

After the break, Comiskey O'Keeffe leads Lynn into his lending history and his relationship with bankers. This is the nub of the issue. The story Lynn has waited so long to tell. What he says next will change the trial – and his fate – irrevocably.

Lynn starts with how, just two months after setting up in Blanchardstown and still with a college loan, he was shown the inside track by the banking friends he was making. He explains how they taught him to buy and 'twist' properties on for immediate profit without even registering them – or the loan used to fund the investment. If Lynn was prepared to give an undertaking on a wink and a nod, they were prepared to lend.

This is the voodoo economics that has led him to this courtroom. It is the drug-filled syringe that ignited his ambition and greed.

He describes his first ever property investment, involving the 1997/98 purchase of a house in Balbriggan with a mortgage loan from the Blanchardstown branch of Permanent TSB. The purchase price had been €110,000 but Lynn was allowed to borrow €135,000 and 'flipped the property in two months for €195,000'.

'I would have paid the mortgage monthly in relation to it,' he tells the court. 'But there would have been no mortgage signed and there would have been no documents lodged in the land registry at the time.'

He has a phrase for this unofficial practice: undertaking-only loans. Even though they have nothing to do with the charges he faces, Lynn admits conspiring with his bankers in this fashion for years before he was ever caught.

By now Lynn is passionately defending himself. He is animated, emotional and fighting for his freedom. Well used to using a microphone and putting on a show, his performance is riveting. He looks and speaks directly to the jury members across the room. He has some entirely in the palm of his hands. Completely engrossed in his drama, one or two nod and shake their heads in unison. They watch him intently as he explains how his bankers introduced him to shadow banking practices not available to the general public.

'This was absolutely understood by the bankers I was dealing with and it was permitted,' he says. 'I am a solicitor myself, so I also understand my duties, but at the time it was about business and fluidity – and that's the truth.'

He continues, 'I had no idea where it would get to at that time. I was learning at that time, but I was introduced to these processes by bankers. I would also say that I didn't refuse them. I embraced them. I was a young person who was learning about business, but I did embrace them.'

Lynn tells the court that not only did he embrace bankers – he employed them, too. He speaks of hiring directly from banks to ensure he had staff who spoke the language of bankers. 'These people hardly spoke English,' he says of the language used in the banking world, 'so I needed bankers.' He offered these employees – who came from First Active, Bank of Scotland and Bank of Ireland – salaries of up to €90,000, a company car, a pension and a 25 per cent profit share deal. They then worked their magic, helping Lynn to build his perilous castle of sand ever higher.

Judge Nolan does not often intervene in the testimony of witnesses. Typically, he only does so to make something clear for the jury if it is in some way ambiguous. But there are times during Lynn's testimony when he appears completely taken aback by what he is hearing – so much so that he has to make sure he has not misheard.

Each time, he suddenly perks up, swivels his judge's chair to face Lynn in the dock below and holds out his hand like a traffic cop. He wants to pause these parts of the race and watch a replay.

What Lynn clarifies in these moments defines the entire trial. One such turning point comes when – after months of tedious documentary evidence and cross-examination – Lynn suddenly reveals that he had secret arrangements with his bankers. They let him pretend to borrow to buy houses in Ireland knowing the money would really be siphoned abroad.

'So, let's be very clear here,' Judge Nolan interrupts. 'Basically, the paperwork is saying that every loan given by a financial institution was given for a particular purpose – for purchasing a piece of property, a house, an apartment – and what you're saying, basically, is that you had permission from these bankers to apply the monies received as your needs dictated. Is that what you're saying?'

'What I'm saying is the banks permitted me to utilise these monies for property development abroad and I would have told them that myself.'

'What you're telling the jury is that you had permission from these bankers to use it as you wanted,' Judge Nolan follows up.

'I wasn't allowed to use it as I wanted,' Lynn explains. 'They would have understood it was being used to purchase a specific asset for a specific period of time and I was to repay it within a specific period of time.'

Judge Nolan has another double-take moment when Lynn tells the court he had a secret 'profit share' deal with former Irish Nationwide chief Michael Fingleton.

'I had an arrangement with Michael Fingleton that he was to have a profit share with me in relation to my development in Portugal,' Lynn tells the court. 'He lent the money to me, which was purportedly for Glenlion but was actually for my development in Portugal.'

Holding up his hand again, Judge Nolan halts traffic again.

'Let's be clear. You are saying that Michael Fingleton had a personal profit share with you to profit from this, even though it was the institution of INBS [Irish Nationwide] who lent you the money?'

When Lynn confirms this, Judge Nolan tips his head to the side, makes a note, settles back into his chair and, rocking gently, appears to be deep in thought.

Later Lynn speaks of 'direct payments to bankers'.

'To be very clear at this point,' Judge Nolan calls a halt again, 'you're saying individual bankers received monies from you or your companies – they weren't paid through their banks indirectly?'

'That's correct, Judge,' Lynn replies.

'Indirectly would mean they got bonuses from the profits they made. You're saying they received monies from you?'

'Absolutely, Judge,' shrugs Lynn.

In his bid for freedom, Lynn is leaving nothing hidden – not even deceptive practices such as bribery that would, in different circumstances, see him jailed.

'Look in business there's nothing for nothing,' Lynn explains as he outlines how bankers sought 30 per cent apartment discounts for themselves. 'A number of bankers would have received direct payments ... and they would also have been interested in apartments.'

Then, pausing for a second as if he can't believe his own actions, Lynn tries to contextualise the bribery of which he is speaking. 'In 2022 I know it seems odd, but during the Celtic Tiger you were vying for position with the banks,' he tells the jury. 'I was in my thirties and I wanted to get on and so did they, but when you look back you wonder who was riding the coat-tails of whom.'

Now, suddenly, Lynn's surprising defence is clear to all. He has kept his powder dry for twelve weeks – as the trial meandered through vast tranches of documents and witnesses. He has said nothing about this throughout years of discovery hearings, and his team has never put any of it to the dozens of bankers, legal professionals and former Lynn employees who have given evidence. Now though he is laying everything on the line.

37

The Wrong People

I HAD BOUGHT THE NOTEBOOK IN February 2008, en route to Budapest. Purchased in the departures lounge of Dublin Airport, it was a slim, hardback pad with yellow, lined pages and a magnetic leather clasp to keep it closed. In Budapest I had filled those pages with names as Michael Lynn detailed the corrupt deals he claimed to have agreed with Ireland's boom-time bankers. Some of those he had identified were household names: Michael Fingleton, for example.

According to my notebook, Lynn claimed that Fingleton had personally sought 20 per cent of profits in Cabanas in return for Irish Nationwide agreeing to finance developments abroad. 'A gentleman's agreement' Lynn had called the deal. He'd explained how the arrangement was reached because Lynn needed funds to complete developments in Portugal and Budapest, and Fingleton had agreed to lend in return for a kickback.

Other names had been new to me and soon after receiving them I'd tried and failed to get in front of some of them in Ireland. I couldn't ever have known then that thirteen years later I'd be sitting in a courtroom in Dublin listening to Lynn list these names off once again – this time as he testified in his own trial. One thing hadn't changed, though. When he'd first mentioned these bankers to me there'd been no proof to back up his assertions. That was still the case. It was Lynn's word against theirs.

'We should have the right bankers here – they are not the people I dealt with – they are not the people who gave me the money.'

It is Wednesday 11 May and Michael Lynn, on his third day of direct evidence, is dismissing the relevance of the thirty-one bankers who have so far been witnesses at his trial. I had listened and watched carefully throughout the trial as the names of the bankers Lynn had spoken to me about bribing more than a decade earlier were repeatedly referenced in documents and the testimony of others. Although they featured prominently in the paperwork presented to the trial, none had been called to give evidence directly.

One such person was Billy Loftus, a school and family friend of Lynn's from Mayo who'd become a relationship manager in the Ballina branch of ACC. It was to Billy that Lynn had gone to borrow €3.8 million for Glenlion – one of three loans he received against that particular property.

'The Lynn family are all well-known customers and have always proven to be exceptional in their ability to make money,' Loftus had written in a lending application presented to the court. Further files showed how Loftus, now the manager of the Mayo–Sligo Livestock Mart in Ballina, had argued for a better lending rate for Lynn. Frustratingly, though, Loftus had not been called to testify.

Ciaran Farrell's name had also featured in the many Permanent TSB documents put into evidence – but he too was not on the witness list. When Lynn had failed to clear an existing loan as agreed with the proceeds of a new loan, it was Farrell who wrote to Permanent TSB's credit committee to explain this breach of his undertaking.

'Due to confusion in Michael's office, this was only done last week and he is embarrassed and annoyed about it,' Farrell had written to his superiors. 'I questioned him on it and it was down to clerical error. I do believe the genuinely [sic] of the delay in redeeming the mortgages and his embarrassment in being told of this. This is based on meeting him and the fact he has little or nothing to do with the running of his practice and would be out of the country for weeks and months at a time.'

Despite this breach of previous conditions, the bank then promptly lent Lynn millions more, something its executives struggle to explain in court.

It was Farrell who had assured his bosses, in March 2007, that Fiona McAleenan was independent of Lynn when the Permanent TSB legal department had sought reassurance that Lynn wasn't signing his own loan undertakings.

'Mr Lynn has contacted me and explained his partner … is independent from him,' Farrell emailed his bank's legal department. 'Obviously he does not want to incur additional costs by utilising a solicitor from a different firm.'

The following month, in April 2007, Farrell had reassured the legal department again. 'I am satisfied from my knowledge of the company that Fiona does indeed look after the legal practice,' he wrote. 'Michael concentrates his efforts on the property development side.'

The court also heard and saw documentary evidence that in May 2007 Farrell had personally collected a €3.7 million loan cheque from Permanent TSB's head office in St Stephen's Green and hand-delivered it to Lynn's office. Farrell, though, had not been called to testify in Lynn's trial.

'I have gone through nearly a million pieces of paper and I have not been able to find a statement from Ciaran Farrell. He is alive and well, is he?' Feargal Kavanagh had asked another witness from Permanent TSB early on in the trial.

In fact, none of those I'd listed in my notebook in 2009, as Lynn detailed those he claimed to have bribed, were in court. Either they were indisposed – such as Michael Fingleton – or they had not been put forward by the banks to give statements to gardaí.

Ironically, this is an area where Lynn and the gardaí who investigated him are close to agreement. Lynn's view is the banks wanted to keep a lid on the secret deals he had. He testifies that Fingleton and Seán FitzPatrick told him to flee and seek bankruptcy in the UK rather than come to court and reveal all on that fateful day on December 2007 when he'd run.

Meanwhile, those tasked with investigating Lynn's dealings with his bankers encountered a strange omertà. Most of the banks were slow to make criminal complaints against Lynn. Interestingly, Irish Nationwide only moved to lodge its formal garda complaint a year after Lynn had fled and three days before the Irish government moved to guarantee the doomed bank.

This behaviour meant fraud detectives on the case had to get court orders to compel most banks to hand over relevant files. In everyday terms that is the equivalent of forensics showing up at the scene of a burglary and being told by the homeowner they can't come in to take fingerprints without a court order.

38

Comrades in Arms

'THE ALGARVE IS A VERY BEAUTIFUL spot and quite a number of the bankers would have travelled to the Algarve and we would have put them up free of charge and flown them out to Portugal.'

It is Thursday 12 May and Lynn – on his fourth day of direct evidence – is explaining precisely how he kept his bankers onside. I'd first heard these claims from him more than a decade ago at our secret meeting in Budapest, but he'd never since backed them up with any tangible proof and my efforts to confront those identified had been stymied by legal threats. Now, protected by court privilege, Lynn is free to detail his claims about how he rewarded his bankers.

'Billy Loftus would have travelled to Portugal,' he tells the court. 'Maurice Aherne and his daughter and myself went to Portugal, and two months later they went to Budapest.'

'Where did they stay?' Comiskey O'Keeffe asks.

'We would have put them up in accommodation and looked after them,' Lynn replies.

'When you say, "looked after them", what do you mean by that?'

'We would have paid for their hotels, we would have paid for their flights and we would also have ensured they got tours of the city,' Lynn explains. 'Look, it's the way it was at the time. You were developing relationships, you were preserving relationships and bankers expected benefits in kind.'

'What do you mean by benefits in kind?' Lynn's lawyer asks.

'The way business was done, bankers received payments over a period of time,' Lynn says. 'They saw you making money – they wanted to make some money as well.'

Guided by Comiskey O'Keeffe, Lynn explains how some bankers would put him under pressure to provide kickback discounts on apartments in return for a loan. 'On a €185,000 apartment, they would expect a 30 per cent discount,' he says. 'That's what was going on at the time.'

He adds that cash payments to various bankers, none of whom are yet witnesses in the case, included €5,000 to €10,000 in spending money during trips abroad.

This direct testimony from Lynn turns the trial on its head. Under the terms of his extradition, he cannot be convicted for anything other than theft. Though he is now openly admitting deception and bribery, he can never be prosecuted for this. He has a free get out of jail card for everything except theft. If he'd murdered someone in 2007, the Irish State would not be able to prosecute him without first getting permission from the Brazilian authorities.

Three months into his trial – after all the witness testimony and evidence has concluded – Lynn is now telling the court that nothing heretofore presented in his trial matters. That signatures were forged is moot. That statements of affairs were hopelessly inadequate and undertakings were ignored is entirely irrelevant. The paperwork was only a charade. A front. According to Lynn he was going to get the loans regardless.

'These loans were being permitted – they were going to be allowed,' he says. He tells the court his 'heart goes out' to the dozens of banking witnesses who spent twelve weeks trying to explain to the court the often hopelessly shoddy loan applications submitted on his behalf when they knew nothing of the real circumstances.

'No bank could not have known what was occurring,' Lynn now tells the jury. 'Firstly, because it was discussed, and secondly, it was occurring openly … I worked alongside the banks.'

When it comes to his turn to cross-examine Lynn, Patrick McGrath finds himself in the absurd position of questioning a man who admits to all sorts of wrongdoing bar the crime for which he is being tried.

Lynn even agrees under cross-examination that virtually anything could have been put on his applications and he'd have got the loans. 'I gained from it and I wasn't right and I have paid dearly for a long time,' he says.

Now he is gambling that this admission of his participation in a secret, shadowy world of side deals and kickbacks will keep him from going back to jail. In Lynn's view, the bankers he dealt with – none of whom have been called to court – were not being misled or deceived by him. Instead, he tells the jury, they were 'comrades in arms'.

'The banks did not put forward the correct people nor did they tell the truth about the arrangement,' he tells McGrath. If enough members of the jury believe him, he will be acquitted.

Lynn's ploy is a high-stakes one. He is openly admitting to corruption, believing he can't be prosecuted for it. And in doing so he is naming his co-conspirators, none of whom have yet been called to court.

If Lynn is telling the truth, he has steadfastly protected his corrupt financiers all these years. If he is lying, he has casually pulled the pin and tossed a hand grenade into the offices of innocent professionals without a care for the collateral damage it will cause.

Lynn wants the jury to believe he is the victim of a deep conspiracy in which all the banks have closed ranks to protect their Celtic Tiger secrets. He is belatedly portraying himself as a complicit but regretful whistleblower, who is finally betraying the omertà of a corrupt system. In tandem, he is condemning the garda investigation against him as fundamentally flawed. He wants the jury to believe that under political pressure and faced with banks' reluctance to divulge their dirty laundry, the probe never got beyond the veneer of Lynn's falsified loan applications.

Stunned with this development, there is only one thing the prosecution can do. Lynn hasn't called any of those he claims were complicit in the charade of which he claims to have been a part. He was entitled to force them into court, but he chose not to. So the prosecution must now call Lynn's bluff.

McGrath asks him outright who got paid 'illegal payments or bribes'. Lynn repeats the names he's already given during his direct evidence: Michael Fingleton, Maurice Aherne, Ciaran Farrell, Billy Loftus and Stephen McCarthy – an Ulster Bank lender in Cork.

McGrath also asks Lynn for the names of those bankers who were not paid bribes or otherwise incentivised but knew his loan applications were a charade. Those named by Lynn in this category include former Permanent TSB credit committee member Martin Huggard, former Bank of Scotland lender Berni O'Farrell, and former NIB lenders Annemarie Straathof, Nicholas Hamilton and Micheál McHugh.

Lynn testifies that former Bank of Ireland lenders Sean Dooley and Gerry O'Gorman were also aware of his secret banking arrangements. He tells the court that Maurice Harte, a former director of Irish Nationwide, was aware of the secret profit share deal he had with Michael Fingleton – so much so that he was set to become a director of Lynn's Kendar firm as Fingleton's eyes and ears.

Sitting in his corner at the back of the courtroom with the rest of his team, Detective Sergeant Coomey jots down each name and consults with his colleagues. They all know exactly what Lynn's surprise testimony means – their weekend has just been cancelled. Now they must fan out across the country to track down, interview and take statements from those Lynn has just named.

39

The Fox

A COUPLE OF HUNDRED METRES TO the west of the court building, morning traffic has ground to a halt opposite a derelict garage forecourt.

Above the site, on the old canopy that once sheltered fuel pumps, a sign covered in blue and white bubbles advertises a long-gone car valeting service. 'Squeaky Clean' it reads, above what is now a boarded-up, graffitied-over car showroom used only by addicts and pigeons.

I mull over the events of the trial and the odyssey that has been the Michael Lynn story as traffic moves on. Precious little of it has been squeaky clean.

Just past the Cunningham Road bus depot, traffic is stopped once again at the lights outside the court building. As ever, photographer Paddy Cummins, dressed in a biker jacket with a canvas bag strung over his shoulder is photographing everyone who enters the building with the long lens of his camera. I roll down the window to take a picture of him in action as the lights turn green. For some reason no one ever snaps the snappers.

Just beyond the lights, traffic comes to a halt again. I spot Lynn to my left, holding hands with Brid, striding past the Guilty Bean Café en route to another day in the witness box. It is Wednesday 18 May – this will be his last full day on the stand. Soon he will know his fate.

When he reaches Cummins, Lynn will pause, stand back and pose for the lens with Brid. Since she began attending court, Cummins has noticed a change in Lynn. He poses more willingly now, proud and defiant.

I give Lynn a thumbs up and he points to something ahead of me. By the side of the road, between the sidewalk and the bicycle lane, a tattered and emaciated fox is gnawing at a black plastic rubbish bag. The starving creature is completely oblivious to the busy vehicle and foot traffic just feet away. Passers-by in cars and on foot alike pause to take pictures.

Once inside, I duck into the bathroom beside Court 19. Lynn is at the urinal. I divert into the first cubicle. Court rules mean witnesses on the stand cannot speak about the evidence they are giving to anyone, not even their own lawyers or their wife. They are free to talk about anything else, but, in reality, everyone avoids them so as not to be seen potentially breaching the rule. It is a lonely station being on the stand.

'Did you see the fox?' Lynn hollers across the bathroom.

'Yeah – something else,' I answer.

'It's a sign of something,' says Lynn. 'God knows what, though.'

I don't have an answer, but later it comes to me. It is a sign of desperation.

The following day Brid swears in. Noticeably absent for most of the trial, she first attends court only when her husband takes the stand. At the start of each of Lynn's nine days in the witness box, the pair sit closely together at the back of the court until the jury has filed in and seen them.

The move is tactical. They want the jury to know they would be splitting up a loving couple if they send Lynn to jail. But it is also instinctive. They have survived by sticking together. Lynn's story is Brid's story. His downfall – or resurrection – will be hers too. Lynn has already given his truth. Now, immediately after Lynn's testimony concludes, it is his wife's turn.

'What county woman are you?' Feargal Kavanagh eases his witness in with a deliberately casual query.

'I'm from Clare – born and bred,' she says before explaining how she first met Lynn in 2000 after a GAA match. A 'fleeting romance' then ensued, followed by a continued friendship until the pair 'found each other again' in 2004 and married in 2006.

Dressed in blue jeans and a simple black cardigan, Brid comes across as softly spoken and timid. But as her testimony reveals, she is made of titanium within. Prompted by Kavanagh, Brid speaks of her work as the manager of the high dependency unit of St Vincent's Hospital until she took a career break in 2007 to nurse her dying father.

At the back of the room the garda team, out of view of the jury, would rather vomit than listen to this. On the prosecution bench, Patrick McGrath props his head up with one hand and listens. He bears the expression of a worn-out husband impatiently waiting for his wife to stop shopping.

Little of what Brid goes on to say about her private life is in any way relevant to the charges against Lynn. This is a heartstrings play. Nothing more. Nevertheless, to interrupt or object might be seen as callous by the jury, so the prosecution must check their cynicism.

Ears prick up, though, when Kavanagh asks Brid about Glenlion House and if she had met or spoken to any of Lynn's bankers. Answering, Brid remembers a 'personal call' between her husband and ACC banker Billy Loftus, Lynn's childhood friend. She also remembers arriving home from a thirteen-hour hospital shift and being asked to sign loan documents to which she did not pay any attention.

'I signed that and that was it,' she tells the court.

When asked if she was involved in any of the Kendar businesses, she replies, 'Not at all. I was a nurse ... Michael had his job. I had mine.'

Kavanagh then raises the matter of civil cases brought against Brid that resulted from the multiple Glenlion loans in her name and that of her husband. Now the prosecution – and Judge Nolan – listen intently. Brid's testimony has just been weaponised and trained on a dangerous target.

In 2008, ACC reached a settlement with Brid that saw the bank recover €4.2 million from the sale of Glenlion, with €450,000 going to her. But Bank of Scotland, which had also lent money for the home, had also sued Brid, and now Kavanagh asks how that was resolved.

'I'm bound by a confidentiality agreement,' Brid begins, before adding that her team learned, through discovery, that the bank 'knew it was a bridging loan'.

Bullseye. Whether deliberately or not – and whether it is actually true or not – Brid has just told the jury that Bank of Scotland accepted its loan for Glenlion House was an unofficial bridging loan to Lynn for other purposes. This notion that the banks participated in the charade with Lynn to provide bridging finance for his developments abroad, while the paperwork said otherwise, is something the defence has been trying to suggest throughout the trial.

'Stop that,' demands Judge Nolan sternly, ushering the jury out. This is the most angry he has been during the trial.

'She's not a lawyer,' Kavanagh begins to explain, once the jury has departed.

The judge cuts him off with a steely sharpness. 'Your witness should not have said that for many, many reasons.'

'It's completely wrong,' Patrick McGrath chimes in, adding that Brid was 'trying to give the impression it was a bridging loan'.

'She got quite a lot out accidentally,' Judge Nolan remarks coldly.

'Maybe not accidentally,' McGrath adds.

As the to and fro continues, Brid glances at her husband in the dock below her, appearing dazed by the furore she's unleashed.

'Apologies, I'm so sorry,' she tells the judge after he delivers a firm rebuke and instructs the defence to 'be very careful from now on'.

With the jury back Kavanagh resumes, putting it to Brid that the Bank of Scotland matter was resolved with a settlement.

'Bank of Scotland never accepted it was a bridging loan,' Kavanagh begins to clarify.

'They received money,' Brid takes over. 'And they were happy and I was told …'

'STOP,' Judge Nolan demands in a tone that would bring a raging Pamplona bull to a skidding halt.

I look over at Lynn. He pulls a face like a child who's just accidentally put a football through a windowpane.

The remainder of Brid's testimony is about the personal sphere. But her performance enthrals the jury.

Just as they were with Lynn, they remain transfixed on the human drama and emotion unfolding before them.

'You had other reasons for going to Brazil,' Kavanagh leads her into a planned segue. 'It's difficult for you but be as open as you can about your own personal circumstances.'

This is Brid's invitation to explain how she had been diagnosed with cervical cancer at the age of twenty-six, how she and Lynn had struggled for five years – even with IVF – to have children and how they had given up all hope.

Then, as Lynn travelled to and from Brazil, a friend had recommended a specialist at São Paulo's Albert Einstein Hospital.

'We went over in October 2010 and got pregnant,' Brid tells the court, presenting a neat alternative narrative to that of Lynn fleeing from justice to Brazil.

'During that time the pregnancy was very tense,' she testifies. 'I was bleeding a lot and wasn't sure if I was going to be able to keep it.'

On 8 August 2011 their first son – described as 'a little miracle' by Brid – was born. Months earlier, Lynn had tweeted to seek legal advice on how to obtain permanent residency in Brazil based on having a child born there. The tweet was regarded by those pursuing him as a taunt. As the parent of a child born in Brazil, Lynn had felt beyond the reach of the law. Yet Brid tells the court the family had never been on the run and had never attempted to avoid police.

Then she tells of the day her husband was arrested. 'I remember the day clearly,' she says. 'That's one day we won't forget ... our son was two and I was seven months pregnant.'

The second pregnancy was also difficult, she tells the court. 'My blood pressure was low. Every time I stood up, I fainted.'

The court hears that in these circumstances Lynn went out on an errand and arrived back an hour later in the custody of 'five armed undercover police' asking to say goodbye to his son before being whisked away. Brid tells how several hours later she received a call to attend the police station where her husband was being held.

'Look! He wasn't beaten here,' officers there told her, displaying Lynn's naked torso before transporting him to COTEL prison.

'For five days I didn't know if he was dead or alive,' an emotional Brid tells the court.

Listening raptly, the jury is completely absorbed in the drama of the story. Lynn too is impacted by seeing his wife recall this trauma. He appears emotional and picks nervously at the side of his head.

Kavanagh then leads Brid to tell the jury about COTEL. She speaks of Lynn sleeping on the floor for months until she could get him a mattress. She describes the 5kg food allowance she was allowed to bring him each week – half of which went to the inmates Lynn had to keep onside.

Judge Nolan calls a halt to this. 'Mr Kavanagh, this historical detail is somewhat interesting, but food is not the issue at this trial. Move on please.'

Kavanagh does so, but only to the matter of conjugal visits during which two further children were conceived.

'There is light in darkness – we had two beautiful children,' Brid says, adding that in a place like COTEL, 'conjugal visits are there to keep peace'.

'To keep a lid on the cattle, so to speak,' Kavanagh elaborates.

He then gets Brid to explain how Lynn could not see his newborn children in prison until a new governor allowed the family to have a day together in the prison church.

'Michael had gone through two of our children where he didn't get to see them for the first year of their life,' Brid says. 'He didn't hold them.'

Afterwards, as ever, Lynn is anxious to get an independent view of the day.

'Brid was strong,' I tell him. 'A tough day for you both.'

'Yes,' he replies. 'She's a great lady.'

40

Rebuttal

Just after lunch the next day, a set of keys rattles in the lock of the door behind Lynn in the dock. If he is found guilty, it will be through this door that he will be escorted in cuffs to holding cells downstairs and onwards to prison.

Lynn pulls a mock face of fear, burying his chin in his chest and glancing back dramatically.

'You've come too early,' he jokes as a uniformed prison officer pokes his head through before realising he has come to the wrong court. Even the officer laughs.

This is classic Lynn. It is just days before the end of his trial, and he is giddy. Gallows humour aside, the court is mid-way through a full day's legal argument caused by his admissions on the stand.

Having astonished the court with claims of bribes and payments to bankers, Lynn's defence team is now objecting to the fact that the State intends to call those named as rebuttal witnesses. They are doing so because they have just been provided with the statements these witnesses have given to gardaí in recent days, and none of them back up Lynn's version of events at all. Lynn's bluff has been called and now, in an effort to prevent the jury hearing this, the defence tries to argue that the rebuttal witnesses have been unfairly foisted on them at the last moment without adequate notice.

All morning, with the jury absent, Kavanagh has been arguing that the prosecution team and the gardaí should have chased down and interviewed these witnesses as part of their original investigation. The authorities should have known all along what Lynn's surprise defence would be, he says. He even goes as far as producing my 2009 interview with Lynn to support this argument.

It is a stretch of logic to argue that Lynn admitted secret, corrupt arrangements with his lenders in that interview – though he did so later, privately. But with the benefit of hindsight, it is fascinating to look back and read between the lines.

'The banks couldn't get enough of me,' he had said in the interview. 'And if you were to get sight of certain decisions by credit committees you would see that they discussed openly my property portfolio abroad. When they were considering the merits of giving me a loan for an asset at home, they would know about my development abroad. That's their decision. They were their choices and it was all of our choices to borrow the money.'

In the interview Lynn had added that 'other parties' had also been involved. 'They didn't conspire; we were all part of a mythical illusion,' he'd said. 'It's true that the borrowings I had were extensive against the portfolio. But in order to understand that, it's critical that you understand the agreements which were in place with the banks and that's a matter between me and the banks.'

Now, thirteen years later, he'd finally outlined in public just what he meant by this.

Having listened to both sides all day, Judge Nolan rejects the defence's application to have the rebuttal witnesses excluded.

'Anything is remotely possible but is it reasonable?' he asks before concluding there was 'no material evidence' to suggest the State could have foreseen Lynn's defence. 'It might be possible for Leitrim to win the All-Ireland,' Judge Nolan observes, dryly. 'But that doesn't mean anyone should anticipate it happening.'

Lynn, as ever, is the first to laugh.

One by one they deny everything. Each and every rebuttal witness the garda team has tracked down and taken statements from in the past few days leaves the jury with a simple choice: believe Lynn or them.

First up, when the trial resumes before the jury, is Stephen McCarthy from Ulster Bank.

'Did you ever take money from Mr Lynn?' McGrath asks him outright.

'No,' comes the response. 'I assisted in a mortgage application and when I found out the bank had been defrauded, I nearly fell off my seat with shock,' he adds. 'I never received any benefits or any cash from Mr Lynn of any description.'

Next up is Ciaran Farrell of Permanent TSB, whose name has featured frequently throughout the trial, though until now he has not been called to testify. 'That is categorically false and I deny it,' he responds when McGrath asks if he received money from Lynn.

'I have absolutely no idea what a special deal is,' Farrell adds, referring to the off-book arrangements Lynn claims to have had with lenders. 'But if there is any inference that monies lent were lent for any other reason than the purpose on the letter of agreement, I totally refute that.'

Retired NIB employee Nicholas Robert Hamilton also refutes Lynn's evidence. Lynn had testified that he met with a Nicholas 'Patrick' Hamilton (he got the name wrong), an NIB credit committee member who was aware of his secret loan deals.

'I never met with Mr Lynn,' Hamilton tells the jury. 'I was never a member of the credit committee in NIB.'

Asked if Lynn was lying, Hamilton replies, 'I just think he's mistaken.'

Next, Bank of Ireland lender Sean Dooley denies his bank would ever have lent for one purpose knowing the funds were going to be used for something else.

The following day Brian Fitzgibbon from Irish Nationwide takes the stand. Lynn had testified about having a good relationship with Fitzgibbon, describing him as Michael Fingleton's 'right-hand man'. Lynn said he'd met Fitzgibbon several times.

'That is a lie,' Fitzgibbon testifies. He also tells the court he did not believe Lynn was ever friendly with Fingleton. 'Mr Fingleton never mentioned him.'

Another banker named by Lynn – NIB's Michael McHugh – also denies ever meeting or speaking to him in any capacity. So too does Gerry O'Gorman, a Bank of Ireland lender Lynn had described as a member of the credit committee. 'To be blunt, I have never been anywhere near that level in the bank,' he testifies.

Next, Detective Sergeant Ger Coomey takes the stand. After sixteen weeks of hearings, he will be the last witness in this trial. He tells the court that Michael Fingleton is unable to attend and that several other bankers, approached to be rebuttal witnesses, have declined to give statements. Those unwilling to provide statements include Bank of Scotland lender Berni O'Farrell, who is indisposed for 'family reasons', and NIB lender Annemarie Straathof, who is in Marrakesh and believes she 'has little to offer'. Former Permanent TSB credit committee member Martin Huggard also declines to testify, as does former ACC banker Billy Loftus. So too does former Irish Nationwide director Maurice Harte. Lynn had claimed, in his own testimony, that Harte knew of his secret deals and was even set to become a director of Kendar.

Lynn's team questions Detective Sergeant Coomey about why the DPP did not issue subpoenas for these witnesses to force them into court. But Judge Nolan informs the jury that the DPP 'hardly ever summons a witness if they don't have a statement from them'.

It was also always open to Lynn to call any banking witnesses he wished. Instead, he'd used the stand to besmirch the reputations of those not present with his own testimony. This very point is driven home as Patrick McGrath delivers the prosecution's closing speech. He tells the jury that Michael Lynn 'doesn't care about the reputation of anyone else – doesn't care what he says about anyone else to save his own skin'.

McGrath points out that Lynn, represented by 'some of the best criminal lawyers in the country', decided to 'sit on his hands' and never sought to compel anyone to come to court. Lynn did not have to testify at all or put forward any defence, McGrath adds.

'This is not catch me if you can. This is not cat and mouse,' he thunders. 'If he chooses to put forward this defence, then he has an obligation to engage and he has not engaged,' McGrath says, beckoning towards Lynn in the dock with the spectacles in his hand. 'And why has he not engaged? Because there is nothing behind it. It is a mirage.'

In a speech that lasts the entire day, McGrath sums up the case and brands Lynn a liar. 'If they have told the truth,' he says of the rebuttal witnesses, 'you can be certain he has told a pack of lies. He has told a pack of lies – and that should be the beginning and the end of it.'

He portrays Lynn as 'not a simple man who is at sea in these courts or some small bit-part player who does not know what is going on'. Instead, he tells the jury, Lynn is 'a very clever man', 'a qualified, experienced solicitor' who is 'at ease with the offences committed'.

'He saw a gap which he could exploit and he manipulated the system,' McGrath says. Lynn was a man who saw 'these great opportunities' abroad but couldn't get the money he needed to 'make a fortune'.

'So what does he do? He just siphons the money off. He gets multiple mortgages on the same properties.'

McGrath describes how for 'years and years and years' Lynn never made anyone aware of claimed secret deals with bankers. Instead, he avoided being interviewed by the authorities, 'fled to Brazil and resisted extradition tooth and nail'. Now, forced to face his actions, McGrath says, Lynn is blaming the courts, the authorities, bankers, 'the world and his wife'.

'None of these people are to blame,' McGrath continues. 'The person who is to blame and the person who refused to take ownership of the fact he stole this money in 2007 is the man sitting in the dock and no one else.'

In his closing speech the following day, Paul Comiskey O'Keeffe is more subdued than his opponent. There is no military service in Ireland, he tells the jury. Voting and jury service is as close as most Irish citizens will ever come to truly serving their country. Now he tells the jury they must cast twenty-one votes – one for each charge against Lynn.

'The twenty-one votes you are going to cast are going to affect Mr Lynn's entire life – and his children's lives,' he says.

But unlike in a general election, Comiskey O'Keeffe tells the jury, they can't come back to vote again next in a few years if they are not happy with their decision. 'You cast that vote and have to live with it, as Mr Lynn will have to live with it.'

He asks the jury to think about important decisions in their lives and how often they might pause for thought before making them. 'A pause for thought is a doubt,' he says. 'You stop and have pause for thought. In a courtroom, that's doubt. Your obligation is to give the benefit to Mr Lynn.'

Then he chips away forensically at the State's case, taking most of a day to do so and taking each bank in turn.

'They never issued one letter of demand to comply with an undertaking or to register a mortgage … Not one institution,' he says. 'The reality of it is, they received the undertakings and they stopped there … This is a situation where recklessness leads to imprudent practices.'

The following day, Judge Nolan takes the morning to sum up and direct the jury. He tells them they are twelve different people of different ages, backgrounds and genders who must now assess another. 'That's your function,' he says. 'If there is one thing people are capable of doing, it's assessing other people. We do it all the time.'

He tells them they must do so in a 'cold and dispassionate manner' and that it is up to the State to prove its case. Lynn 'does not have to prove anything', he warns. It is the State that must meet the 'burden of proof beyond reasonable doubt'.

'If you have reasonable doubt, acquit,' Judge Nolan says simply. 'If you don't believe the State's case, acquit.'

He tells the jury that Lynn did not have to take the stand but did so.

'Mr Lynn gave evidence,' he says. 'If you find that explanation capable of reasonable belief, you acquit him.'

But he instructs that 'consent obtained by intimidation or deception is not consent'. The jury must decide whether Lynn deceived his bankers and robbed them, or conspired with them in a charade they all knew about.

Finally, at 12.22 p.m. on Friday, 27 May 2022, the jury retires to deliberate. There is nothing more anyone can do but wait. In the lull afterwards, each side gathers to assess their chances. It is a pointless but unavoidable exercise, part of human nature.

Ultimately, Patrick McGrath, who has experienced more jury decisions than most, puts it best: 'We might as well slay a goat, slit its stomach open and examine the entrails for all the good it will do.'

41

Impasse

No one expected this. After three days of deliberations the jury files back into the court for the last time. It is 16.15 on Wednesday 1 June. Each and every one of them looks strained. Unable to reach a unanimous majority, they have already been informed by Judge Nolan that he will accept a ten–two majority.

There is complete silence as the clerk passes a note from the jury foreperson forward. Judge Nolan unfolds it and reads to himself. As he does so, for a fleeting moment, his mouth drops open. He didn't expect this either. Recovering his composure, he reads out loud. 'We would like to inform you that we cannot reach a ten–two majority.'

The meaning is clear, but it is nevertheless one of those moments when everyone's mind starts to spin. Have we heard right? Has there been a mistake? What? How?

Everyone has been expecting the verdict to be a lance, a pin that pops one of two balloons and releases the tension in the room. Guilty or not guilty. One or the other. Now it feels as if the court has been enveloped by a deflating hot air balloon that is enfolding it.

In the witness box, Lynn initially looks confused but quickly realises he won't be going to prison today. That door behind him will remain firmly shut. No keys will rattle in the lock.

'If I gave you more time, would that help the situation?' Judge Nolan asks the jury, more in vain hope than anything else.

Twelve heads shake in unison. They have reached an impasse they cannot overcome.

'It has been long and difficult, but you've reached a conclusion – of sorts,' Judge Nolan says as he discharges the jury.

Lynn is remanded on continuing bail and the case is listed again for the first day of the next court term. In between now and then the DPP must decide if it wants to go through this again. Right now, it is something no one can face.

Reality sinks in for Lynn.

'Thank you, thank you,' he gushes, shaking hands with his team. 'Thank you very much.'

On the prosecution bench and among the garda team at the back of the room there is silence.

A short stroll from the court building, Ryan's pub on Parkgate Street has a U-shaped bar counter dividing the two sides of the premises. Ceiling-high drinks shelves in the middle ensure those on one side cannot see anyone on the other, except fleetingly through a gap that allows the barman to serve both. On the left side, the prosecution gathers for a glum post-verdict drink. No one will stay for long. This was their case to win and they have not done so.

On the other side of the counter, Lynn is gleefully ordering a hefty round. This was his case to lose and he has not done so. It will be a big night out in Dublin for Lynn – one he will later admit to regretting. In hindsight he thinks it was unfair not to go straight home to his children with Brid.

As Lynn accompanies Brid to the front door after saying goodbye for the night, the prosecution team turns to watch. Through the front window they see the pair hug and kiss with wild abandon on the street outside. This is a couple who could have been torn apart again today. Instead, they have been granted a sweet reprieve.

Turning back to their pints, the State side resolves to double down and go again. On the first day of the next term, that decision is formalised in court and a new trial date is set for October 2023.

For six months all communication to me from Lynn stops. Then, in December 2022 he resumes contact via the secure Telegram app and we agree to meet in early January 2023.

Now that the Lynn saga has a fresh twist and another trial imminent, I am anxious to pursue a documentary project about his odyssey. Discussions with Emmy-nominated producer Trevor Birney from Fine Point Films prove positive. But we would need Lynn to cooperate, and tying him down is, as ever, tricky.

Eventually, after many setbacks, a face-to-face meeting with Lynn is agreed for 11 July. With no apparent cognisance of the irony involved, he asks to meet in the grounds of Wicklow Gaol, a historical jail museum. Also present is Fine Point Films producer Eimhear O'Neill.

It is immediately apparent that the hung jury has bolstered Lynn's confidence, while the possibility of a documentary plays to his ego. For an hour he speaks of the injustices he has faced and his plans for the retrial. This is not a man who feels lucky to have escaped jail. Instead, he feels aggrieved that he had to face such a possibility in the first place. He is now doubly determined to see out the second trial.

Lynn appears amenable to an interview and likes the idea that his story can demonstrate aspects of the Celtic Tiger that remain buried. He asks for a memo of understanding to be drawn up about filming, but, ultimately, he does not commit.

Watching him speak to Eimhear with his self-engrossed sense of having been wronged by the world, it strikes me that little has changed since I first tracked him down in 2009. Years in exile, a stint in Brazilian prison, life on bail and a four-month trial have done nothing to reduce Lynn's determination. Instead, his self-conviction has grown immeasurably stronger.

42

For What?

'STARTING A JURY TRIAL IN IRELAND is like starting an old tractor. You know it will get going eventually – you just don't know when.'

It is 11 a.m. on Wednesday, 25 October 2023 and Michael Lynn is in typical form as he wisecracks about a last-minute delay to his retrial caused by the need to replace two jury members. It has been a year and four months since Lynn's first, inconclusive trial concluded and all sides are now poised on the precipice again.

This time, though, things feel different. There is a familiarity between both teams and an expectation that proceedings will quickly advance to the core of the issue. The raw tension of the first trial has morphed into something more routine.

One way or another everyone expects a verdict by Christmas. In just sixty days' time Lynn's children will either have their father back for the holidays or face the prospect of a new year without him.

Whatever the outcome, Lynn's claims of bent dealings with Ireland's boom-time bankers are no longer secret. As the falling autumn leaves outside reveal bare branches and tree trunks, this claim, which Lynn kept close to his chest for more than a decade, has now been exposed. It cannot now be used with the same effect to which it was deployed in the dying days of the first trial. Lynn's last-minute ploy might have swung the last jury, but it also came with consequences. Now, if he is not sent down as a thief, he will go down in history as corrupt. Clearly, this is a price he is willing to pay for his freedom.

Nearby, a now retired Paddy Linehan is in relaxed form. After so long on the case, he remains invaluable. He may no longer be a policeman, but Lynn remains unfinished business for Linehan. He will be in court until the end.

That won't be the case for the prosecution's lead barrister, Patrick McGrath, who is unexpectedly absent from the courtroom when the retrial gets underway. He has just been nominated as a High Court judge by the government and must relinquish his cases. McGrath was present for the pretrial legal argument and jury selection, but as the retrial proper begins on the top floor, he quietly leaves the building by the front steps. Dressed in casual jeans and suede ankle boots he doesn't even look back before driving away in his polished, blue Jaguar. McGrath's next appointment will be with President Higgins as he receives his seal of office and is formally appointed to the bench.

There are other changes too. Feargal Kavanagh is absent on Lynn's side, replaced by Mark Lynam. One of the country's top criminal legal aid lawyers, Lynam, a senior counsel, has recently defended Hutch family associate Paul Murphy. In April, Murphy was found guilty at the Special Criminal Court of acting as getaway driver during the notorious Regency Hotel attack in 2016, when Kinahan Cartel member David Byrne was murdered.

But as with the first trial, it will be Paul Comiskey O'Keeffe who does most of the heavy lifting, despite still being a junior counsel. Like Paddy Linehan, Dermot Mara – Lynn's 'library' – has also retired. Nevertheless, he too is back, this time as a consultant for Lynn's team. He is joined on the defence by junior counsels Alison Fynes and Simon Crowley.

Lynn has also changed solicitor and is now represented by Irish-speaking, Belfast-born Ciarán Mulholland. An award-winning human rights lawyer, Mulholland is a bold and brash, media-savvy criminal defence solicitor with a lightning-fast wit. He demonstrates this admirably when he hears a member of the prosecution remark that McGrath's departure means the State's team is 'down a counsel'.

'That's not what I heard,' Mulholland quips cheekily in his Belfast accent. 'I heard you're up a judge.'

On the prosecution side, the State is represented by Jonathan Antoniotti, a solicitor with the DPP's financial fraud division. Rather than replace Patrick McGrath, the prosecution decides that Karl Finnegan, who has taken silk as a senior counsel since the last trial, will now take the lead. John Berry remains and is accompanied by Junior Counsel Joe Mulrean. Also on the team is AnnNoelle Bennett, a former school principal embarking on a new career, who is devilling for Berry.

The garda team has changed too. Sergeant Sean O'Riordan, who was part of the previous trial team, remains. But Detective Ivor Scully has been promoted to organised crime and is absent from the proceedings. So too is Detective Sergeant Ger Coomey, who has also been promoted. In their place, Detectives Laura Barton and Daniel Queeney have been propelled into the world of Michael Lynn's nebulous affairs for the first time. Detective Queeney becomes witness manager, while Detective Barton is the trial's exhibits manager.

The retrial begins in earnest with an opening statement from John Berry for the prosecution. Standing up, Berry makes a solemn promise to the jury that his opening will be 'done by four'.

I look at the court clock. It is 14.58.

Inside Court 22 the minutes and seconds tick by in red on the face of the digital display beneath the clerk. Berry will fulfil his commitment with a few minutes to spare. He wants the jury to know they can trust him when he tells them something; that he will deliver the truth and can be relied upon to be accurate.

Peering through his round tortoiseshell glasses, Berry tells the jury there is no room for prejudice or sympathy in the court. They must assess the facts coldly, calmly, clinically. Any bad or good experiences with solicitors or bankers have to be left outside the door. He tells them documents will play an important role because they 'speak to obligations'.

Then Berry addresses the charges Lynn faces. Theft is stealing he tells them, like a boy in an orchard or someone pilfering a shop till. 'But theft can be more complicated than that,' he says. 'Theft can be done by way of deception.'

He gives an example: someone comes to the door to collect the milkman's money but he's an imposter. 'That's theft.'

He also deals with the issue of consent. In Ireland theft is defined as taking something without the consent of the owner. 'Consent is important here,' he says. 'Because consent that's obtained by deception isn't consent ... Anything that creates or reinforces a false impression isn't consent.'

Next, he deals with the notion that the banks were sloppy and may have brought this on themselves. 'People who are the victims of crime still remain the victims of crime even though the manner in which they behaved wasn't the wisest,' he explains. 'Just because somebody placed themselves in a vulnerable position doesn't mean you can take advantage.'

He gives an example: it is no excuse to say you stole something because 'the car was unlocked or there was no alarm on the house'.

Now he moves to the scale of Lynn's actions. 'When we talk about deception in this case, we are not talking about small-time deception,' he says. 'We are not talking about a small-time investor here. We are talking about a qualified solicitor who described himself as a property investor – and who stole €27m.'

Berry then goes through various examples of Lynn's deceit: for Glenlion House in Howth, which was worth €5.5 million, he tells the jury Lynn secured €11.7 million from three banks in little over two weeks in April 2007. For 11 Cowper Street, in Dublin's Stoneybatter district, Berry tells the jury that Lynn borrowed €508,000 that was never used to buy the house at all.

'He drew down that money – but he never bought that property,' Berry says. 'The property was never sold.'

Berry tells the jury the banks didn't know Lynn 'was approaching multiple institutions' for loans on the same properties and that when they discovered this, they 'were unable to recover their funds'.

Then, just as he promised and with time to spare, Berry hands over to the jury. 'Mr Lynn is guilty of nothing,' he tells them, 'unless – and until after hearing all the evidence – you and you alone are satisfied that he is guilty.'

The next morning Karl Finnegan takes over the mantle for the State as the first witness – retired NIB Business Banking Manager Noel McCole – is called. This time, with Lynn's defence in the open, things move faster, particularly as the defence aggressively challenges each witness under cross-examination.

'I'm going to put Michael Lynn's position to you,' defence barrister Paul Comiskey O'Keeffe begins after Finnegan has led the banker through Lynn's lending for an hour and a half. 'He disputes everything.' In this fashion, McCole is forced to deny he knew of secret deals with Lynn. He also denies any knowledge of Lynn's unorthodox borrowing practices. By the end of the day, Lynn is bored.

'Hi,' he messages on Telegram after court. 'Is it like you never left?'

'Apart from one brief moment of lucidity just before lunch,' I respond.

'Yes,' he agrees. 'It's a challenge.'

Then, before I know it, he's on the phone. I'm in the car ferrying various children between evening activities and I put him on loudspeaker. He's at home, and Brid, the dogs and children can be heard coming and going in the background. He's been up since 5 a.m., travelled from Wicklow to Dublin, had his usual breakfast meeting with the team, been through the first full day of evidence in his retrial, talked strategy to various members of his team from the car on the way back home and still he wants a sounding board.

'I wouldn't like to have a client like me,' he tells me, 'because I'd have to be on my toes. There'd be days you'd be going, "I wish he'd fuck off." Not every client will want to read every line of the document and analyse it.'

In his position, I think I would simply want to cuddle up to the kids, crack open a cold one and try to get some sleep. I might even have pled guilty years ago just to be done with it. Not Lynn though. The dynamo within him is spinning fiercely. Its momentum is maintained by his sense of injustice as he complains that the banks are 'covering up' their sins by not providing adequate records.

'We are talking here about something called fair play – and we are talking about a person having the right to a fair trial,' he says. 'The banks have suppressed information left, right and centre.'

I've been listening to claims of banking corruption from Lynn since 2009 and have repeatedly sought solid proof – to little avail. In many ways I wish the proof had been forthcoming. It would have been a great scoop. Nevertheless, I listen. If Lynn wants a sounding board, I'm happy to provide it.

For a moment, there's an interruption from Brid and Lynn apologises. 'Brid is gone to get balloons for our youngest,' he tells me. 'It's her birthday tomorrow.'

Again, I marvel at his priorities. I would not be on the phone to me in these circumstances.

'On a human level,' I ask him, 'can you see beyond this or are you completely engrossed?'

'I can't wait for it to be over,' he says without hesitation. 'I can't wait. I'm sick and tired of it. I am really sick and tired of it, and this time for some reason I'm more at peace. I don't know why. Maybe I'm fucking nuts, but I feel very much at peace, regardless of what it is.'

When I ask about the prospect of prison, Lynn expresses the view that imprisonment remains a possibility because the 'establishment' wants to punish him. 'I think they need to cut the bollix off me, so I think that's a possibility, yes. But what can I do? I can only do my best and that's it.'

The conversation turns to the essence of his case.

'This whole thing is quite simple,' I tell him. 'You are perfectly willing to admit your part in what you say was a corrupt system – you just don't want to be sent down as a thief.'

'In essence, exactly,' he agrees.

'It's a shame we just can't stand up in front of everybody, tell them that and let them decide,' I say.

Lynn agrees. He would have loved to be able to negotiate a lesser plea – some corporate offence or other – so long as it's not theft. He begins to count up the legal costs of his trial and reaches a daily total of 'at least €10,000 a day for another fifty-day trial'.

'It's serious dosh,' he says. 'A lot of money has been wasted – for what? To prove that Lynn was bold, naughty, corrupt and that the banks weren't. That somehow he took advantage of the banks on his own – all seven of them – for fucking five years. Jesus.'

When the call is finally over, my daughter turns to me.

'Why does he talk to you?' she asks, incredulous.

'Because I listen,' I tell her.

43

Fightback

THROUGHOUT BOTH TRIALS MICHAEL LYNN HAS claimed that the banks have not been entirely forthright – something his defence tries to demonstrate at every opportunity in the retrial.

Lynn is not alone in that view. It is shared too by the man who led the investigation against him. After the verdict, Paddy Linehan, whose investigation was initially frustrated by the necessity to secure court orders from banks, will say so publicly.

'We thought it was a bit ironic – contradictory in many ways,' Linehan will tell me in a post-trial interview. 'It didn't help and it slowed down the case because access and information was not expedited. Obviously, if you had to get information about a customer – and if the bank was not a complainant – you had to get a court order, but this was the injured party requiring a court order.'

This, Linehan will tell me, was like the owner of a burgled home saying, 'If you want to come in and examine the scene and dust down the windows, you have to get a warrant.'

During the first trial, Lynn had sat back for months watching the State try to prove its case with the records it got from the banks. This time he is proactive from the start. His aim is to put the banks on trial. He does so using a small, potent arsenal he has put together since the first trial.

When he rises to cross-examine Lynn's former NIB lender, Noel McCole, Paul Comiskey O'Keeffe draws a weapon from this stockpile. It is a data subject access request from NIB. Everyone has the right to request data relating to them from businesses and Lynn has now done so from each and every bank.

To his disgust, most banks told him they no longer held any records about him. In most cases, there are no available emails to or from Lynn and his lenders left, no internal communications about the chaos his borrowing activity must have generated. Nothing.

But on NIB's systems, certain data remained. It will now become the first defence exhibit.

Comiskey O'Keeffe displays a record from NIB's 'internal portal' and tells the jury it was not among the files the bank disclosed to gardaí. He points to a heading: 'collateral'. This details the security the bank had against Lynn's borrowings.

'Solicitor's U/t over 4 properties,' is the only form of security listed.

Is this single, abbreviated note proof that the bank conspired to lend to Lynn on nothing more than a solicitor's undertaking?

'I don't really know what I'm looking at,' says McCole.

Comiskey O'Keeffe then points to another page. It indicates that certain, unspecified information about Lynn must be 'kept off' the NIB portal 'at the request' of the bank's 'Steering Committee'.

'There was a committee made up of senior management at the bank who was keeping information off portal,' Comiskey O'Keeffe proposes to McCole.

'I was never aware of anything withheld from the portal,' McCole replies.

There is little context for this document, amongst the million-plus other files in this case. It could, perhaps, be explained, were the full context known. McCole may not be the right man to be putting this to at all. But that is not what matters to Lynn. The data access file allows him to raise a query and perhaps a doubt in the minds of the jury.

He seeks to use data access files received from Bank of Ireland in the same way. In this way Bank of Ireland underwriter Arthur King finds himself being asked about a €1.5 million 'bail out' Lynn provided in 2003 when he 'took over' a Bank of Ireland loan for which he had no responsibility. The issue, backed up by the data files Lynn has secured, involves a struggling development in Carrick on Shannon for which Lynn did not have to take responsibility.

The 'favour' was not an 'entirely altruistic gesture', Comiskey O'Keeffe suggests to the witness. 'He was trying to develop a relationship with personalities in Bank of Ireland and one way of going at that was to do them a favour.'

Asked if such a 'bail out' was normal, King says he has no idea.

Judge Nolan has a view and he interjects, 'I think the jury can accept there are very few people out there who would take on responsibility for a loan that was not theirs,' he observes. 'If it happened that would be very unusual.'

Bingo. Sitting in the dock Lynn looks delighted. The context is not clear. There could be a reasonable explanation, but seeds of doubt are being sown. Lynn just needs them to sprout.

Lynn has a second salvo ready for Bank of Ireland. He has repeatedly said that for years before he was caught, he was able to borrow from Irish banks without ever securing loans against a property as required by his undertakings. Now he's about to demonstrate this was true – at least at Bank of Ireland.

The defence asks Arthur King – and later Bank of Ireland lender Jim Madden – if they know of any previous loans Lynn had failed to secure before the 2006–7 loans he is accused of stealing were approved. Both deny any knowledge of this possibility.

They may not have known, but the new data Lynn has secured from Bank of Ireland shows the jury that others in the bank did. To prove this, Lynn's defence produces two internal emails. In the first, two Bank of Ireland officials are seeking to understand the bank's exposure to Lynn when his story first erupted in October 2007. 'Back in 2004 we highlighted to you that the solicitor [Lynn] was not registering their ownership of the properties and also the bank's mortgage was not being registered,' one executive told another in the email. 'I think we succeeded in getting out clean at that point … Looks like a timely escape.'

The second email, dated 31 March 2004 – long before the Lynn scandal emerged – is far more damaging to the bank. In it, Mary Tuck, from the Bank of Ireland's Business Banking Shared Services Centre, is writing to a superior, Michael G. Griffin.

'I think you will need to talk to Michael Lynn again,' Tuck wrote. She had just completed an exercise to check if Lynn's solicitors' undertakings had been properly registered and it was clear something serious was amiss. The list of improperly secured loans to Lynn that Tuck produced back in 2004 runs to more than a full page.

'I think you have more than enough here to call Michael Lynn back in and ask him to explain how he has not complied with the undertakings given,' Tuck concluded. 'He should be referred to the Law Society.'

For the bank, in the absence of an explanation, this is damning. The possibility that Bank of Ireland lent on solicitors' undertakings is backed up by further records secured by Lynn. One such document is an October 2007 email to Bank of Ireland from Thomas Brophy in the office of the Financial Regulator. 'Is it the bank's normal procedure to grant loans secured solely on the back of a solicitor's undertaking?' he wanted to know as news of the Lynn scandal was erupting. 'If so, what procedures are in place to review same?'

Once again, this document could, in the correct context, have a different meaning to that Lynn attributes – or it could simply have been ill-phrased. But none of that matters if Lynn can use it to create doubt.

Lynn is not finished yet. He still has a dangerous left hook to throw, one that is left to Mark Lynam to deliver. Lynam questions King about his role in preparing a claim that saw Bank of Ireland recover €4.5 million relating to Lynn's loans from its insurance company in September 2014. Once again, this information has come from Lynn's data request, and thanks to it the jury now know that ultimately Bank of Ireland lost nothing from Lynn's deceptive borrowing.

After King confirms he helped prepare the insurance claim, Lynam asks him about Mary Tuck's 2004 email and the 'extremely abnormal borrowing' it details.

'Is this the kind of email that would cause concern?' he asks King.

'Yes, I would expect so,' King replies.

Why then, Lynam wants to know, did Bank of Ireland not tell its insurers when it made the insurance claim? Did the bank not have 'a duty of the utmost good faith' to tell its insurers? 'Is this issue potentially relevant to the insurance claim?' Lynam continues. 'There's material in the bank that supports that they ought to have had a level of knowledge.'

In the witness box, King agrees that the 2004 email was 'potentially relevant' to the insurance claim.

The prosecution counters that theft is still theft, regardless of who actually bears the ultimate loss. But Lynn has scored a few points here, for sure. The jury may now think twice when it comes to considering Bank of Ireland.

Michael Fingleton occupies a unique place in Lynn's trials. Not able to attend – even if he would have been minded to – his shadow nevertheless looms large. In his testimony Lynn presents Fingleton as the most corrupt of all his lenders; someone who allegedly agreed secret 'off-book' arrangements to use the bank he ran to fund Lynn in return for a personal cut of the profits.

Lynn even details for the court an alleged 2006 meeting with Fingleton in the Berkeley Court Hotel, during which he claims to have signed a memorandum of understanding with the banker. According to Lynn, the deal – drawn up by Fingleton's London lawyer – saw the banker secure a personal stake in the third stage of Lynn's Cabanas development in return for off-the-book lending from Irish Nationwide. Lynn also presents to the court pretrial correspondence with Irish Nationwide's London lawyer in which his defence unsuccessfully sought a copy of the claimed memorandum he had signed with Fingleton.

'The signature was him tying me down, not the other way around,' Lynn tells the court when challenged on why he did not keep a copy of the document himself. 'Michael Fingleton was an extremely astute man ... I wasn't even allowed to make a copy of it.'

He has no documents to support his claim and Fingleton cannot be put on the stand. Nevertheless, all Lynn needs is to create a doubt in the minds of three members of the jury that his claims could be true. To this end, Lynn secures testimony from others at Irish Nationwide who speak to the dominance and power Fingleton held. For example, Irish Nationwide lender Olivia Greene testifies that Fingleton personally approved the €4,125,000 Lynn secured for Glenlion House. Greene also testifies that when news of Lynn's practices broke, Fingleton told her, 'Someone else was going to take the blame for it.'

He might not have a copy of his claimed deal with Fingleton, but Lynn's team has secured evidence – via an extraordinary Irish Nationwide board resolution – that Fingleton was powerful enough to have done such a deal. Although the resolution had, in the past, been reported to exist, it had never before been seen in public. The resolution, delegating power to Fingleton, is dated 25 August 1997 and confirms he had complete control. This included the power to 'vary and alter interest rates, fees, terms, conditions of all loans whether secured or unsecured' and to 'make arrangements with individual borrowers, investors and depositors in the normal course of business'.

Reading the document on the court screens, a memory of Lynn's voice pops into my mind from years back. It's Lynn calling unexpectedly during Christmas 2019.

'How is he by the way?' he'd inquired of Fingleton before adding that eleven of the twenty-one charges he faced involved Irish Nationwide.

Now, precisely because Fingleton is not present, Lynn can freely accuse him of serious corruption without any comeback. Unlike others whom Lynn accuses of being corrupt, Fingleton cannot be brought by the State as a rebuttal witness. In addition, Fingleton's reputation – as one of Ireland's most incorrigible boom-time bankers – is such that the jury is likely to give some credence to Lynn's claims. If enough of them think Fingleton could have struck the deal Lynn has outlined, he will escape eleven of the charges he faces.

There is something different about Ciaran Farrell. Something lively. Something edgy. Something irreverent. The vast majority of the lenders called by the State to testify against Michael Lynn have been grey-haired and terribly dour. But Farrell is different. His thick hair may be fading, but it's doing so from a shade of red. And unlike most appearing here, he still works as banker, in his case, for Permanent TSB – which has just rebranded as PTSB.

A true Dubliner, Farrell does not sound like a banker. His voice and approach are more that of a man selling scarves and headbands on All-Ireland Final day. But he is initially nervous when called to the stand and he overdoes the faux deference.

'That is correct, sir,' he repeatedly replies as Karl Finnegan introduces him to jury. It is a tone so different to all those who have come before that it immediately piques the attention of everyone in the room.

Today Farrell is a business development manager in HQ for Permanent TSB, though, in his own words, 'I do be on the road as well.'

In years past, Farrell once hand-delivered a €3.7 million loan cheque to Lynn's office. 'Sure look, instead of paying to get a courier, I'll deliver it down to you,' is how Farrell explains his motivation for this to the jury.

With no data access documents in his possession from Permanent TSB, the approach of Lynn's team will be simple: hit Farrell hard – above and below the belt – and keep pummelling. Farrell was, after all, a name that featured prominently throughout the first trial, though he was only called at rebuttal stage, where he was on the stand briefly.

Knowing this, the prosecution seeks to cover all the bases first. Led by Finnegan, Farrell denies '1,000 per cent' that he ever received money or tickets for Wembley Stadium or a 30 per cent discount offer on a foreign apartment from Lynn.

Finnegan then asks about Farrell's social relationship with Lynn.

'There was two tickets for a Dublin match sent to the branch,' he confirms, adding that no one in the office wanted them, so he had gone to the game himself.

'Mr Lynn had invited me to a concert, which I turned down,' he continues.

'He invited me to a second one and then he invited me to a third one. This was over a period of time. It was Meatloaf – which isn't my scene,' Farrell says. 'I'd be more Dermot Kennedy, now.'

In cross-examination, Paul Comiskey O'Keeffe switches focus. 'You've been accompanied to court by some colleagues,' he says, pointing to two figures at the back of the court who had also been present a day earlier when another Permanent TSB witness, John O'Brien, had testified.

'One of them was coming and going from court and speaking to you during Mr O'Brien's testimony, isn't that right?' he asks Farrell.

It is forbidden for witnesses to speak of their evidence to anyone while on the stand – something trial Judge Martin Nolan has repeatedly stated.

'We spoke about fantasy football,' Farrell responds, without any hesitation whatsoever. 'We didn't actually talk about the case.'

The remark sparks laughter throughout the courtroom and among the jury. Lynn laughs too, but he looks incredulous.

44

No Joy

THERE ARE NO CHRISTMAS DECORATIONS IN any of the public areas of the criminal courts. No place for joy in the administration of justice. God might be good enough for swearing in witnesses but marking his son's birthday with tinsel and baubles would not be appropriate.

If you walk the building and look closely, you will spot an occasional clue of the time of year so prevalent everywhere else in the city. But these are tucked away in areas not accessible to the public.

On the top floor, a lone foot-high plastic tree atop a desk divider between reading lamps can be seen through the Law Library window. The Bar of Ireland also has an artificial tree placed at the back of its reception area, and the information point on the ground floor has a tiny white tree placed on the counter. Other than that, the courts are Christmas free.

'Do you think we should ask Judge Nolan if we can hang some decorations?' I ask Lynn during a break. Outside in the real world the festive season is in full swing.

He chuckles. This is just the type of inane, no-harm natter he loves in between the heavy lifting and focus required for hours on end in court.

'Do you know,' he says, 'my first year in prison in Brazil I asked for a tree. They looked at me as if I was loo-la.'

I laugh at the thought of Lynn trying to bring seasonal cheer into the hellhole of COTEL. I would not put it past him for a second.

'I tell ya,' he continues, 'by year three we had one, just in our little area,' he assures me.

As the retrial nears its conclusion, it must weigh heavily in Lynn's mind that he could be back in prison before Christmas. On a human level it is a sobering thought to think he and Brid have put up a tree with their four kids this year and decorated the house, not knowing if he will be there with them on Christmas morning. It's not a hard guess what those children have wished for from Santa.

After court, I bump into Lynn again as I head for my car and we stop to talk for a few minutes below the twinkling festive lights above the door of the Ashling Hotel. One of the things he brings up is the insurance money Bank of Ireland got back.

'I'm convinced they all got all the money back,' he says.

There is no proof of this one way or the other. But in court the assertion is a useful one for him. In Lynn's view the Bank of Ireland insurance claim shows his misdeeds ultimately had little consequence for the bank.

It is easy, when engrossed in the technical detail of the charges against Lynn, to lose sight of the real victims: the people his actions devastated. Part of this is because for more than five years, since he was charged in 2018, the press cannot write anything that might prejudice a trial. Lynn cannot be called a 'fugitive' or a 'rogue lawyer' as every headline once screamed about him when he went on the run. For years now – and until the trial is over – he is referred to simply as a man on trial for the theft of millions from seven named banks. No further detail can be published, not even the fact that he was extradited.

Cushioned by these restrictions, Lynn may have forgotten about the victims of his actions. Perhaps he has had to do so to carry on. They may be silent for now, but those victims remain and when the trial is over, they can speak up again. They are people like Killarney publican Sean O'Mahony.

In late 2007, when Lynn's Byzantine world was imploding in Dublin, Sean was nursing his cancer-stricken wife, Kathleen, in her Cork hospital bed. At six o'clock on Tuesday, 16 October 2007, Kathleen handed her husband the remote and asked him to put on the news.

'She was dying and she gave me the remote for the television and we turned on the *Six O'Clock News* and Kendar Properties came out on it,' Sean told me when we first spoke.

On the TV, a report flashed up with footage of Lynn leaving the High Court in Dublin with Brid.

'He appeared on television with his wife. She had long black hair,' Sean recalled. 'It was Kendar Properties and this Michael Lynn. I never met him. I never knew him.'

But the name Kendar rang a bell and a horrific thought dawned on Sean.

'I have an association with Kendar, I thought. Have I? And my wife was dead before the news was over. She got a heart attack and they had told me they wouldn't revive her if she got it.'

Kathleen O'Mahony was forty-five when she passed away that evening. She left Sean with two daughters, aged ten and thirteen.

Sean was right. He did have an association with Kendar.

Kathleen, who had worked for the Department of Justice until she got sick, used her €45,000 illness retirement payout to leave a legacy for the children. She had paid Kendar for an off-plan apartment in the Bulgarian ski-resort of Bansko.

'She wanted it for the girls,' Sean told me. 'That when they grew up, they could go to a holiday village and, you know, that she'd be thought of.'

Like many others, Sean filed a criminal complaint, but the DPP decided not to prosecute any cases involving private investors. Instead, Sean was told his case would be forwarded to the Bulgarian authorities for investigation, but nothing ultimately ensued. In all, according to Lynn when I interviewed him in 2009, he owed hundreds of investors like Sean approximately €13 million.

This time there is no testimony from Brid Murphy. Unlike the first trial, she does not take the stand to support her husband. But the day after Lynn begins his own testimony – late on Monday 11 December – Brid attends the second trial for the first time. As before, the pair sit together at the back of the court as the jury is about to file in. They want to be seen together. But Judge Nolan beckons Lynn up to the witness box and it doesn't appear as if any jury members noticed Brid. That will change after lunch.

From the witness box at the beginning of the afternoon sitting, Lynn summons his wife as the jury takes their seats. 'Brid ... BRID,' he whispers, loudly enough for the whole room to hear, his hand raised in a drinking gesture.

Lynn accepts the bottle of Ballygowan his wife brings him and takes a sip. Amongst the jury, twelve heads turn to watch Brid retake her seat. On the desk before Lynn a court-supplied jug of water beside a stack of plastic glasses remains untouched.

Lynn's testimony is much shorter this time – just over two days, compared to more than a week for the first trial. It feels like he wants to get this done now. He seems ready for whatever awaits.

After Lynn's upbringing and career are briefly outlined, he is quickly led by Comiskey O'Keeffe into discussing the attitude of the banks. 'The emphasis was on getting money out the door,' Lynn says. He explains how he hired former bankers 'who speak bankalese' to smooth the progress of his loan applications. These staff were always 'incentivised in terms of profit', Lynn says. 'It's what makes people get up in the morning, if you're sharing the spoils.'

He appears at his most determined and dogged when speaking of the stark contradiction between his evidence and that of his bankers. Either he is lying or they are. So Lynn gathers every ounce of his willpower when addressing this.

'There isn't one banker who has come in to explain what happened,' he insists. 'I'm not surprised by that. I'm disappointed they couldn't have told the truth. I admit I'm many things and let myself down in many ways. But I'm not a thief. I had no intention to deceive or steal money from any banks.'

He denies deliberately evading planned meetings with gardaí as he prepared a move to Brazil. Instead, he says, he simply followed his legal advice – that his 'right to silence was important'.

'When you're in the dentist's chair, you rarely do your own fillings. So, I would have depended on legal advice concerning a criminal process.'

Lynn briefly describes his fruitless efforts to recover in Europe with a 'black mark' to his name and accounts frozen by court order. 'It is essentially a commercial tsunami which occurs and you are drowned, but you do your best,' he says.

Then he is surprisingly candid about his own personal need to move on. 'From my perspective,' he says of his move to Brazil in 2011, 'I needed to try to get on with my life economically. I had been in Europe for three and a half years at that stage.'

It is clear Lynn wanted back in the game. He'd put the past behind him. He tells the jury how, with the help of his former Portuguese associates, he had begun seeking development land in São Paulo before moving to Recife. The reason for the move: a new port development near Recife had created 'major, major investment and consequently there were a lot of opportunities likely to occur', he says.

It is never made entirely clear how he funded this new chapter of his life. Listening to him, I think of those whose money vanished when they placed deposits on Kendar apartments. I recall the paper trails I pursued as Kendar assets in Portugal, Bulgaria and elsewhere were siphoned away via offshore firms in tropical havens. These thoughts are interrupted as Lynn begins describing his first week in a squalid COTEL holding cell.

'I'm dealing with guys who are, I suppose, strung out,' he is telling the jury. 'Also, you're encountering people who are armed and I'm the gringo. So, I suppose I would say that what happened to me in October 2007 when I lost my practice seems like the worst thing in the world. And it was. But that weekend, I suppose you really achieve a level of serenity in terms of life.'

Lynn tells the court that 'regard for human beings was dreadful' in the

Brazilian prison. 'They have the front of the house painted, but it's extremely depraved in how it's run and my heart goes out to them [the inmates],' he says. 'I understand. People are in those prisons for particular reasons, including myself, but the treatment of human beings is dreadful and the conditions are deplorable.'

Then he glances at Brid, who is listening intently.

'Brid visited me every weekend, in fairness,' he says.

Then, far faster than anyone expected, Lynn's direct evidence is over. Just a cross-examination remains.

'Greed got the better of you, didn't it?' Karl Finnegan immediately challenges Lynn for the prosecution.

'I would say all of us, including the bankers, were carried on a wave of property speculation and that time I wasn't alone,' Lynn replies. 'It wasn't a one-way street,' he adds. 'We were both dating.'

It is a fascinating battle to watch. Lynn is stronger when openly challenged like this. He rises to the bait but is too cute to get caught on the hook. But Finnegan acts like he doesn't care, as if Lynn's responses don't matter. He asks something, then refuses to acknowledge Lynn's response at all. He deliberately avoids eye contact with Lynn, looking instead over his shoulder, and cuts in again before Lynn's answer is finished. It's as if Finnegan has simply decided to throw insults at someone not worth looking at or listening to at all. He wants the jury to feel this way too. Soon he will know if he has succeeded.

45

Change of Status

THE CHRISTMAS LIGHTS, WRAPPED AROUND THE palm tree by their gate, twinkle in the early morning darkness as Michael and Brid Lynn leave their Wicklow home and their children behind.

It is Wednesday, 20 December 2023 – two days since the jury retired to consider a verdict.

On the gable wall of the house more festive lights hang, meeting in the middle at a large, tied red ribbon beneath the eaves. It is almost as if this home itself is a present, wrapped up for Christmas Day.

This is a new home for the Lynn family, recently renovated and prepared for them since the first trial concluded. Just across the road and over the sand dunes, the white sands of Brittas beach stretch for miles. In the other direction the garden offers an unrestricted view of the foothills of the Wicklow Mountains. Beside the freshly laid driveway, a new swing set and slide sit adjacent to a trampoline. This, for the Lynn children, is where Santa will deliver his gifts this year. No one knows if Lynn will be there for Christmas and, in truth, it is probably the only thing the kids want. But Lynn's fate now rests entirely in the hands of the twelve members of the jury.

After another morning's deliberations there is still no sign of a verdict and the jury breaks for lunch. For Lynn the waiting must be insufferable. Holding hands with Brid he pushes through the exit turnstiles at the entrance to the courts complex and goes for a walk. He does not know if or when he will be free to do so again.

Inside an empty and silent court 22, the garda team waits in their corner. They are happy with their case.

So too is Lynn. He's fought harder than last time. Given it his all.

Outside the court door, Dermot Mara sits on the marble bench built into the wall and talks to anyone who will listen. When this is over he will retire properly, although it doesn't look like he wants to.

Mara runs to get Lynn. Having resumed deliberations for about an hour after lunch, the jury now wants to inform the court of something. They had previously asked one or two questions of the court and received clarity. But no one knows what's afoot now.

The foreperson passes a note to Judge Nolan, who reads it out loud. The jury has reached a unanimous decision on seven of the twenty-one counts. Guilty or not guilty, no one knows. But this will not be a hung jury.

The jury is asked to leave. Judge Nolan asks Finnegan what he thinks. Comiskey O'Keeffe too. All agree.

The jury is summoned back.

'There are fourteen charges left,' Judge Nolan begins. 'If I gave you more time, could you come to a unanimous verdict on those?'

'I don't think so,' the foreperson replies. His fellow jurors shake their heads. Judge Nolan tells them he will accept a majority verdict on the remaining charges. Now just ten of the twelve jurors must agree.

Outside, to the left of the courtroom, Lynn huddles with his entire team. He leans up against the wall looking worried.

A short distance away, in another huddle, Paddy Linehan calls it. A hung jury is one thing. But he cannot fathom that any group of twelve people could agree unanimously that Lynn was not guilty on seven counts.

Sixteen years after he was first assigned this case, Linehan breaks away from his team and strides towards Lynn. He offers his hand. Lynn accepts.

Lynn's huddle breaks up. They leave him with Brid and the couple begins to walk in a slow circle around the top floor, hand in hand. They have hardly gone 10 metres when the clerk calls everyone back into the courtroom.

Lynn and Brid enter the court and sit together, one seat from the back waiting for the jury to enter. They do not notice, but for the first time there are two uniformed prison guards waiting in the back corner behind them.

'All rise,' the clerk announces for the last time. 'DPP and Michael Lynn,' she reads for the court record.

The jury enters. Lynn kisses Brid and takes his place in the dock.

The note is passed to Judge Nolan. He reads, 'We have reached a verdict on ten counts. We are not going to reach a decision on the remaining counts.'

'If I gave you more time?' Judge Nolan asks.

'No.'

The foreman hands over the issue paper to the clerk.

'Mr Foreman, please answer yes or no,' the clerk begins. 'Have at least ten of you agreed on every verdict?'

'Yes.'

'Have you recorded the verdict on the issue paper?'

'Yes.'

'Have you signed the issue paper?'

'Yes.'

There is a long moment's silence as the clerk scans the document. Lynn shifts and clears his throat loudly.

'You say the accused, Michael Lynn, is guilty on Count No. 2,' the clerk reads.

Everyone remembers to breathe again.

Lynn remains rigid, hardly registering any flicker of emotion. But he visibly exhales and his shoulders drop.

In the corner, prison guard number WD673 rises, walks to Lynn in the dock and sits down facing him. Brid is silent, but her shoulders shake. The other guard takes up a position behind Lynn at the door through which he will be led away.

'Is the verdict on Count No. 2 the verdict of you all or a verdict by majority?'

'It's the verdict of all of us.'

In this way, one charge at a time, Lynn learns his fate. He has been found guilty of ten counts of theft – seven unanimously and three by a majority – from six banks amounting to almost €18 million. The only silver lining is that when he used the weaponry in his arsenal, his fightback worked. The jury has been unable to reach a decision on the only charge relating to Bank of Ireland, after Lynn revealed the bank's internal files to his benefit. Similarly, the long shadow of Michael Fingleton remains to Lynn's advantage, and of the eleven charges relating to Irish Nationwide, the jury could agree on only one, involving a home for which Lynn borrowed but never bought. For all the other banks Lynn is found guilty on all charges.

Judge Nolan thanks the jury. 'It's not easy to render a judgement on a fellow human being.' When the jury members have left, he asks Finnegan for the state's position.

'My instructions are that the gardaí will be objecting to bail pending sentencing and on that basis I would ask that Mr Lynn remain in custody until sentencing,' Finnegan says.

Comiskey O'Keeffe rises with an application for bail. He asks that the court take into consideration the 'considerable period of time since the offences in question'.

'Mr Lynn is someone who has attended two lengthy trials, he has observed his bail conditions in relation to that. He is not somebody who is likely to reoffend,' Comiskey O'Keeffe begins. 'He has surrendered his passport. His entire family has surrendered their passports.'

Then he concludes, 'Given the time of year it's a matter the court could review in the new term if it so wished.'

Judge Nolan waits for Comiskey O'Keeffe to finish and then speaks.

'Obviously Mr Lynn's status has changed,' he begins. 'He no longer enjoys the presumption of innocence in this matter. I'm aware of prison time spent in Brazil. The question is, is there a chance this court will extend it? I think there is a chance and I don't think it would be appropriate to grant bail.'

The court then quickly agrees a sentencing date on 15 January before Judge Nolan wraps up.

'That's all I can say on the matter,' he concludes. 'Mr Lynn's status has changed. The jury have rendered their judgment.'

In the dock Lynn stands to face prison guard WD673 and his colleague. He greets them in a friendly fashion. Typical Lynn to the last.

'Can I talk to my wife?' he asks, beckoning Brid over. For a few moments the couple hug tightly. Lynn is calm. Brid is in tears. Her fiftieth birthday is in five day's time, on Christmas Day. They share a last kiss. Then Lynn clears his jacket pockets, hugs his wife again and is led away in cuffs.

46

Déjà Vu

I should have known there'd be a twist. There always is with Michael Lynn. In the months before his retrial, Lynn moved his family into a new home in an idyllic seaside location in Wicklow. Checking the ownership of the property was always on my to-do list. But I'd neglected to get to this until midway through the retrial. When I finally did, the results of that Land Registry search opened up a brand-new money trail – even as Lynn's trial continued.

Lynn's new home had been bought in January 2022 for more than €450,000. It had then been renovated before his family took up residence after the first trial ended. There was no mortgage on the house. It had been bought outright. But the property was not in Lynn's name – or that of Brid. Instead, the owner was a new Irish company being run by someone whose name I recognised immediately. It was a go-to Bulgarian associate of Lynn's. Over the course of more than a decade I had seen this associate's name pop up repeatedly in locations across the world. Now here it was in Ireland, linked to the very house Michael Lynn was living in.

The discovery stunned me and sent me scurrying to pull out my files and recordings. In the evenings after court sittings, I compiled all the evidence I had about the Bulgarian. I'd first seen his name on records from 2009, created even before I'd caught up with Lynn for that first interview. At the time Lynn's Kendar assets in Europe were being packaged up into anonymous companies and moved beyond the reach of creditors. When I'd interviewed Lynn he denied knowing who the mysterious new owners of these firms were, while admitting that he acted as a consultant for them. But companies need bank accounts. And bank accounts need signatories. And deep in my files was a spreadsheet from Lynn's office outlining the creation of these new accounts and the signatures required. One such signature was that of the associate now running the new Irish firm that had bought the house Lynn had just moved into.

There was more. I had a recording of Lynn in 2010 during which he speaks about the associate and promises to put me on the phone with him so he can act as a Bulgarian translator for certain documents. The tape is further evidence of Lynn's relationship with the man.

From 2010 onwards further international company records tend to link the associate to Brid instead of Lynn. These files show Lynn's wife and the associate involved in companies in Brazil, Bulgaria, Slovakia, Panama and elsewhere. For example, I had a copy of a late 2010 share purchase deal involving an offshore firm in the Seychelles. It had been signed by both the associate and Brid. Their names, signed in biro and witnessed by a notary, are side by side on the document. The deal involved the shares of European firms linked to Lynn's former property assets at a time when these were being moved beyond the reach of creditors.

Now, even as Lynn sat in the dock, his associate was running a new network of Irish property companies – including the firm that owned Lynn's new home.

Digging further I discovered that one of the associate's new Irish firms had obtained planning permission for a multimillion-euro apartment complex on a recently purchased development site in Dublin. When I visited the location mid-trial, foundations were being poured and the work was in full flow. Looking at the Dublin site I couldn't help but think of another site I'd visited years earlier – that of Lynn's Bansko development in Bulgaria, where hundreds of clients had seen their money vanish amongst the weeds.

Could it be that the new Dublin project was linked in some way to Lynn's stolen millions or the funds he obtained from private investors? Was he secretly back in business, even as he sat in the dock during his retrial? Or was it someone else's money, and were Lynn's and Brid's links to the associate an unlikely coincidence?

Such questions would have to wait. I didn't have the bandwidth or resources required to attend the trial each day for my newspaper, complete this book and launch the wide-ranging investigation such questions required.

But the gardaí did. Unbeknownst to me they had already begun. Lynn, Brid and the Bulgarian were now the focus of a new money-laundering investigation. Even as the retrial continued, surveillance was being conducted and movements were being monitored. Secret court orders had been obtained to compel banks to provide access to accounts. The gardaí knew exactly how much money was in the accounts controlled by the associate and precisely who had access to these funds via bank cards and otherwise.

Now that Michael Lynn is a criminal, there is an unavoidable question to be asked: where is the money? He is guilty of stealing €18 million. He had access to far more than that. He owed the Irish banks €80 million when he first absconded, never mind the millions more borrowed abroad. By his own admission, private investors were owed another €13 million. So where has it all gone? Has any portion of this been secretly stashed away for a rainy day? Will it be waiting for Lynn when he is released from prison?

In all my dealings with him, Lynn has always played the poor mouth. He portrays himself as a man from whom everything has been taken: his legal practice, property business, houses, wealth and, ultimately, his freedom. Since being extradited from Brazil, he's been on social welfare. He also sought disability benefit on the basis that he suffered severe mental trauma while detained in COTEL. When this disability application was initially rejected, he appealed the matter all the way to the High Court. Lynn's legal battles, including his two lengthy trials, were all funded by free legal aid. There is, Lynn claims, no money. Believe him or not, Lynn insists he is broke. So too does Brid.

In the first trial Brid was quizzed under oath about the possibility of a secret cache of money by Lynn's own defence barrister, Feargal Kavanagh. At the time I found the line of questioning puzzling because the prosecution had never raised the possibility of hidden wealth.

'Lest there be some idea floating around that money has been squirrelled away – that there's 20 odd million or something like that – how are you presently surviving?' Kavanagh had asked Brid. 'Is there any reality to any suggestion that somehow or other there's money offside somewhere?'

Listening to the question, Judge Nolan had also been puzzled as to why the issue was being raised.

'Just to be clear,' he'd interrupted, 'that has never been put by prosecution counsel – that suggestion.'

'Oh, I know that, but lest it be supposed,' Kavanagh had replied.

Then Brid had answered.

'We're on social welfare,' she told the court. 'Our families support us. Michael is on disability allowance. He's on medication.'

Brid had then gone on to describe her own health struggles, how her mother had died from cancer at the age of forty-two – when she was just ten – and how her sister also passed away at the same age from the same cause.

'So as far as finances are concerned, the future is bleak enough. Is that what you're saying?' Kavanagh had prompted. 'There's no stash anywhere of any money or anything like that?' he had asked.

'We don't have any money,' Brid had answered. 'We are on social welfare. We are so fortunate that our families are supporting us in Ireland and we have four beautiful children.'

Brid's testimony in the first trial had set me thinking. She portrayed herself as a nurse who knew nothing of her husband's business affairs – or his thefts.

'Not at all,' she had testified when asked if she was involved in her husband's businesses. 'I was a nurse … Michael had his job … I had mine.'

This went unchallenged. But Brid had been a director and a 50 per cent shareholder of one of Lynn's property companies – Proper T Capel Ltd – which had been associated with some of his fraudulent activities. Furthermore, some of Lynn's criminal actions required her signature on loan documents.

Some of those dud loans for houses had been in her name too. Her testimony that she'd signed loan documents blindly, without knowing what they were, was never contested. But I wondered how many times she might have signed her name blindly like this. And I wondered whether she had continued to do so as her husband went on the run, moving assets beyond the reach of creditors as he went. Now I also wondered what precisely she knew about the role of the associate she is linked to on paper.

I spot him completely by chance. It's 9.48 a.m. on Thursday, 14 December 2023. Walking past the Ashling Hotel on my way to court, a man 20 metres ahead of me glances sideways, showing his face.

I recognise him immediately. It's Lynn's Bulgarian associate.

I'd known his name for more than a decade, but until recently I had never known what he looked like. Now I did, thanks to a LinkedIn profile connected with his Irish companies. When I'd seen the profile, I'd immediately recognised him as someone who had attended the first trial when Lynn was giving evidence. Now, here he is again as Lynn once again takes the stand.

Instinctively, I begin videoing him with my phone. As I do so he turns, rips up a sheet of paper and pauses to throw it into a large wheelie bin. When recovered later – and reassembled – the paper is shown to contain legal notes relating to Lynn's trial. I knew Lynn routinely met his team in the Ashling Hotel each morning. Had the associate just left them – and why would he be privy to such a meeting?

I continue recording as the Bulgarian enters the court building and passes through security alone. As he does so, Lynn and his team appear 20 metres behind him. They enter and go straight to their private consultation room on the first floor. Lynn uses a swipe card to gain entry. Thirty seconds afterwards, the associate, who has been waiting nearby, approaches the door. Lynn, waiting inside, lets him in.

The associate spends the rest of the day at the back of Court 22 taking notes on a yellow-paged notepad as Lynn completes his testimony. Afterwards he goes back into the private consultation room with Lynn's team until the prosecution has left the building.

I position myself on the street outside with photographer Sean Dwyer – who has now been on this case with me for more than a decade and a half. Our aim is to grab a clear photo of the associate – preferably with Lynn – as he leaves. Then we see him heading towards the sliding exit doors of the building together with Lynn, Brid and his solicitor. But Lynn spots us through the glass before they exit. He raises his hand as if to say, 'Don't shoot, I'll come over and pose instead.' At the same time the associate hastily splits off in the other direction. Brid and Lynn then come over to allow Sean to take some photos. Looking over Lynn's shoulder as Sean takes the photos, I watch the Bulgarian disappear into the distance. These will be the last photos Sean will take of Lynn with his wife before he is jailed again.

They wait until after Christmas to carry out the raids and swoop before dawn on Tuesday, 9 January 2024. Unaware of the operation, Lynn remains in prison awaiting sentencing set for 15 January. Armed with district court warrants, officers target Lynn's new home, that of the associate and three other locations. In the pitch darkness, unseen by the search team, Sean and I watch as Lynn's home is swarmed by gardaí. Since this story began in 2007, we've spent countless days and nights like this all over the world. Waiting and watching.

From our vantage point it is clear that Brid is cooperative. It is nothing but sad to see her prepare her children for their second day back at school since the Christmas break as police scour their home and the family car is seized. On the other hand, it could have been worse – the authorities could have decided to seize the house.

An hour away in Dublin, our *Irish Mail on Sunday* colleague, Michael Chester, photographs Lynn's associate being led away from his penthouse by gardaí. By the end of the day the authorities will have frozen significantly in excess of €2 million in Irish accounts linked to his companies. Now they will take their time to examine the phones, computers and documentary records they have found.

We run the story and the photos in the next edition of the newspaper, after I seek clarification from Brid and her associate about their business relationship. Brid does not respond at all; the associate issues a legal letter denying any wrongdoing. It is penned by Ciarán Mulholland – the same solicitor who represents Lynn.

Six days after the raids, on 15 January, Lynn is back in court for sentencing. Once again there's a delay. Led into the court by prison guards, Lynn watches from behind plexiglass as his defence team tells Judge Nolan they need more time so a psychiatric report can be prepared. An adjournment is agreed and Lynn is sent back to jail to await a new sentencing date of 19 February 2024. Another month in jail before he knows his fate.

When the new hearing comes around, Lynn's team makes a 305-page submission to Judge Nolan informing the court that he is suffering from post-traumatic stress as a result of his time imprisoned in COTEL, where, among other depraved acts, he witnessed a beheading. For the first time it is also revealed that in 2023 he was diagnosed with a skin carcinoma as a result of being exposed to direct sunlight in prison in Brazil. Paul Comiskey O'Keeffe tells the court there is now a real concern that Lynn's experience in the Brazilian prison system will ultimately affect 'his overall life expectancy'.

Having listened to the defence submission, Judge Nolan accepts that Lynn is an 'energetic, accomplished and very intelligent' individual, who is capable of reform and contributing to society. But he adds that Lynn has brought his profession into disrepute, and he tells the court that in his view Lynn led the authorities on a 'merry dance' while abroad and had 'no intention of ever being interviewed by the Guards'.

To no visible reaction from Lynn, Judge Nolan hands down a headline sentence of sixteen years, but he reduces this to thirteen years because of mitigating factors – such as the fact that Lynn has no previous convictions. He then allows a further seven and a half years to account for the inhumane conditions Lynn faced while incarcerated in Brazil for four and a half years. This leaves Lynn facing five and a half years in prison. With remission he will serve four.

As he is led away, Lynn pauses for a fleeting moment as he is ushered towards the side door by prison officers. Acknowledging his wife, he holds his hand to the plexiglass that separates him from Brid. She reciprocates the gesture. And then, in a microsecond, he is gone.

This chapter of his life is now closing – though as soon as the sentence is handed down Lynn announces his intention to prolong it by launching an immediate appeal. In a statement issued by his solicitor, Ciarán Mulholland, he even calls for a Tribunal of Inquiry to 'properly investigate' systemic flaws in banking.

Meanwhile, another chapter is already underway. If prosecuted and convicted of money laundering, Lynn, Brid and anyone else involved could face fresh fourteen-year jail terms. For now though, Lynn remains innocent until proven guilty. Again.

Acknowledgements

My work as a journalist is only possible because of the many others who back me.

Some of those, such as photographer Sean Dwyer, have worn down copious amounts of shoe leather and countless sets of tyres alongside me on the road. In the years it took to cover this – and other intervening stories for *The Irish Mail on Sunday* – we have had each other's backs in all sorts of places, under all sorts of duress. We've also had a ball – and I cured him of being vegan.

Another photographer for the newspaper, Michael Chester, also played a key role at vital times. His hearty chuckle is incurable. These photographers rarely get the credit and the bylines they deserve. In fact, they often go unnoticed and are hugely and unfairly undervalued. But to me they are far more than cameramen – they are among the best and most hard-working journalists I know.

Like many of the best things in life – good steak, ice baths and Tequila aside – investigative journalism is best done slowly. Slow news is the oxymoronic way I like to think of it. This can only be achieved if someone pays the bills to keep the presses rolling and the servers online. I am grateful for the management teams who achieve this at DMG Media Ireland – where Paul Henderson is CEO – and in turn at the Daily Mail and General Trust in London.

Those who soldier hardest with me in the news-gathering trenches are the troops in editorial. These include the various layers of editors, journalists, sub-editors, photographers, designers and lawyers who correct my mistakes, suffer my foolhardy doggedness and usually succeed in making me look way better than I am.

Since I joined *The Irish Mail on Sunday* I have worked under more than half a dozen Editors. I apologise for any wear and tear they may have endured working with me. They include Philip Molloy, Ted Verity, Paul Field, Paul Drury, Sebastian Hamilton, Conor O'Donnell and Robert Cox. Each of them in turn provided unfaltering support and cover as I stayed with this story for sixteen years. Sadly, not all of them lived to see the end.

It was Sebastian who first let me loose in 2007, resulting in a considerable dent in his budget and that first interview with Michael Lynn. 'I suppose you want to go to Brazil now,' Conor sighed deeply in 2013 when Lynn was finally detained there. And it was Robert who made it possible for me to cover two lengthy trials in 2022 and 2023 that took me off agenda for many months on end.

News Editors, Deputy Editors and Associate Editors who have allowed me huge latitude for which I am grateful include Neil Michael, Enda Leahy, Eddie Coffey, Christian McCashain, Anne Sheridan, Shane Doran, Aengus O'Hanlon, Nicola Byrne and Helen Rogers.

I also owe a huge debt of gratitude to our in-house lawyers – Michael Kealey and Liz Walsh. They battle in a world where – because of Ireland's draconian libel laws – the odds are often stacked against the truth being published.

Throughout the Lynn saga, as other editors came and went, James Meehan was a pillar of stability and support as Picture Editor. He is old-school and brilliant – and sorely missed now that he's hung up his boots for good. I'll see you for the Mayfly, James.

Thanks to Paul O'Brien and Colin Lawlor for the read-throughs of early drafts, the encouragement and the friendship. To Tim Vaughan, my first ever newspaper editor, for giving me my first job in the *Irish Examiner*. I still remember the Academy Street newsroom shaking as the presses roared into action. To Brian Carroll, who gave me an early lesson in the futility of trying to bullshit a Cork news desk and who cast an eye over this book for me. I am also grateful to the EU Fund For Investigative Journalism and to all those who continue to pay for news and public interest journalism.

Thanks also to my agent, Peter O'Connell, and all at Merrion – including Wendy Logue, Fiona Dunne and everyone else on the team who assisted. To Conor Graham with whom I signed this book deal ten years ago, thinking we'd be done within a year. Thanks for the patience.

To those who must go unnamed in Ireland and elsewhere. Every journalist is only as good as his sources. I am no exception.

To my parents, for their unconditional love and values. 'Money makes people funny,' my father always said. He wasn't wrong. 'People matter' was another oft-cited principle. He got that right too.

To my siblings Anne-Marie, Gilbert and Daniel, who we lost along the way.

And finally, to Krisztina, Oisin, Rian, Ailbhe and Fiachra. My world would be nothing without you.

Index